cover colors
Guy Major

chapter break gray tones by
Arthur Dela Cruz

book design by
Keith Wood

edited by
James Lucas Jones

original series edited by
C.B. Cebulski

Published by **Oni Press, Inc.**
Joe Nozemack, publisher
Jamie S. Rich, editor in chief

This collects issues 1-3 of the miniseries *Sidekicks*
originally published by Fanboy Entertainment as
well as *Sidekicks: The Substitute* published by Oni
Press. "Crash Course" originally appeared in *Love
in Tights* #1 published by Slave Labor Graphics.

Special thanks to C.B. Cebulski, Mutsumi Masuda,
B. Clay Moore, Dan Vado, and Deb Moskyok

ONI PRESS, INC.
6336 SE Milwaukie Avenue, PMB 30
Portland, OR 97202
USA

www.onipress.com

Second Oni Press edition: October 2003
ISBN 1-929998-76-7

1 3 5 7 9 10 8 6 4 2
PRINTED IN CANADA.

SIDEKICKS:™
THE TRANSFER STUDENT

SIDEKICKS:
THE TRANSFER STUDENT

written by
J. Torres

illustrated by
Takeshi Miyazawa

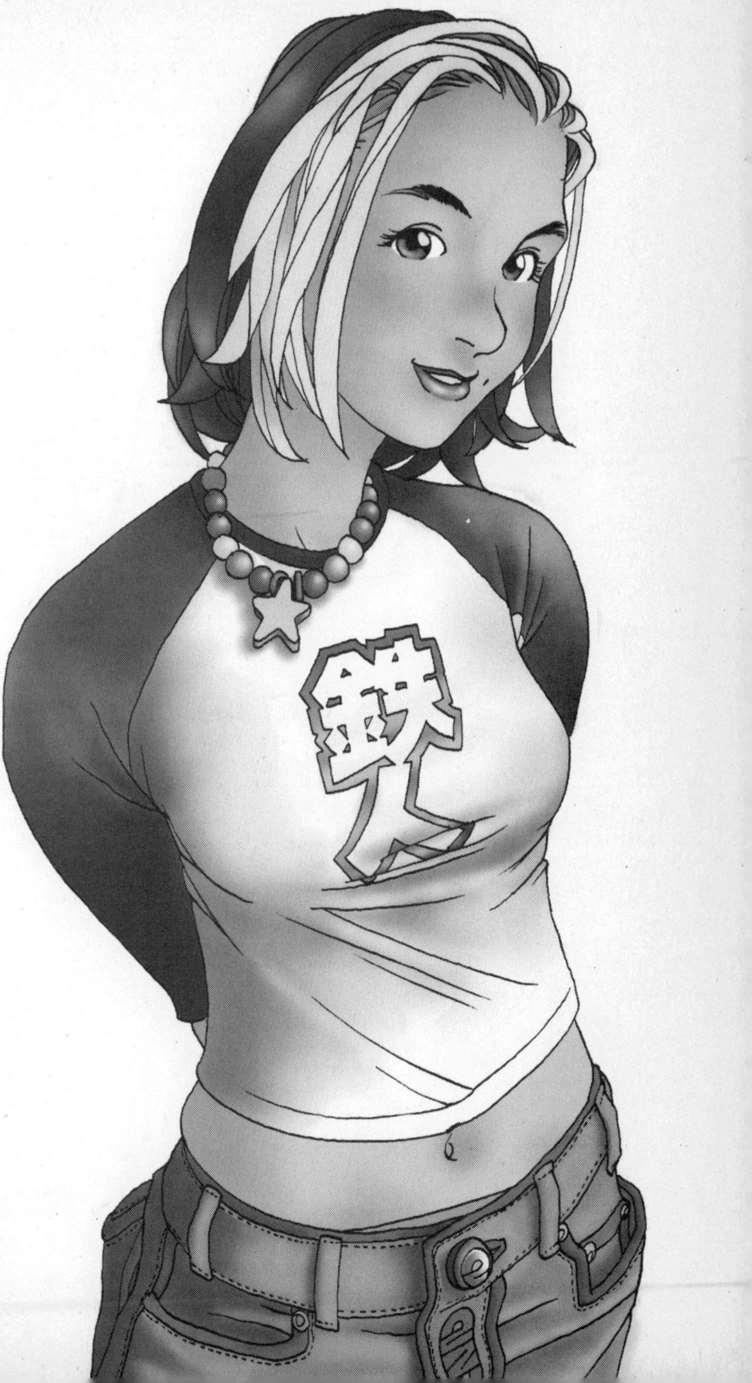
鉄

Chapter one

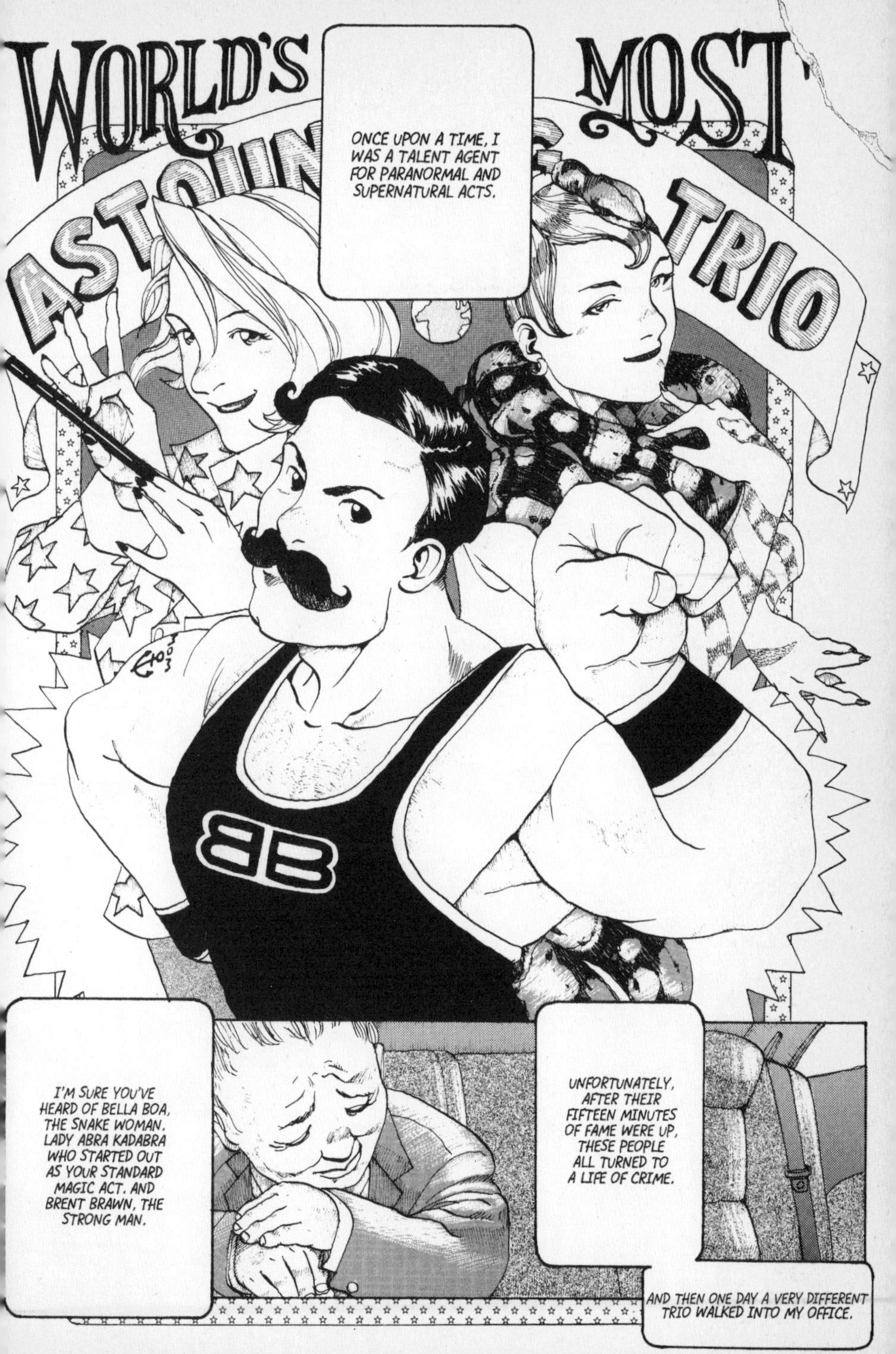
WORLD'S MOST ASTOUNDING TRIO
ONCE UPON A TIME, I WAS A TALENT AGENT FOR PARANORMAL AND SUPERNATURAL ACTS.
BB
I'M SURE YOU'VE HEARD OF BELLA BOA, THE SNAKE WOMAN. LADY ABRA KADABRA WHO STARTED OUT AS YOUR STANDARD MAGIC ACT. AND BRENT BRAWN, THE STRONG MAN.
UNFORTUNATELY, AFTER THEIR FIFTEEN MINUTES OF FAME WERE UP, THESE PEOPLE ALL TURNED TO A LIFE OF CRIME.
AND THEN ONE DAY A VERY DIFFERENT TRIO WALKED INTO MY OFFICE.

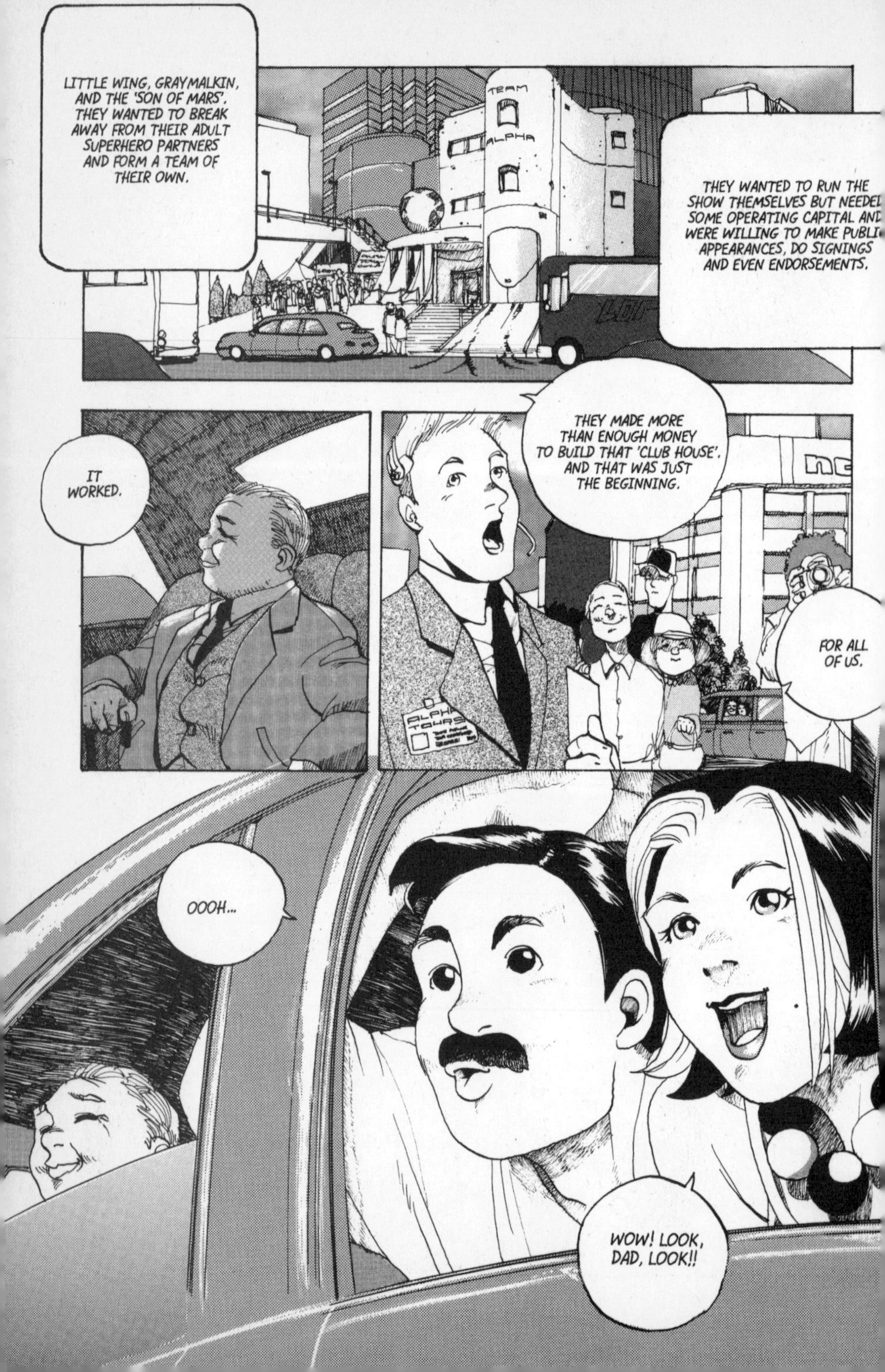
LITTLE WING, GRAYMALKIN, AND THE 'SON OF MARS', THEY WANTED TO BREAK AWAY FROM THEIR ADULT SUPERHERO PARTNERS AND FORM A TEAM OF THEIR OWN.
TEAM ALPHA
THEY WANTED TO RUN THE SHOW THEMSELVES BUT NEEDED SOME OPERATING CAPITAL AND WERE WILLING TO MAKE PUBLIC APPEARANCES, DO SIGNINGS AND EVEN ENDORSEMENTS.
IT WORKED.
THEY MADE MORE THAN ENOUGH MONEY TO BUILD THAT 'CLUB HOUSE'. AND THAT WAS JUST THE BEGINNING.
FOR ALL OF US.
OOOH...
WOW! LOOK, DAD, LOOK!!

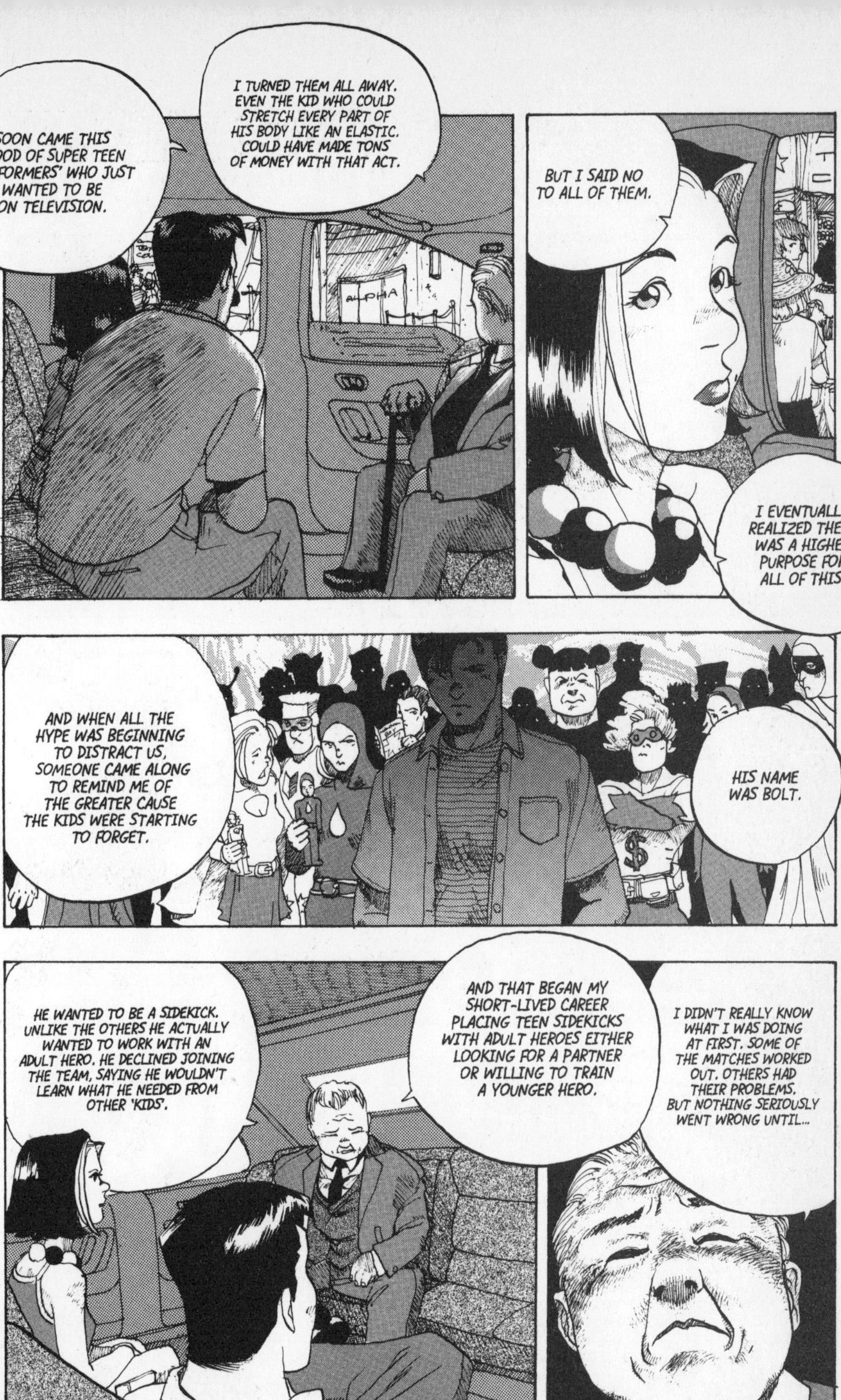
SOON CAME THIS FLOOD OF SUPER TEEN 'PERFORMERS' WHO JUST WANTED TO BE ON TELEVISION.
I TURNED THEM ALL AWAY. EVEN THE KID WHO COULD STRETCH EVERY PART OF HIS BODY LIKE AN ELASTIC. COULD HAVE MADE TONS OF MONEY WITH THAT ACT.
ALPHA
BUT I SAID NO TO ALL OF THEM.
I EVENTUALLY REALIZED THERE WAS A HIGHER PURPOSE FOR ALL OF THIS.
AND WHEN ALL THE HYPE WAS BEGINNING TO DISTRACT US, SOMEONE CAME ALONG TO REMIND ME OF THE GREATER CAUSE THE KIDS WERE STARTING TO FORGET.
HIS NAME WAS BOLT.
HE WANTED TO BE A SIDEKICK. UNLIKE THE OTHERS HE ACTUALLY WANTED TO WORK WITH AN ADULT HERO. HE DECLINED JOINING THE TEAM, SAYING HE WOULDN'T LEARN WHAT HE NEEDED FROM OTHER 'KIDS'.
AND THAT BEGAN MY SHORT-LIVED CAREER PLACING TEEN SIDEKICKS WITH ADULT HEROES EITHER LOOKING FOR A PARTNER OR WILLING TO TRAIN A YOUNGER HERO.
I DIDN'T REALLY KNOW WHAT I WAS DOING AT FIRST. SOME OF THE MATCHES WORKED OUT. OTHERS HAD THEIR PROBLEMS. BUT NOTHING SERIOUSLY WENT WRONG UNTIL...

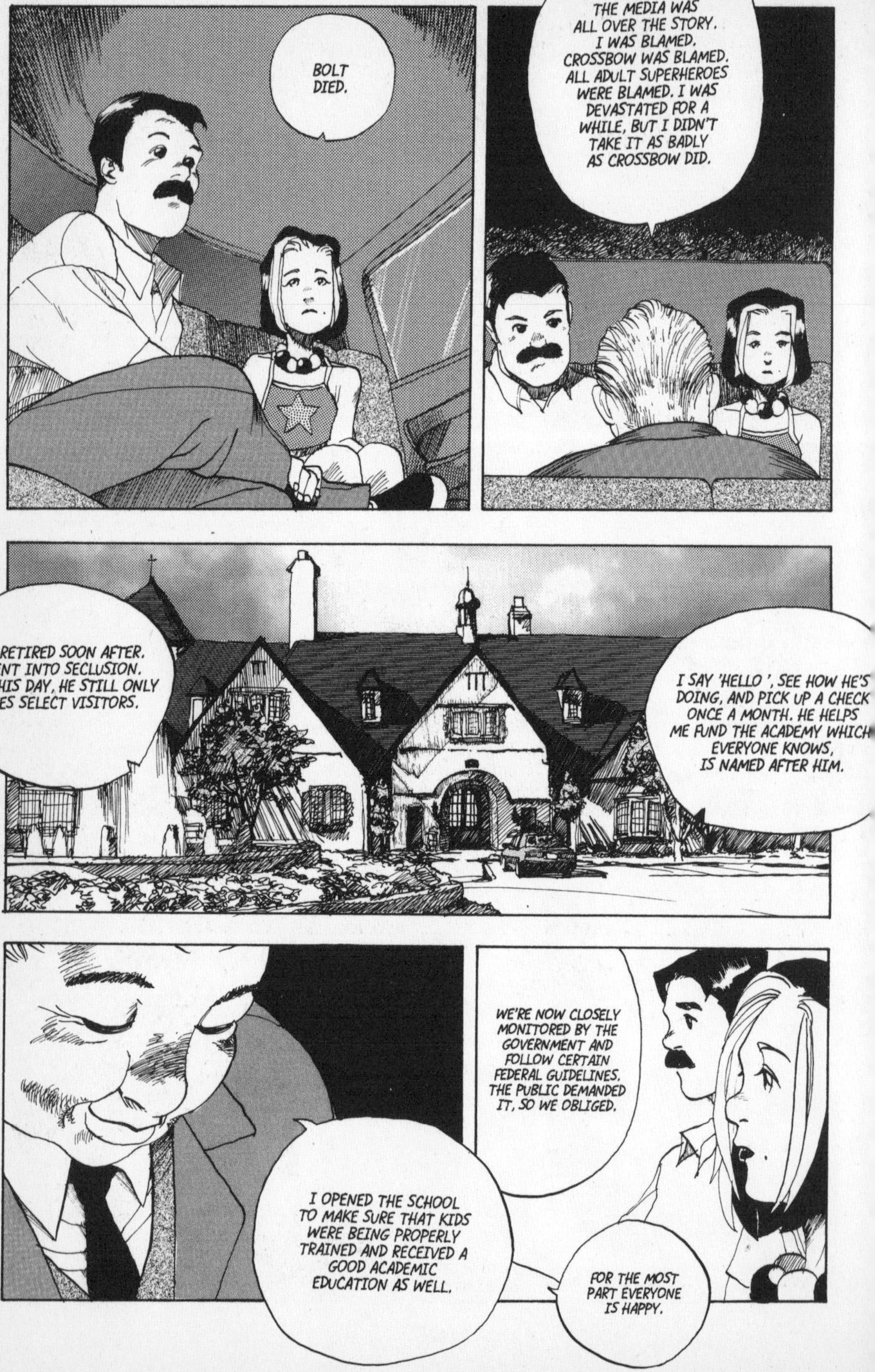
BOLT DIED.
THE MEDIA WAS ALL OVER THE STORY. I WAS BLAMED. CROSSBOW WAS BLAMED. ALL ADULT SUPERHEROES WERE BLAMED. I WAS DEVASTATED FOR A WHILE, BUT I DIDN'T TAKE IT AS BADLY AS CROSSBOW DID.
HE RETIRED SOON AFTER. WENT INTO SECLUSION. TO THIS DAY, HE STILL ONLY SEES SELECT VISITORS.
I SAY 'HELLO', SEE HOW HE'S DOING, AND PICK UP A CHECK ONCE A MONTH. HE HELPS ME FUND THE ACADEMY WHICH EVERYONE KNOWS, IS NAMED AFTER HIM.
I OPENED THE SCHOOL TO MAKE SURE THAT KIDS WERE BEING PROPERLY TRAINED AND RECEIVED A GOOD ACADEMIC EDUCATION AS WELL.
WE'RE NOW CLOSELY MONITORED BY THE GOVERNMENT AND FOLLOW CERTAIN FEDERAL GUIDELINES. THE PUBLIC DEMANDED IT, SO WE OBLIGED.
FOR THE MOST PART EVERYONE IS HAPPY.

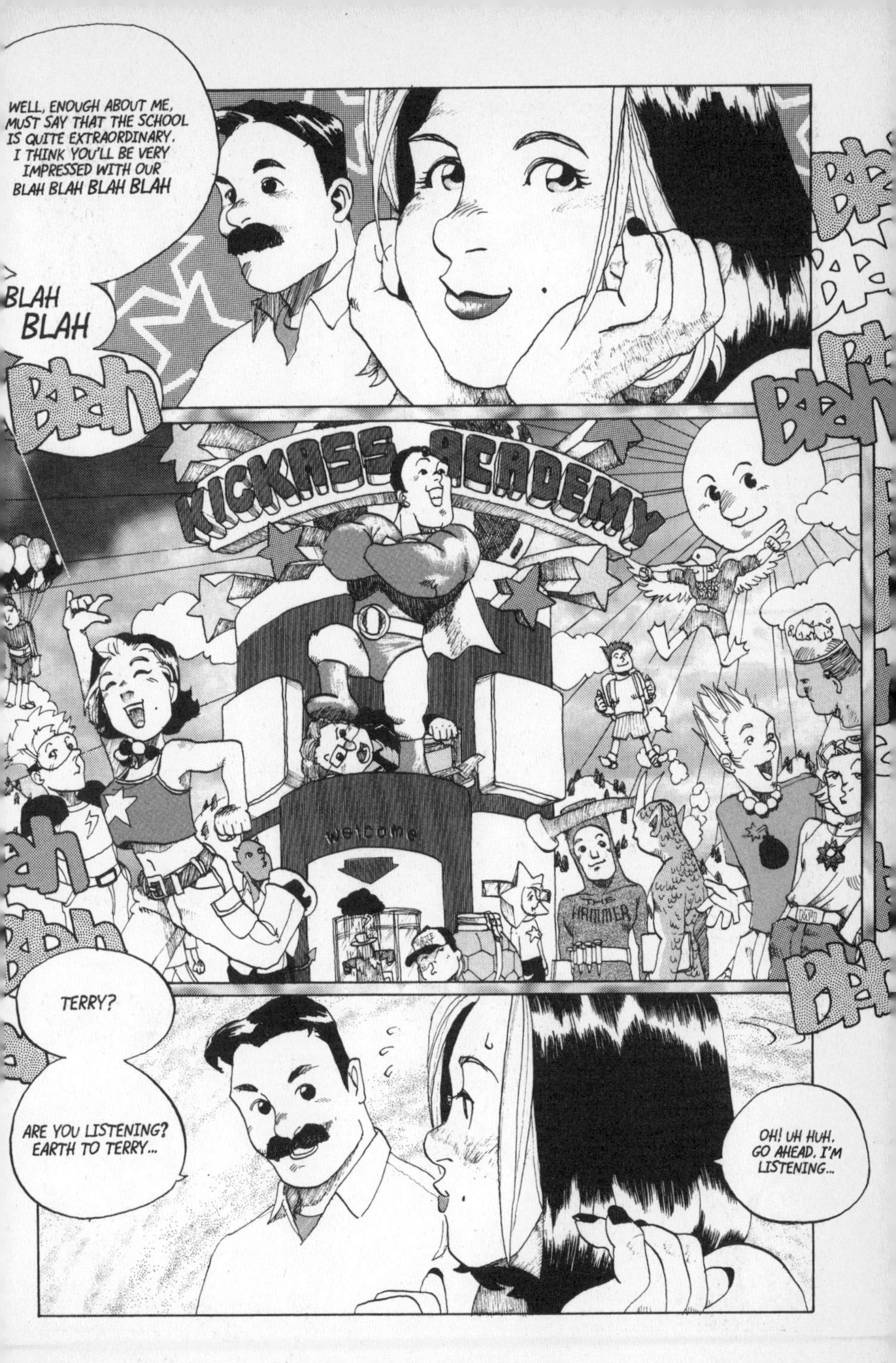
WELL, ENOUGH ABOUT ME, MUST SAY THAT THE SCHOOL IS QUITE EXTRAORDINARY. I THINK YOU'LL BE VERY IMPRESSED WITH OUR BLAH BLAH BLAH BLAH
BLAH BLAH
BLAH
KICKASS ACADEMY
welcome
THE HAMMER
TERRY?
ARE YOU LISTENING? EARTH TO TERRY...
OH! UH HUH. GO AHEAD. I'M LISTENING...

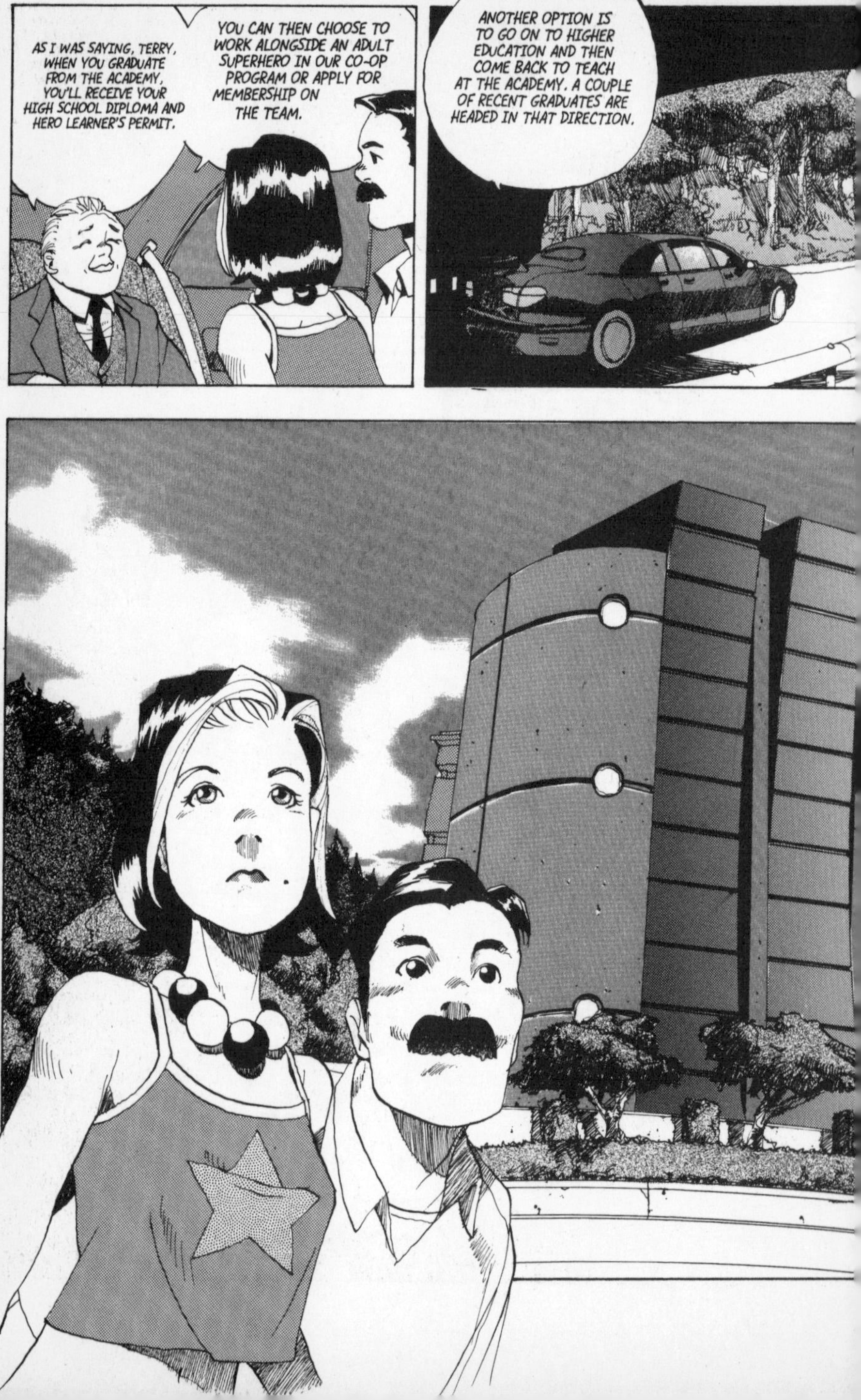
AS I WAS SAYING, TERRY, WHEN YOU GRADUATE FROM THE ACADEMY, YOU'LL RECEIVE YOUR HIGH SCHOOL DIPLOMA AND HERO LEARNER'S PERMIT.
YOU CAN THEN CHOOSE TO WORK ALONGSIDE AN ADULT SUPERHERO IN OUR CO-OP PROGRAM OR APPLY FOR MEMBERSHIP ON THE TEAM.
ANOTHER OPTION IS TO GO ON TO HIGHER EDUCATION AND THEN COME BACK TO TEACH AT THE ACADEMY. A COUPLE OF RECENT GRADUATES ARE HEADED IN THAT DIRECTION.

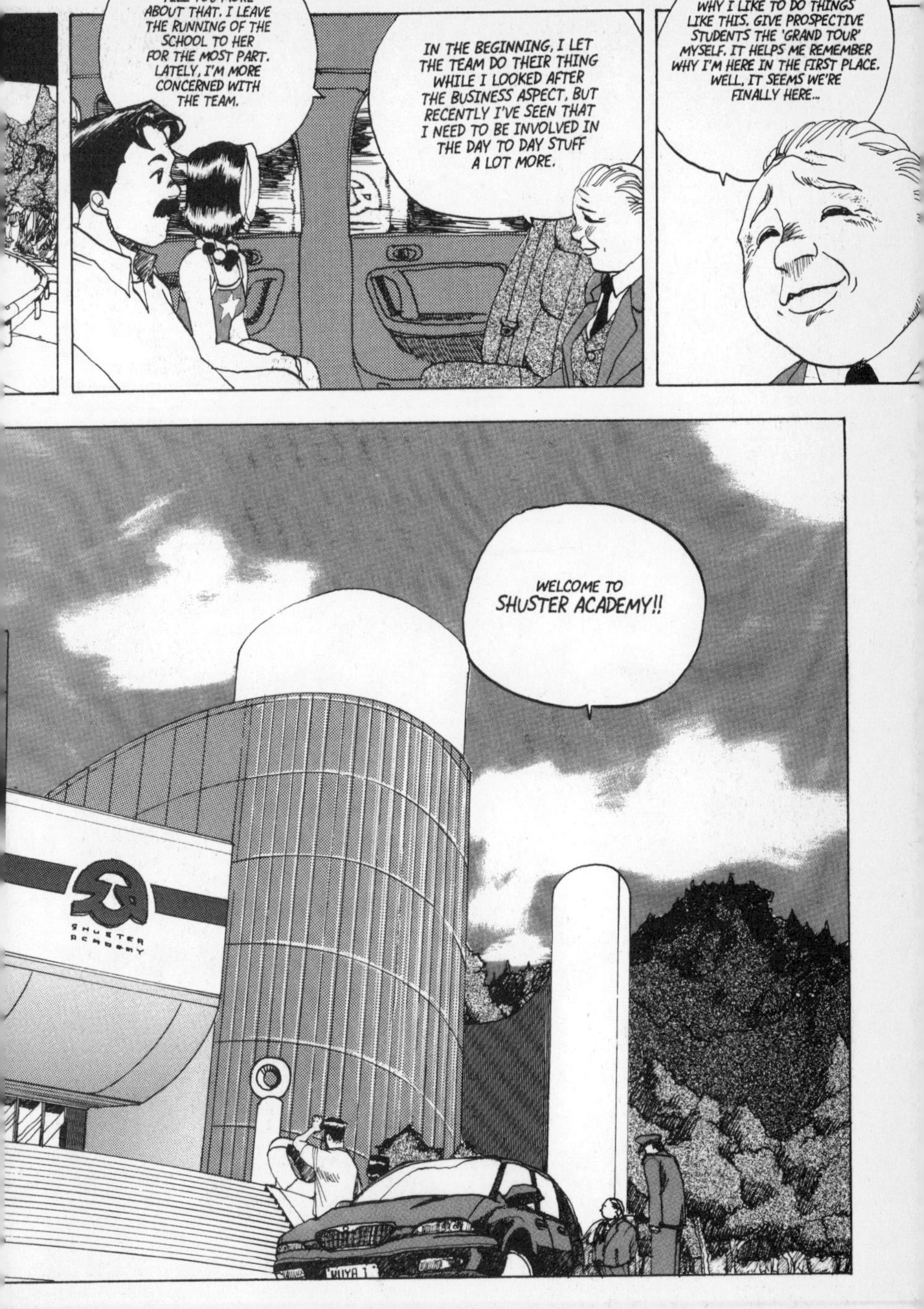
MS. STERNIN CAN TELL YOU MORE ABOUT THAT. I LEAVE THE RUNNING OF THE SCHOOL TO HER FOR THE MOST PART. LATELY, I'M MORE CONCERNED WITH THE TEAM.
IN THE BEGINNING, I LET THE TEAM DO THEIR THING WHILE I LOOKED AFTER THE BUSINESS ASPECT, BUT RECENTLY I'VE SEEN THAT I NEED TO BE INVOLVED IN THE DAY TO DAY STUFF A LOT MORE.
AND THAT'S ALSO WHY I LIKE TO DO THINGS LIKE THIS. GIVE PROSPECTIVE STUDENTS THE 'GRAND TOUR' MYSELF. IT HELPS ME REMEMBER WHY I'M HERE IN THE FIRST PLACE. WELL, IT SEEMS WE'RE FINALLY HERE...
WELCOME TO SHUSTER ACADEMY!!
SHUSTER ACADEMY

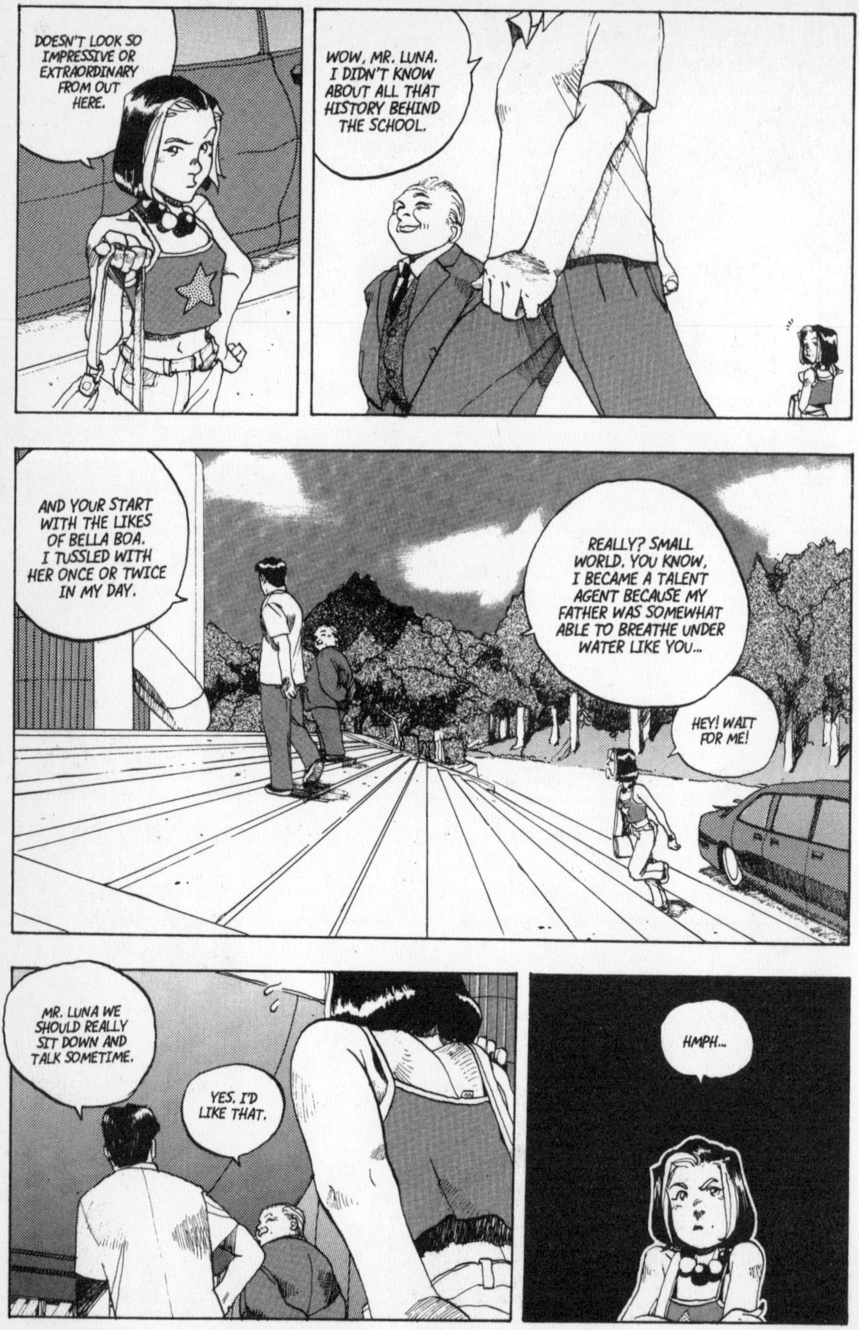
DOESN'T LOOK SO IMPRESSIVE OR EXTRAORDINARY FROM OUT HERE.
WOW, MR. LUNA. I DIDN'T KNOW ABOUT ALL THAT HISTORY BEHIND THE SCHOOL.
AND YOUR START WITH THE LIKES OF BELLA BOA. I TUSSLED WITH HER ONCE OR TWICE IN MY DAY.
REALLY? SMALL WORLD. YOU KNOW, I BECAME A TALENT AGENT BECAUSE MY FATHER WAS SOMEWHAT ABLE TO BREATHE UNDER WATER LIKE YOU...
HEY! WAIT FOR ME!
MR. LUNA WE SHOULD REALLY SIT DOWN AND TALK SOMETIME.
YES. I'D LIKE THAT.
HMPH...

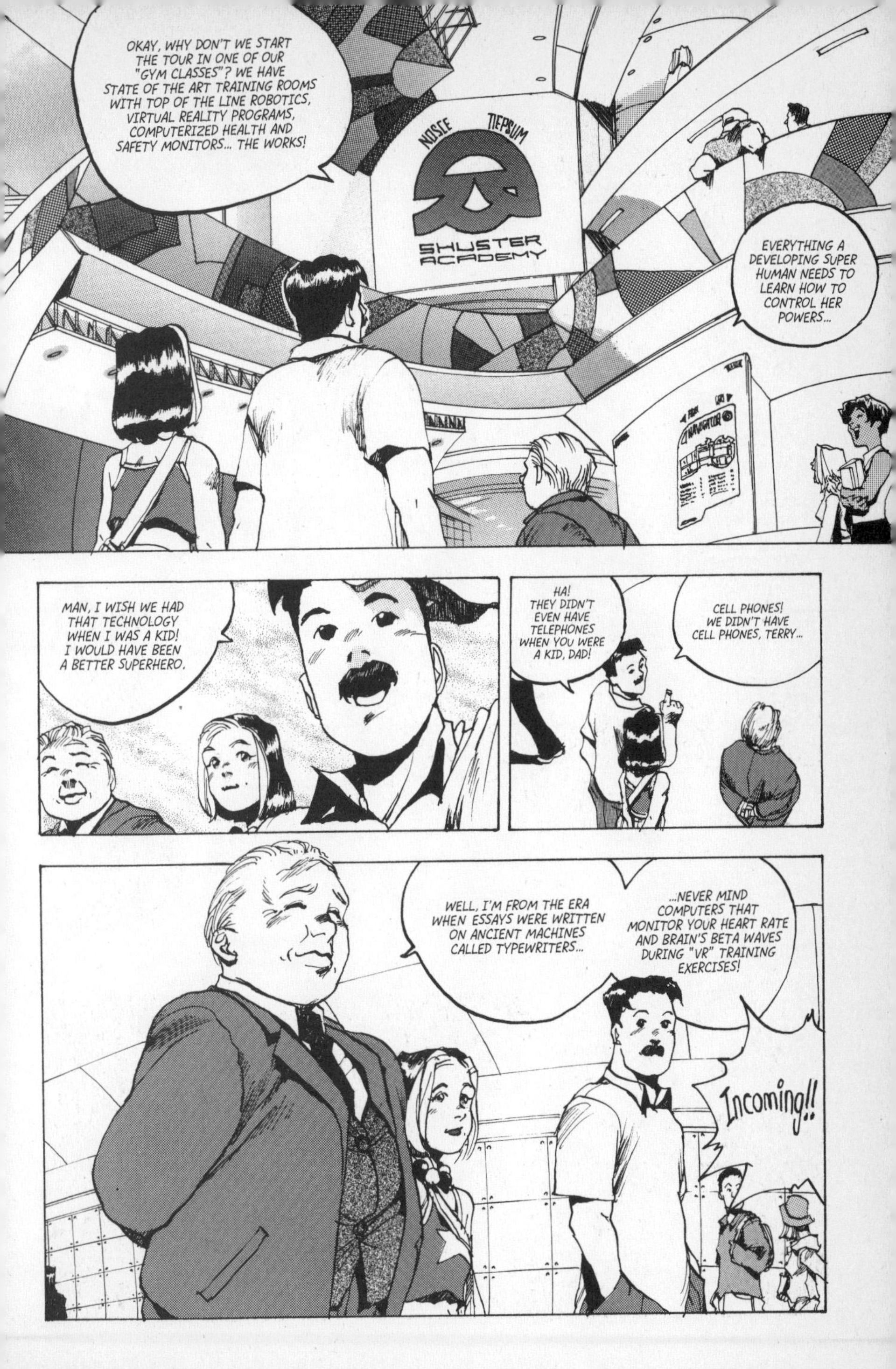
NOSCE TIEPSUM
SHUSTER ACADEMY
OKAY, WHY DON'T WE START THE TOUR IN ONE OF OUR "GYM CLASSES"? WE HAVE STATE OF THE ART TRAINING ROOMS WITH TOP OF THE LINE ROBOTICS, VIRTUAL REALITY PROGRAMS, COMPUTERIZED HEALTH AND SAFETY MONITORS... THE WORKS!
EVERYTHING A DEVELOPING SUPER HUMAN NEEDS TO LEARN HOW TO CONTROL HER POWERS...
MAN, I WISH WE HAD THAT TECHNOLOGY WHEN I WAS A KID! I WOULD HAVE BEEN A BETTER SUPERHERO.
HA! THEY DIDN'T EVEN HAVE TELEPHONES WHEN YOU WERE A KID, DAD!
CELL PHONES! WE DIDN'T HAVE CELL PHONES, TERRY...
WELL, I'M FROM THE ERA WHEN ESSAYS WERE WRITTEN ON ANCIENT MACHINES CALLED TYPEWRITERS...
...NEVER MIND COMPUTERS THAT MONITOR YOUR HEART RATE AND BRAIN'S BETA WAVES DURING "VR" TRAINING EXERCISES!
Incoming!!

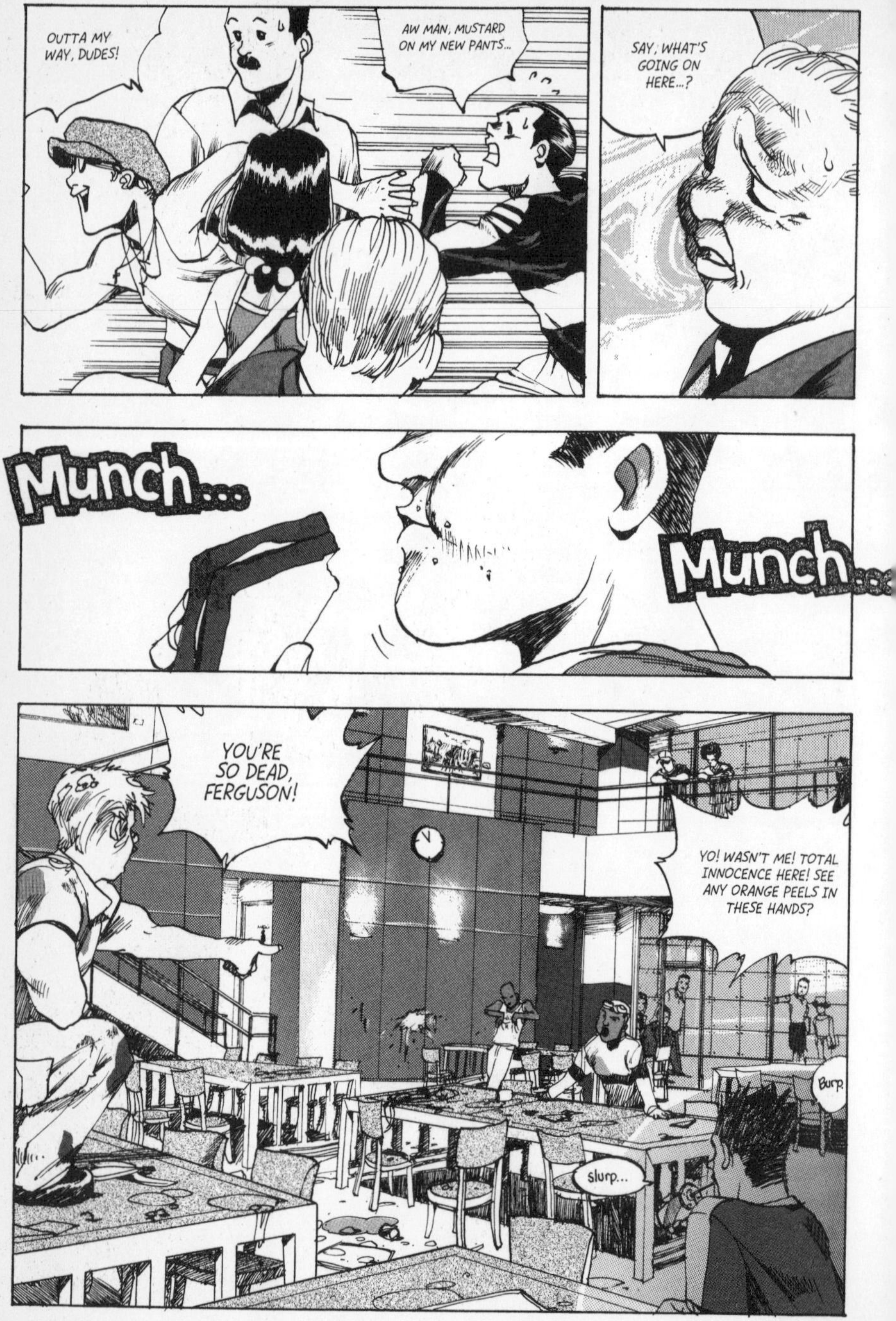
OUTTA MY WAY, DUDES!
AW MAN, MUSTARD ON MY NEW PANTS...
SAY, WHAT'S GOING ON HERE...?
Munch...
Munch...
YOU'RE SO DEAD, FERGUSON!
YO! WASN'T ME! TOTAL INNOCENCE HERE! SEE ANY ORANGE PEELS IN THESE HANDS?
Burp.
slurp...

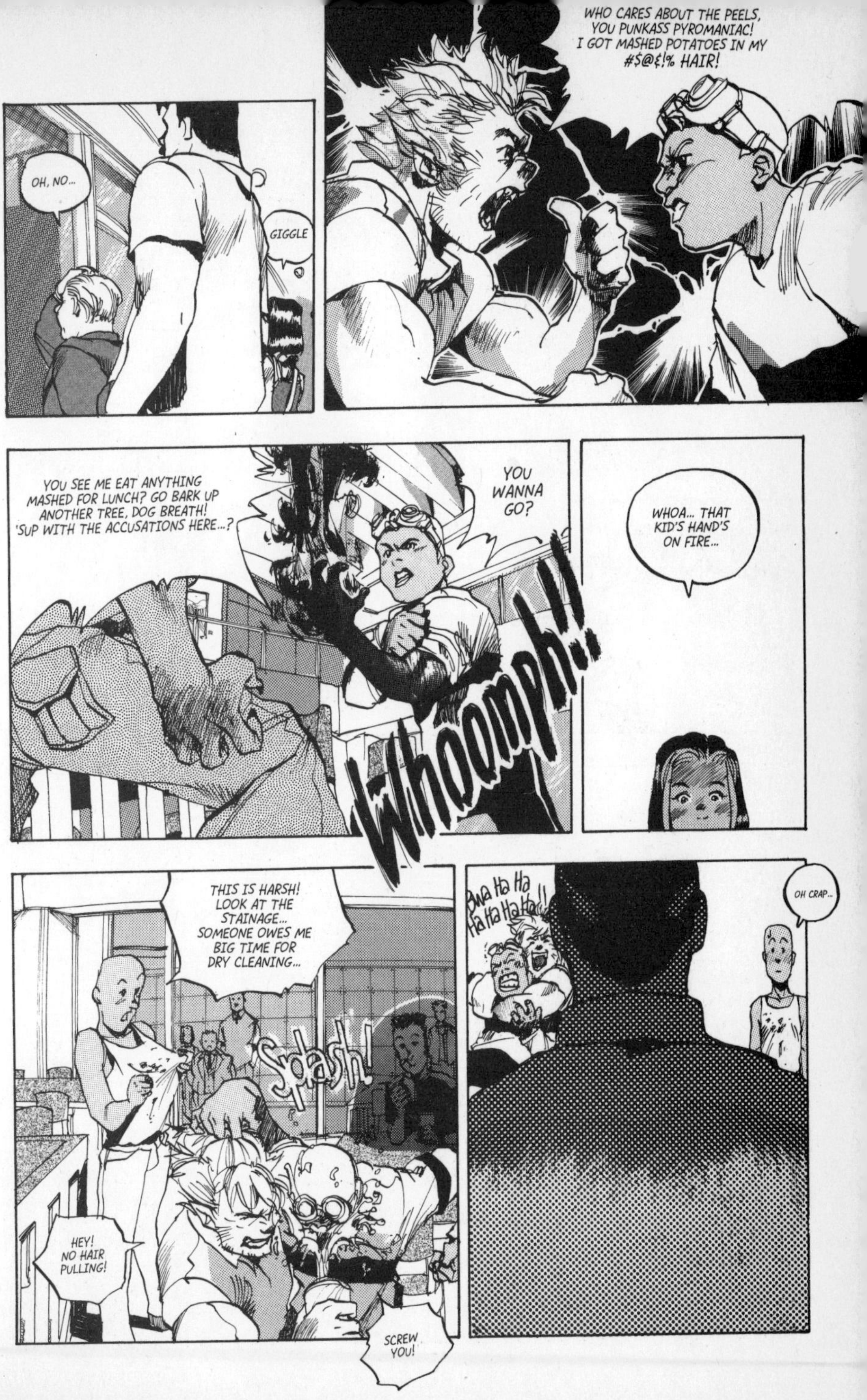
OH, NO...
GIGGLE
WHO CARES ABOUT THE PEELS, YOU PUNKASS PYROMANIAC! I GOT MASHED POTATOES IN MY #$@¢!% HAIR!
YOU SEE ME EAT ANYTHING MASHED FOR LUNCH? GO BARK UP ANOTHER TREE, DOG BREATH! 'SUP WITH THE ACCUSATIONS HERE...?
YOU WANNA GO?
Whoomph!!
WHOA... THAT KID'S HAND'S ON FIRE...
THIS IS HARSH! LOOK AT THE STAINAGE... SOMEONE OWES ME BIG TIME FOR DRY CLEANING...
Splash!
HEY! NO HAIR PULLING!
SCREW YOU!
Bwa Ha Ha Ha Ha Ha Ha!!
OH CRAP...

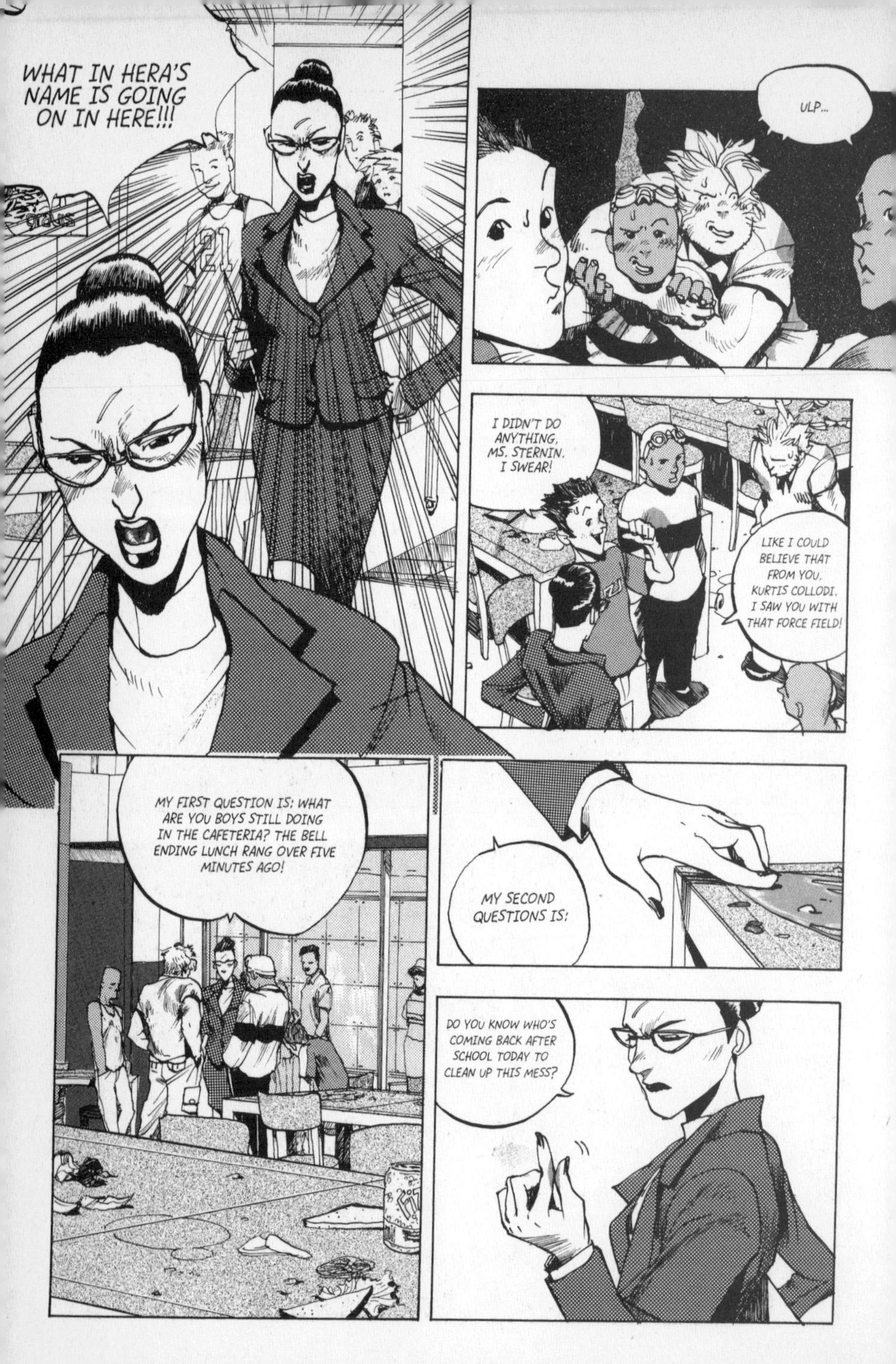
WHAT IN HERA'S NAME IS GOING ON IN HERE!!!
ULP...
I DIDN'T DO ANYTHING, MS. STERNIN. I SWEAR!
LIKE I COULD BELIEVE THAT FROM YOU, KURTIS COLLODI. I SAW YOU WITH THAT FORCE FIELD!
MY FIRST QUESTION IS: WHAT ARE YOU BOYS STILL DOING IN THE CAFETERIA? THE BELL ENDING LUNCH RANG OVER FIVE MINUTES AGO!
MY SECOND QUESTIONS IS:
DO YOU KNOW WHO'S COMING BACK AFTER SCHOOL TODAY TO CLEAN UP THIS MESS?

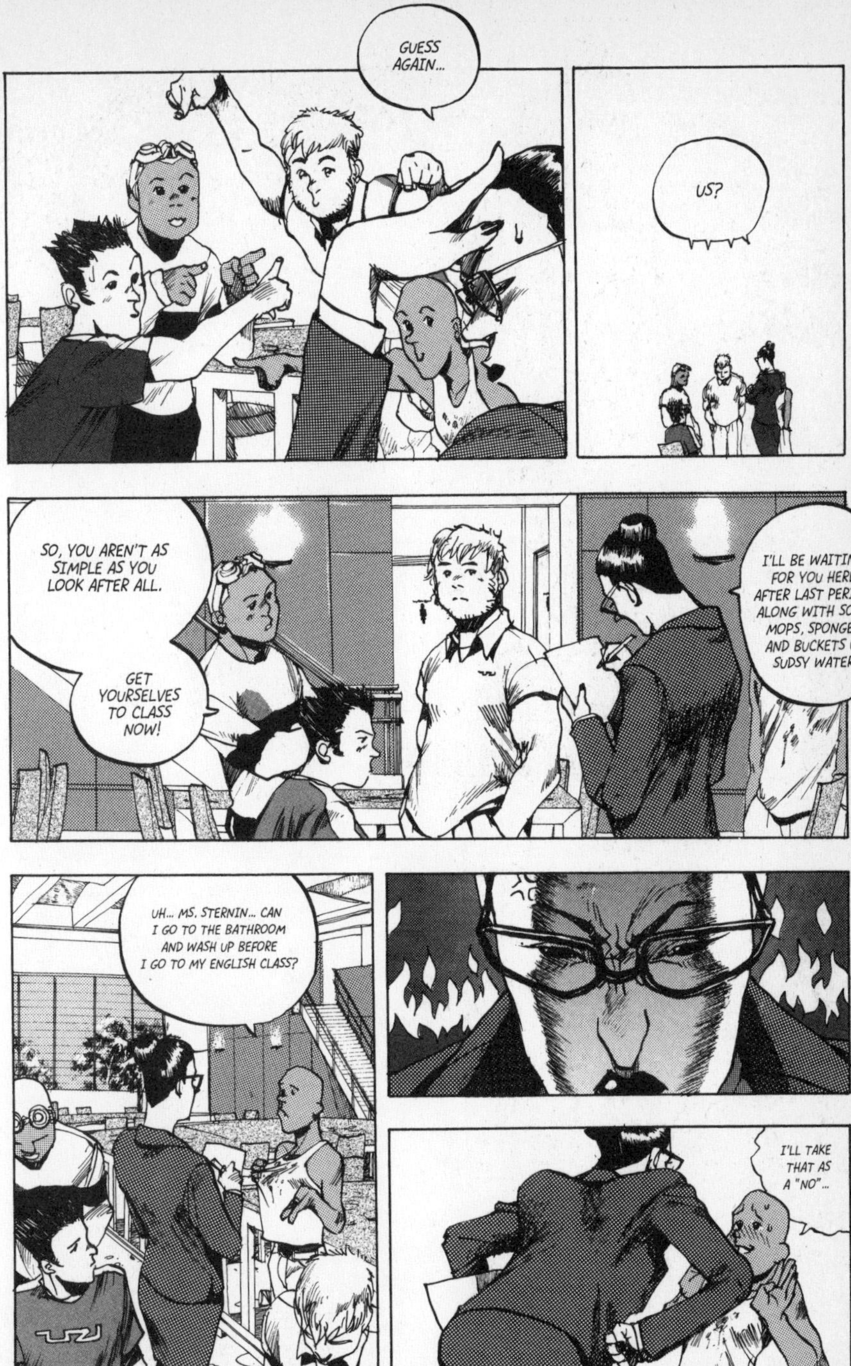
GUESS AGAIN...
US?
SO, YOU AREN'T AS SIMPLE AS YOU LOOK AFTER ALL.
GET YOURSELVES TO CLASS NOW!
I'LL BE WAITING FOR YOU HERE AFTER LAST PERIOD, ALONG WITH SOME MOPS, SPONGES, AND BUCKETS OF SUDSY WATER.
UH... MS. STERNIN... CAN I GO TO THE BATHROOM AND WASH UP BEFORE I GO TO MY ENGLISH CLASS?
I'LL TAKE THAT AS A "NO"...

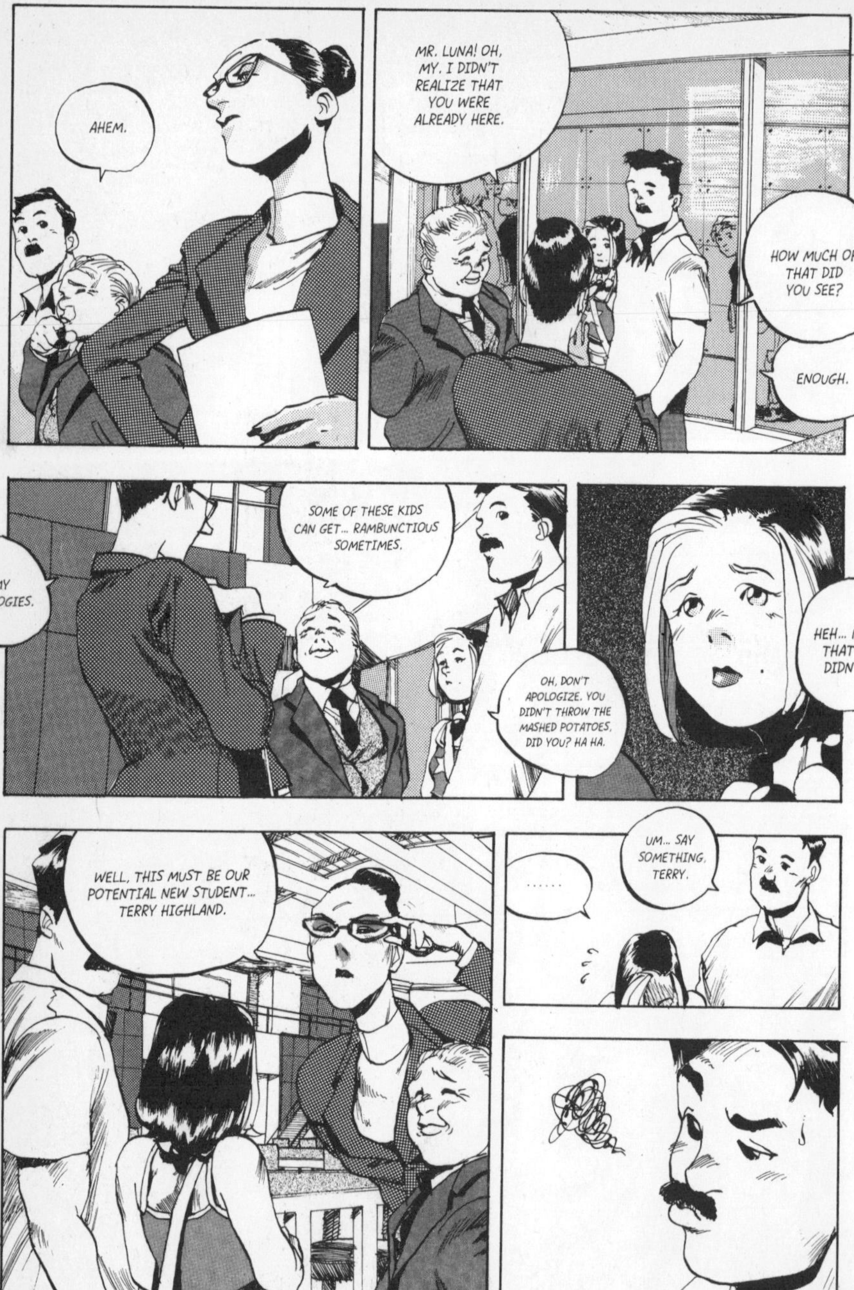
AHEM.
MR. LUNA! OH, MY. I DIDN'T REALIZE THAT YOU WERE ALREADY HERE.
HOW MUCH OF THAT DID YOU SEE?
ENOUGH.
MY APOLOGIES.
SOME OF THESE KIDS CAN GET... RAMBUNCTIOUS SOMETIMES.
OH, DON'T APOLOGIZE. YOU DIDN'T THROW THE MASHED POTATOES, DID YOU? HA HA.
HEH... NO, THAT I DIDN'T.
WELL, THIS MUST BE OUR POTENTIAL NEW STUDENT... TERRY HIGHLAND.
......
UM... SAY SOMETHING, TERRY.

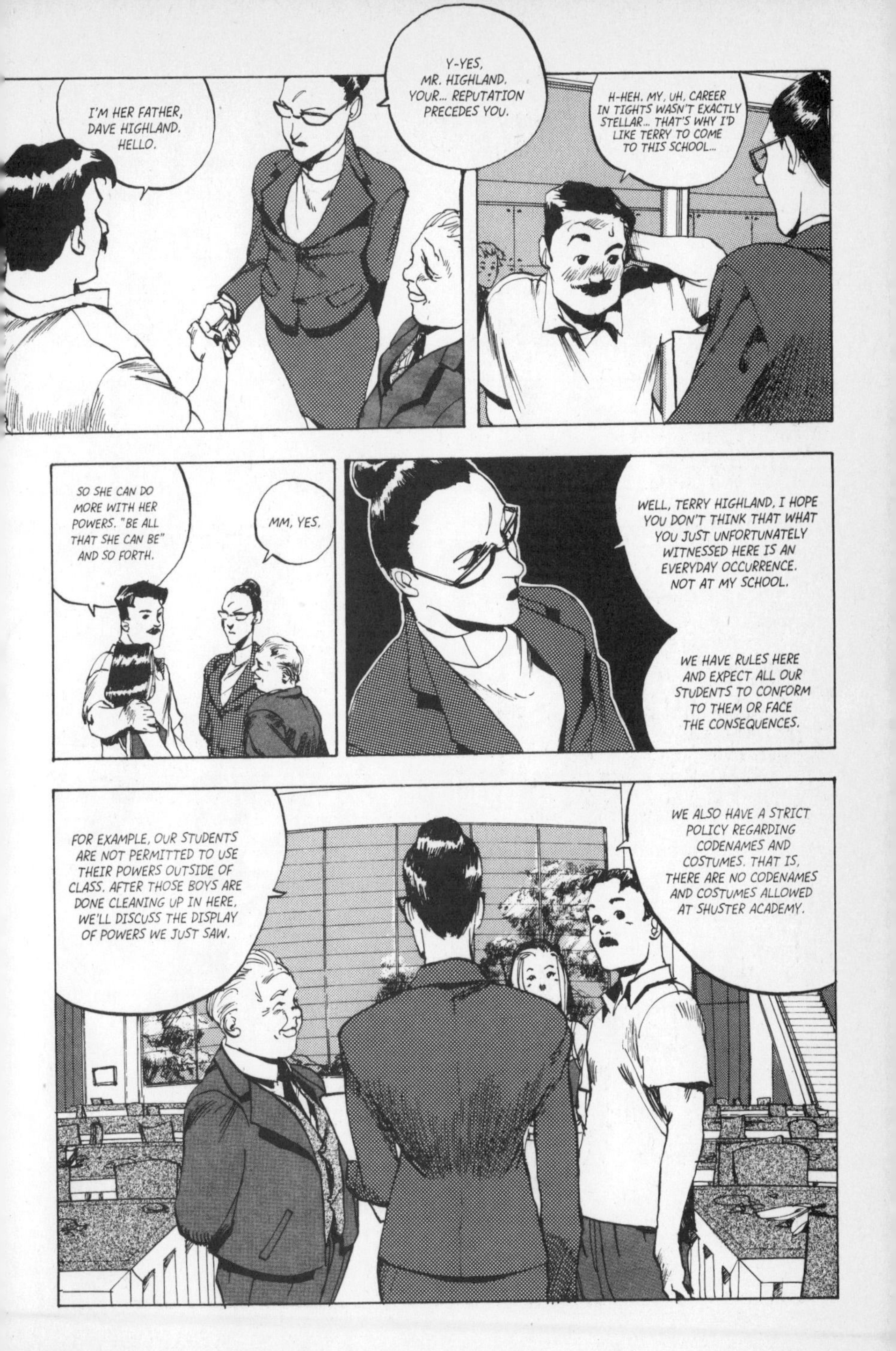
I'M HER FATHER, DAVE HIGHLAND. HELLO.
Y-YES, MR. HIGHLAND. YOUR... REPUTATION PRECEDES YOU.
H-HEH. MY, UH, CAREER IN TIGHTS WASN'T EXACTLY STELLAR... THAT'S WHY I'D LIKE TERRY TO COME TO THIS SCHOOL...
SO SHE CAN DO MORE WITH HER POWERS. "BE ALL THAT SHE CAN BE" AND SO FORTH.
MM, YES.
WELL, TERRY HIGHLAND, I HOPE YOU DON'T THINK THAT WHAT YOU JUST UNFORTUNATELY WITNESSED HERE IS AN EVERYDAY OCCURRENCE. NOT AT MY SCHOOL.
WE HAVE RULES HERE AND EXPECT ALL OUR STUDENTS TO CONFORM TO THEM OR FACE THE CONSEQUENCES.
FOR EXAMPLE, OUR STUDENTS ARE NOT PERMITTED TO USE THEIR POWERS OUTSIDE OF CLASS. AFTER THOSE BOYS ARE DONE CLEANING UP IN HERE, WE'LL DISCUSS THE DISPLAY OF POWERS WE JUST SAW.
WE ALSO HAVE A STRICT POLICY REGARDING CODENAMES AND COSTUMES. THAT IS, THERE ARE NO CODENAMES AND COSTUMES ALLOWED AT SHUSTER ACADEMY.

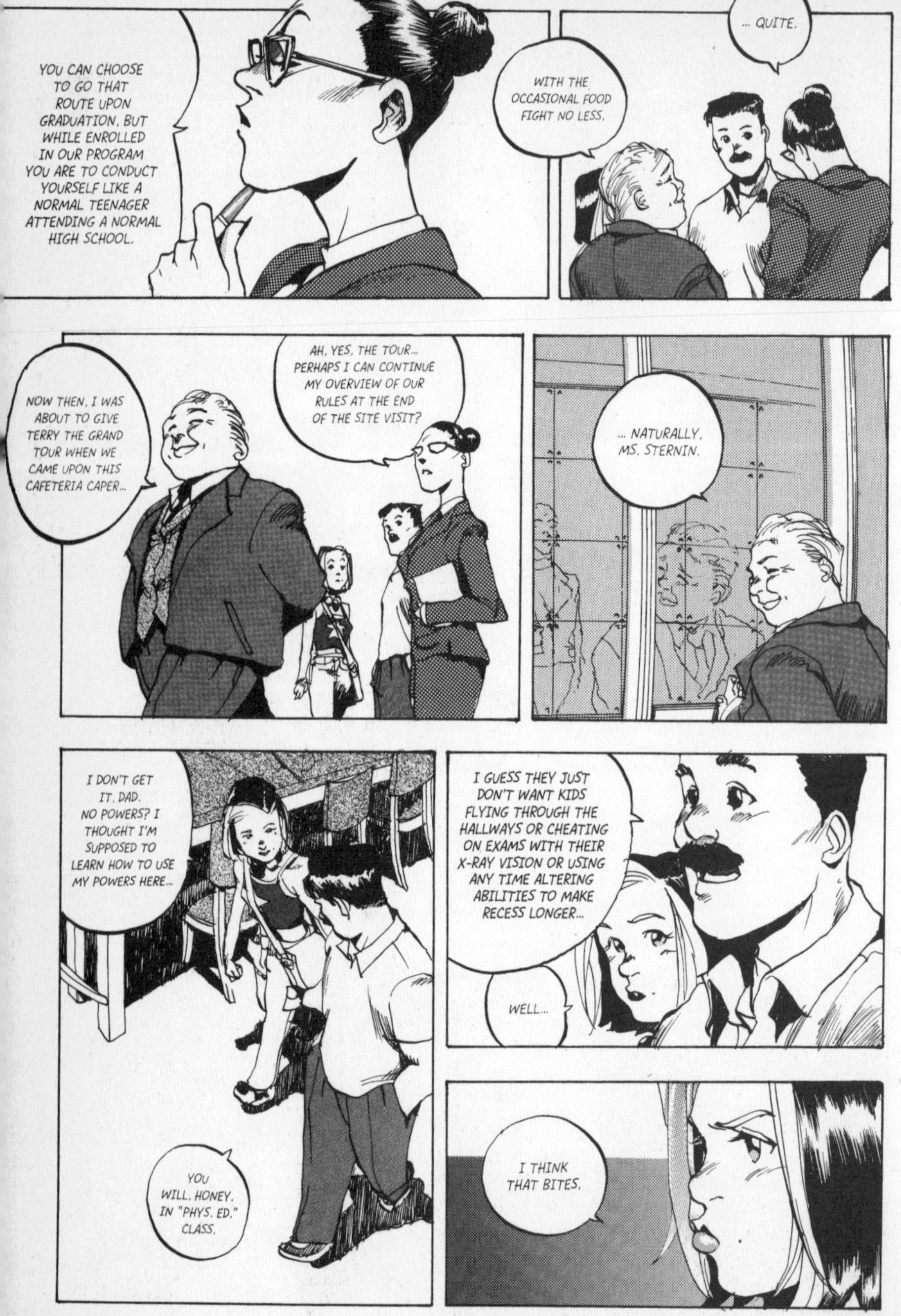
YOU CAN CHOOSE TO GO THAT ROUTE UPON GRADUATION, BUT WHILE ENROLLED IN OUR PROGRAM YOU ARE TO CONDUCT YOURSELF LIKE A NORMAL TEENAGER ATTENDING A NORMAL HIGH SCHOOL.
WITH THE OCCASIONAL FOOD FIGHT NO LESS.
... QUITE.
NOW THEN, I WAS ABOUT TO GIVE TERRY THE GRAND TOUR WHEN WE CAME UPON THIS CAFETERIA CAPER...
AH, YES, THE TOUR... PERHAPS I CAN CONTINUE MY OVERVIEW OF OUR RULES AT THE END OF THE SITE VISIT?
... NATURALLY, MS. STERNIN.
I DON'T GET IT, DAD. NO POWERS? I THOUGHT I'M SUPPOSED TO LEARN HOW TO USE MY POWERS HERE...
YOU WILL, HONEY. IN "PHYS. ED." CLASS.
I GUESS THEY JUST DON'T WANT KIDS FLYING THROUGH THE HALLWAYS OR CHEATING ON EXAMS WITH THEIR X-RAY VISION OR USING ANY TIME ALTERING ABILITIES TO MAKE RECESS LONGER...
WELL...
I THINK THAT BITES.

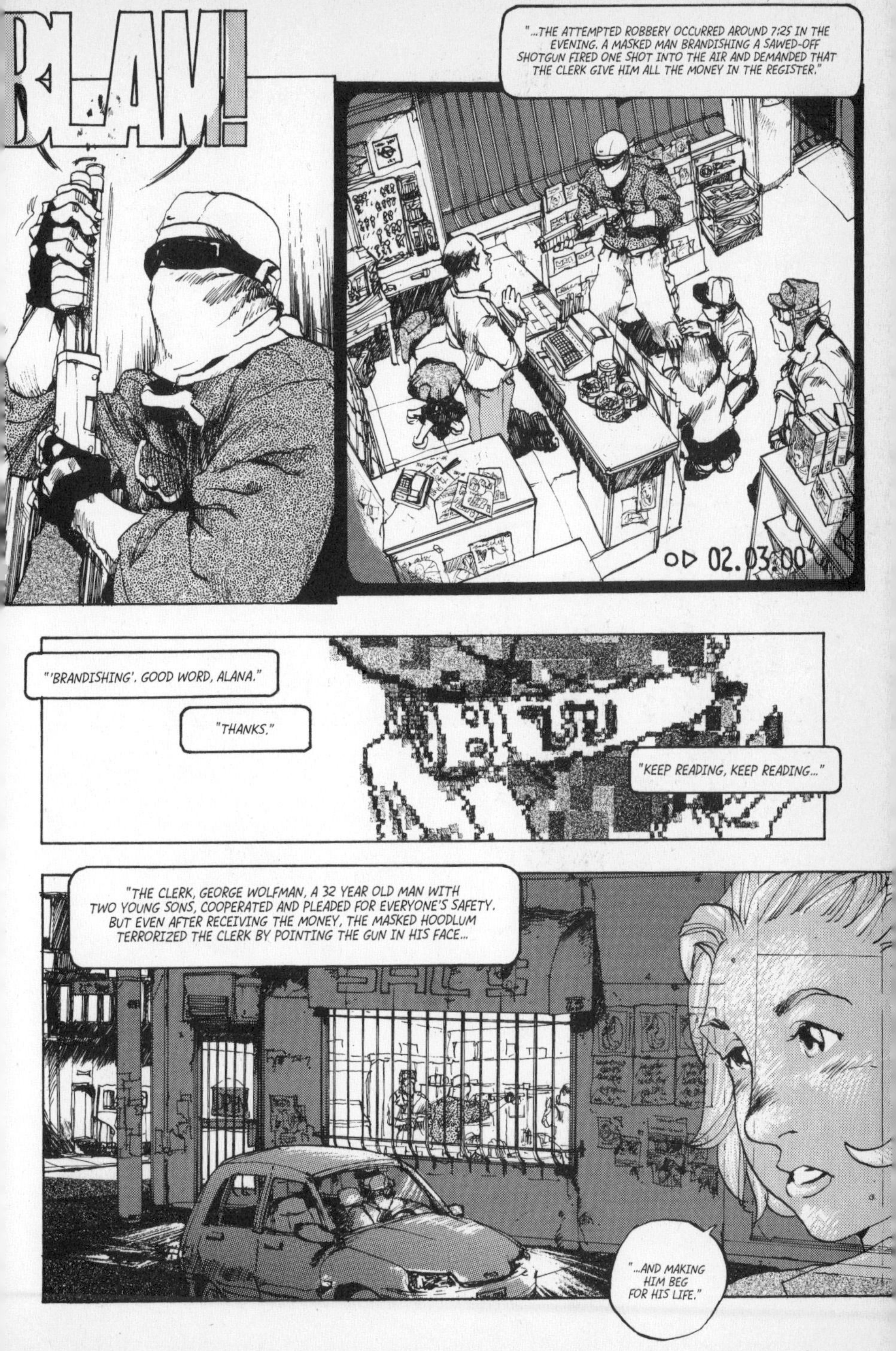
BLAM!
"...THE ATTEMPTED ROBBERY OCCURRED AROUND 7:25 IN THE EVENING. A MASKED MAN BRANDISHING A SAWED-OFF SHOTGUN FIRED ONE SHOT INTO THE AIR AND DEMANDED THAT THE CLERK GIVE HIM ALL THE MONEY IN THE REGISTER."
OD 02.03.00
"'BRANDISHING'. GOOD WORD, ALANA."
"THANKS."
"KEEP READING, KEEP READING..."
"THE CLERK, GEORGE WOLFMAN, A 32 YEAR OLD MAN WITH TWO YOUNG SONS, COOPERATED AND PLEADED FOR EVERYONE'S SAFETY. BUT EVEN AFTER RECEIVING THE MONEY, THE MASKED HOODLUM TERRORIZED THE CLERK BY POINTING THE GUN IN HIS FACE...
"...AND MAKING HIM BEG FOR HIS LIFE."

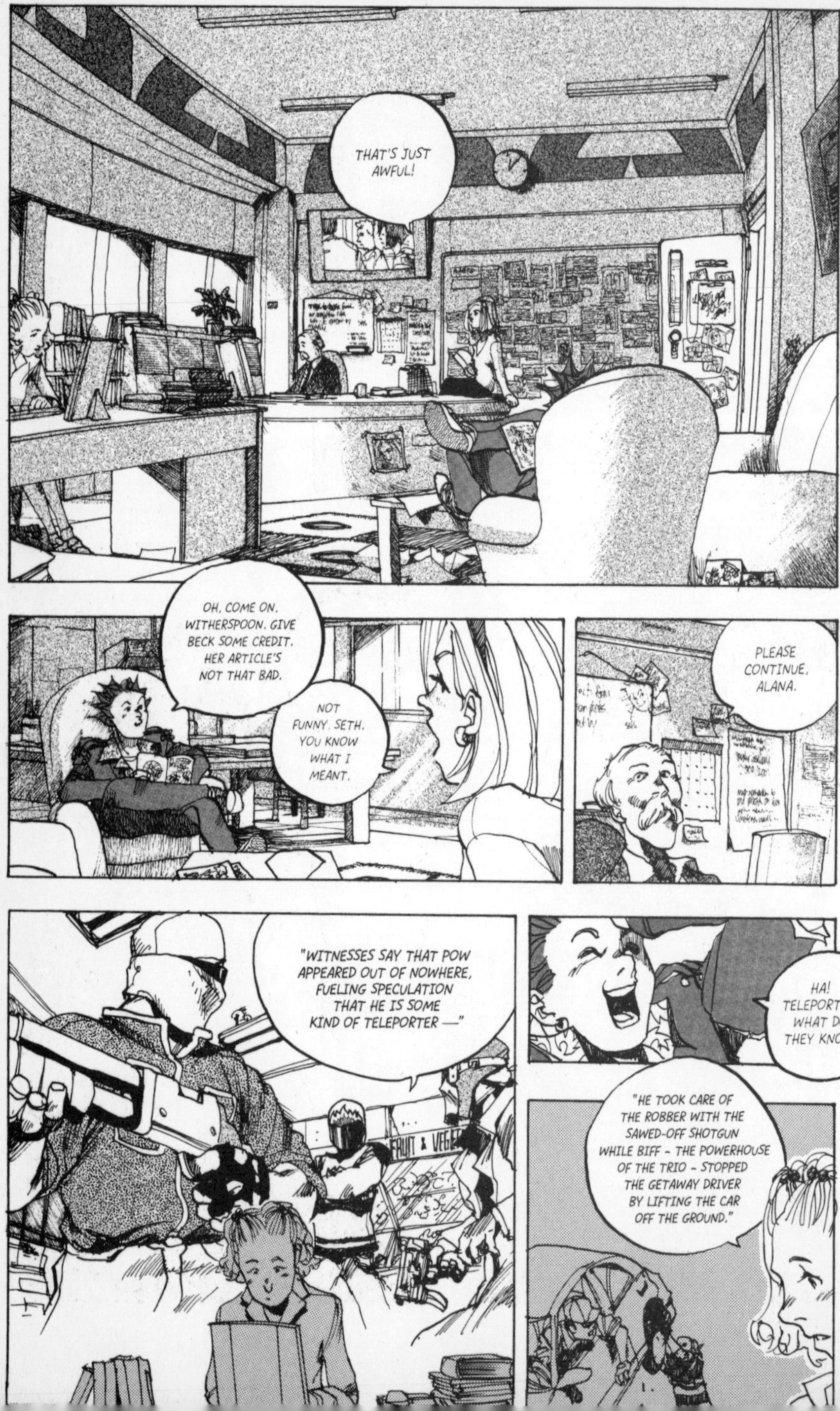
THAT'S JUST AWFUL!
OH, COME ON, WITHERSPOON. GIVE BECK SOME CREDIT. HER ARTICLE'S NOT THAT BAD.
NOT FUNNY, SETH. YOU KNOW WHAT I MEANT.
PLEASE CONTINUE, ALANA.
"WITNESSES SAY THAT POW APPEARED OUT OF NOWHERE, FUELING SPECULATION THAT HE IS SOME KIND OF TELEPORTER —"
HA! TELEPORTER! WHAT DO THEY KNOW?
"HE TOOK CARE OF THE ROBBER WITH THE SAWED-OFF SHOTGUN WHILE BIFF - THE POWERHOUSE OF THE TRIO - STOPPED THE GETAWAY DRIVER BY LIFTING THE CAR OFF THE GROUND."
FRUIT & VEGE

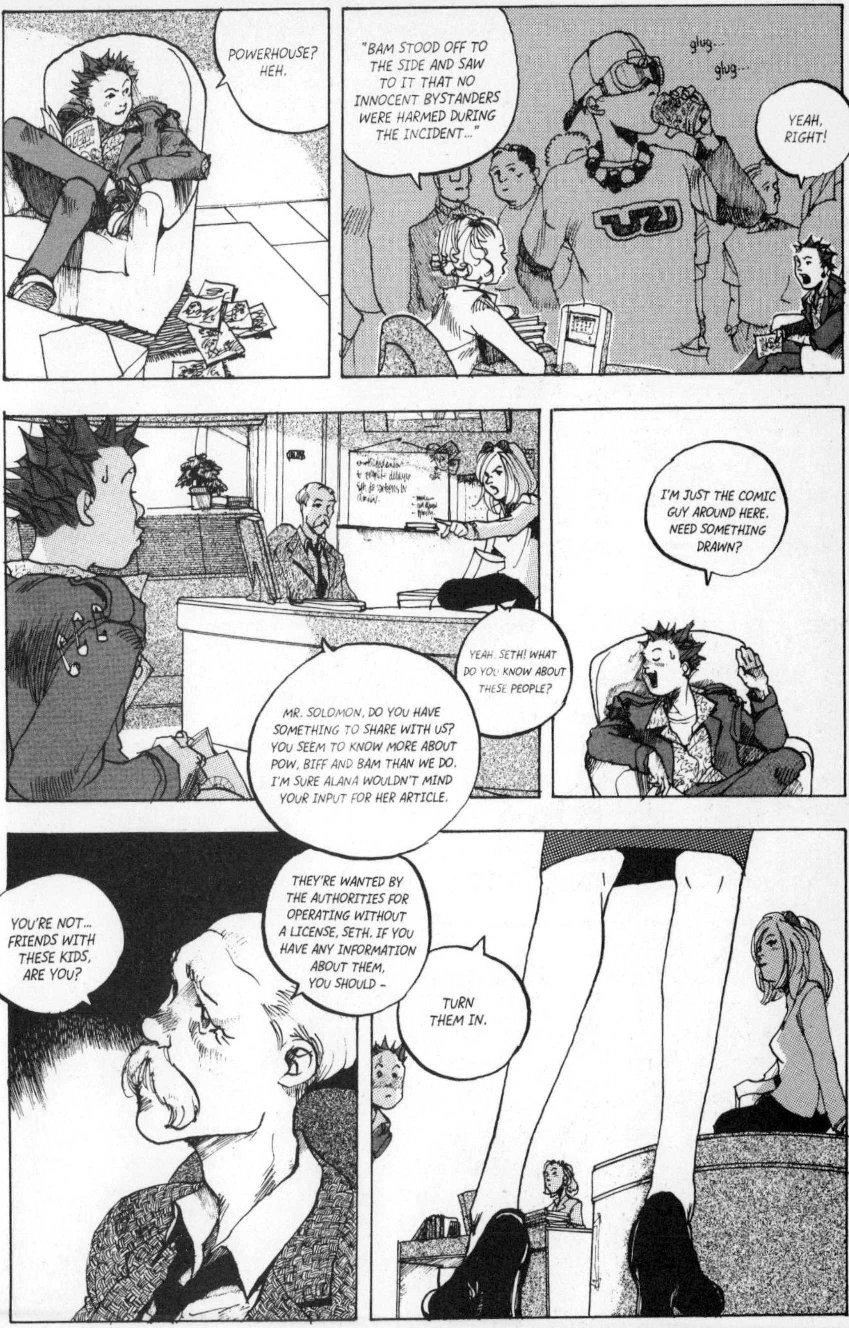
POWERHOUSE? HEH.
"BAM STOOD OFF TO THE SIDE AND SAW TO IT THAT NO INNOCENT BYSTANDERS WERE HARMED DURING THE INCIDENT..."
glug...
glug...
YEAH, RIGHT!
MR. SOLOMON, DO YOU HAVE SOMETHING TO SHARE WITH US? YOU SEEM TO KNOW MORE ABOUT POW, BIFF AND BAM THAN WE DO. I'M SURE ALANA WOULDN'T MIND YOUR INPUT FOR HER ARTICLE.
YEAH, SETH! WHAT DO YOU KNOW ABOUT THESE PEOPLE?
I'M JUST THE COMIC GUY AROUND HERE. NEED SOMETHING DRAWN?
YOU'RE NOT... FRIENDS WITH THESE KIDS, ARE YOU?
THEY'RE WANTED BY THE AUTHORITIES FOR OPERATING WITHOUT A LICENSE, SETH. IF YOU HAVE ANY INFORMATION ABOUT THEM, YOU SHOULD -
TURN THEM IN.

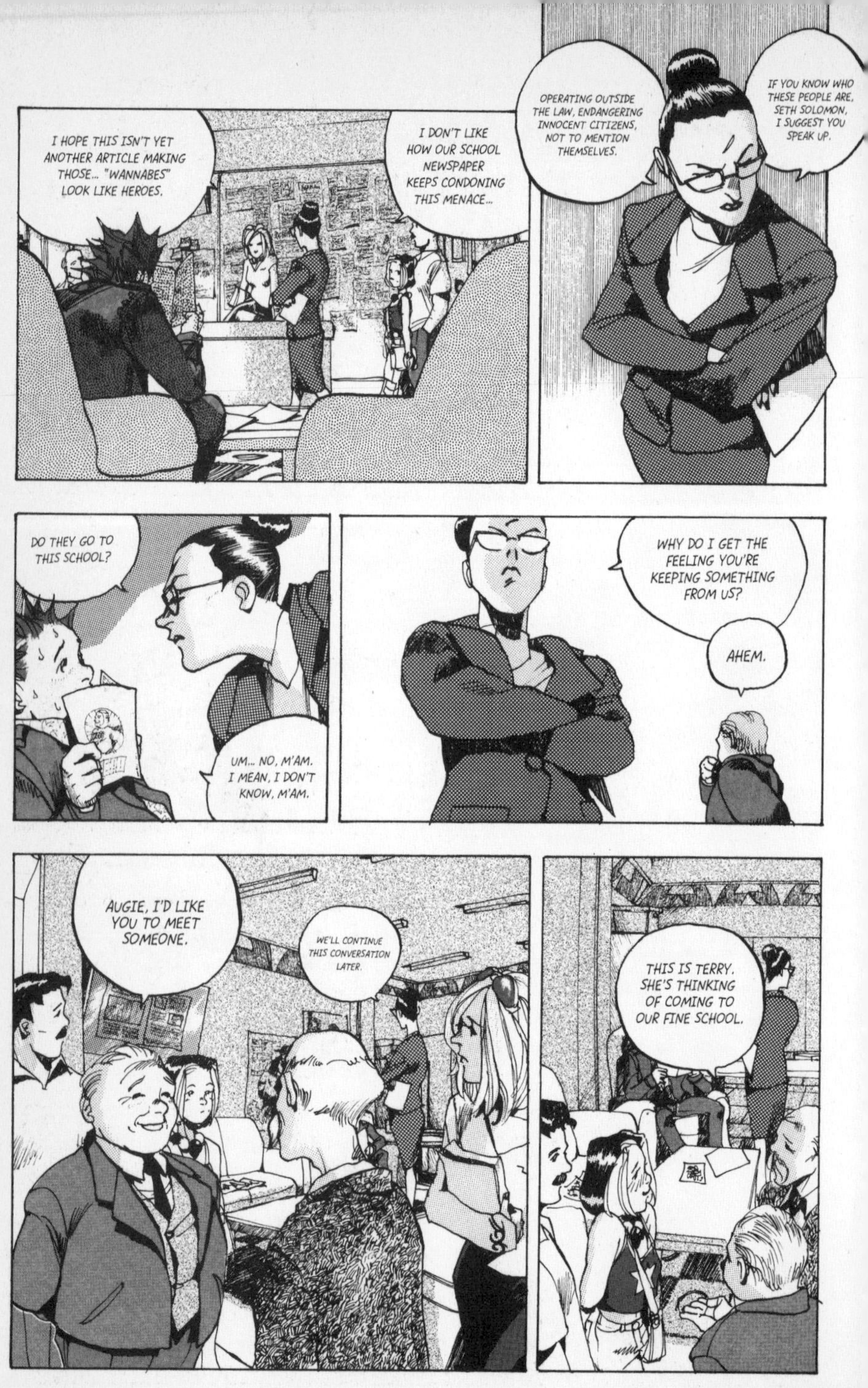
I HOPE THIS ISN'T YET ANOTHER ARTICLE MAKING THOSE... "WANNABES" LOOK LIKE HEROES.
I DON'T LIKE HOW OUR SCHOOL NEWSPAPER KEEPS CONDONING THIS MENACE...
OPERATING OUTSIDE THE LAW, ENDANGERING INNOCENT CITIZENS, NOT TO MENTION THEMSELVES.
IF YOU KNOW WHO THESE PEOPLE ARE, SETH SOLOMON, I SUGGEST YOU SPEAK UP.
DO THEY GO TO THIS SCHOOL?
UM... NO, M'AM. I MEAN, I DON'T KNOW, M'AM.
WHY DO I GET THE FEELING YOU'RE KEEPING SOMETHING FROM US?
AHEM.
AUGIE, I'D LIKE YOU TO MEET SOMEONE.
WE'LL CONTINUE THIS CONVERSATION LATER.
THIS IS TERRY. SHE'S THINKING OF COMING TO OUR FINE SCHOOL.

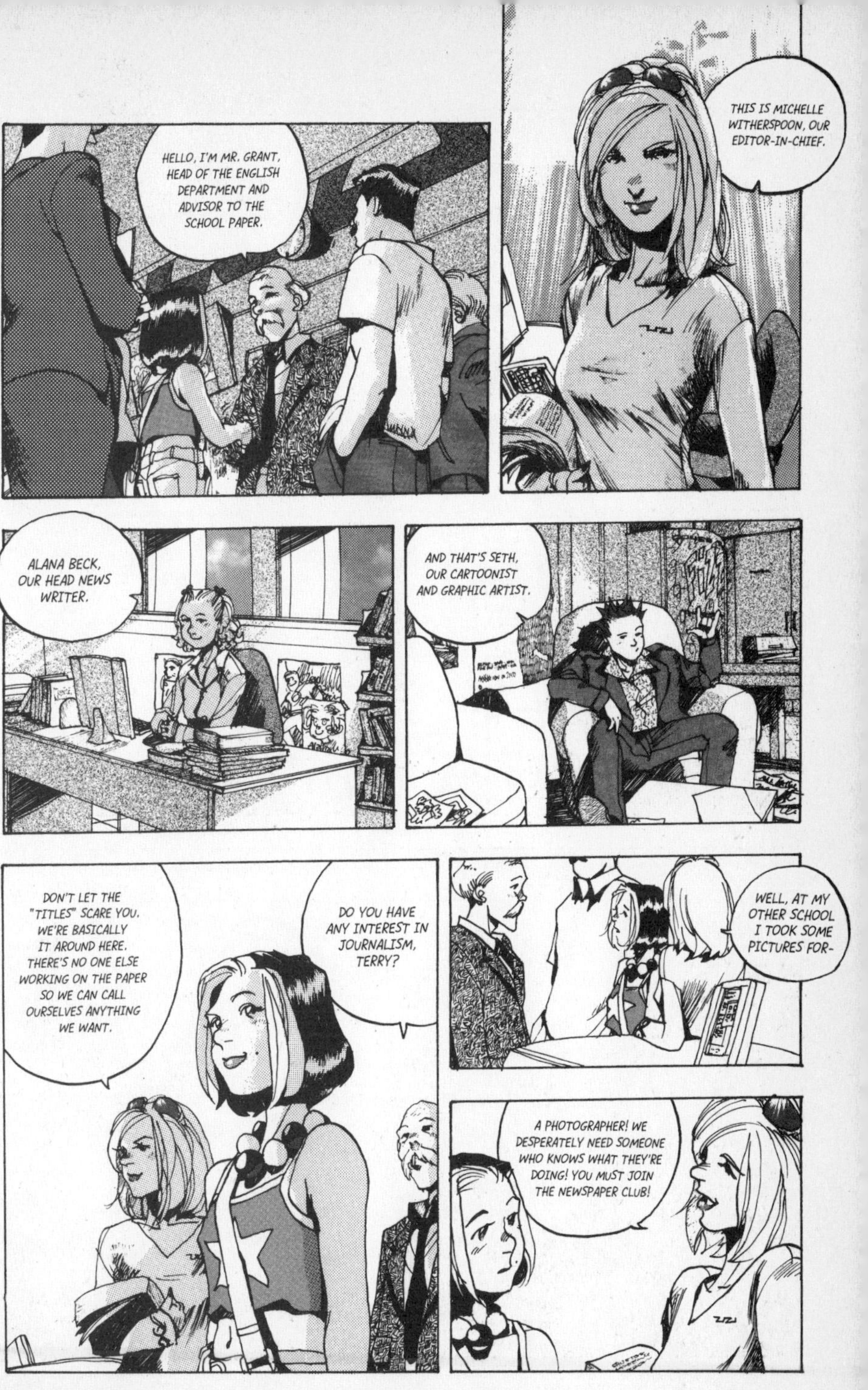
HELLO, I'M MR. GRANT, HEAD OF THE ENGLISH DEPARTMENT AND ADVISOR TO THE SCHOOL PAPER.
THIS IS MICHELLE WITHERSPOON, OUR EDITOR-IN-CHIEF.
ALANA BECK, OUR HEAD NEWS WRITER.
AND THAT'S SETH, OUR CARTOONIST AND GRAPHIC ARTIST.
DON'T LET THE "TITLES" SCARE YOU. WE'RE BASICALLY IT AROUND HERE. THERE'S NO ONE ELSE WORKING ON THE PAPER SO WE CAN CALL OURSELVES ANYTHING WE WANT.
DO YOU HAVE ANY INTEREST IN JOURNALISM, TERRY?
WELL, AT MY OTHER SCHOOL I TOOK SOME PICTURES FOR-
A PHOTOGRAPHER! WE DESPERATELY NEED SOMEONE WHO KNOWS WHAT THEY'RE DOING! YOU MUST JOIN THE NEWSPAPER CLUB!

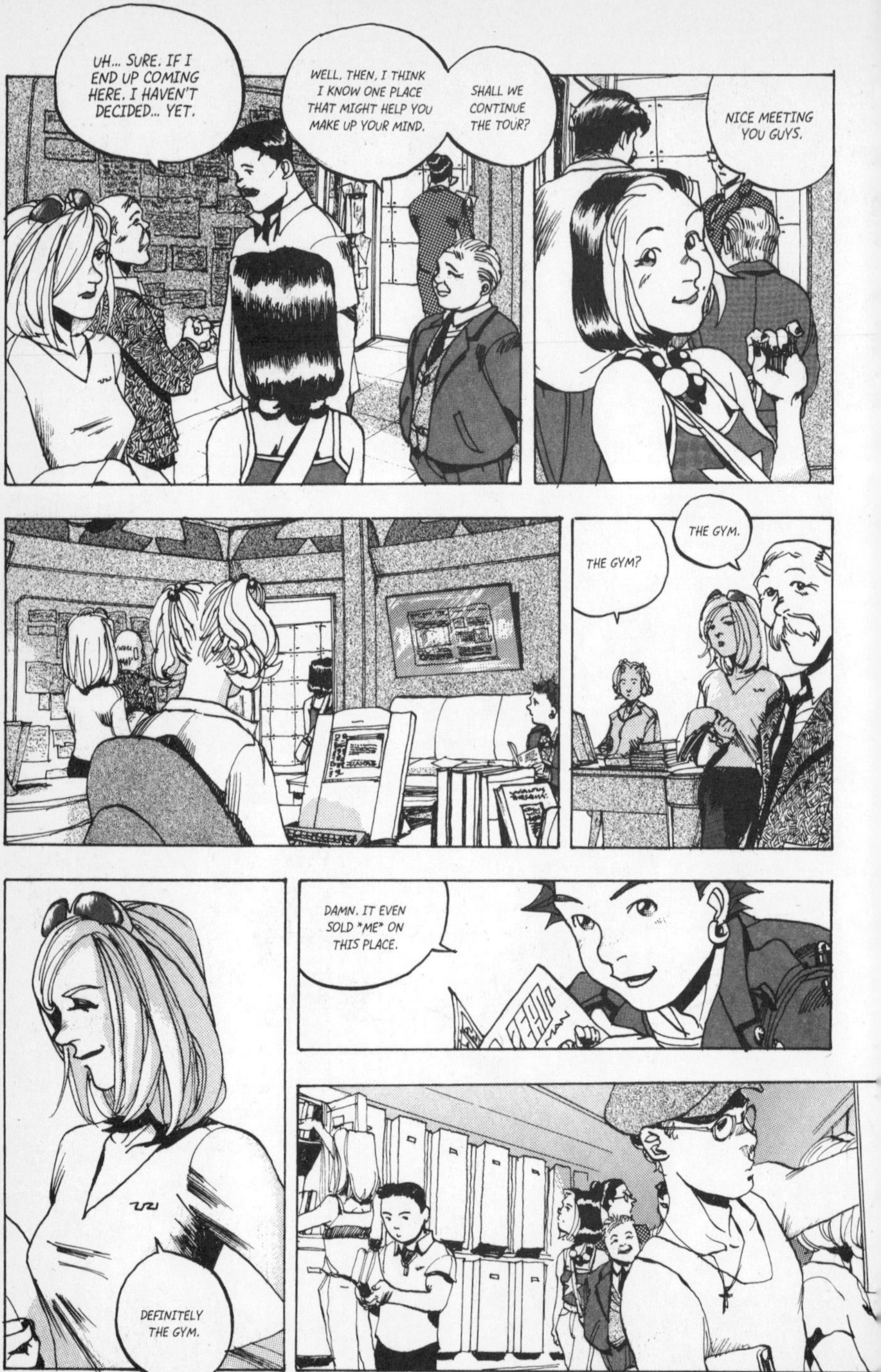
UH... SURE. IF I END UP COMING HERE. I HAVEN'T DECIDED... YET.
WELL, THEN, I THINK I KNOW ONE PLACE THAT MIGHT HELP YOU MAKE UP YOUR MIND.
SHALL WE CONTINUE THE TOUR?
NICE MEETING YOU GUYS.
THE GYM?
THE GYM.
DAMN. IT EVEN SOLD *ME* ON THIS PLACE.
DEFINITELY THE GYM.

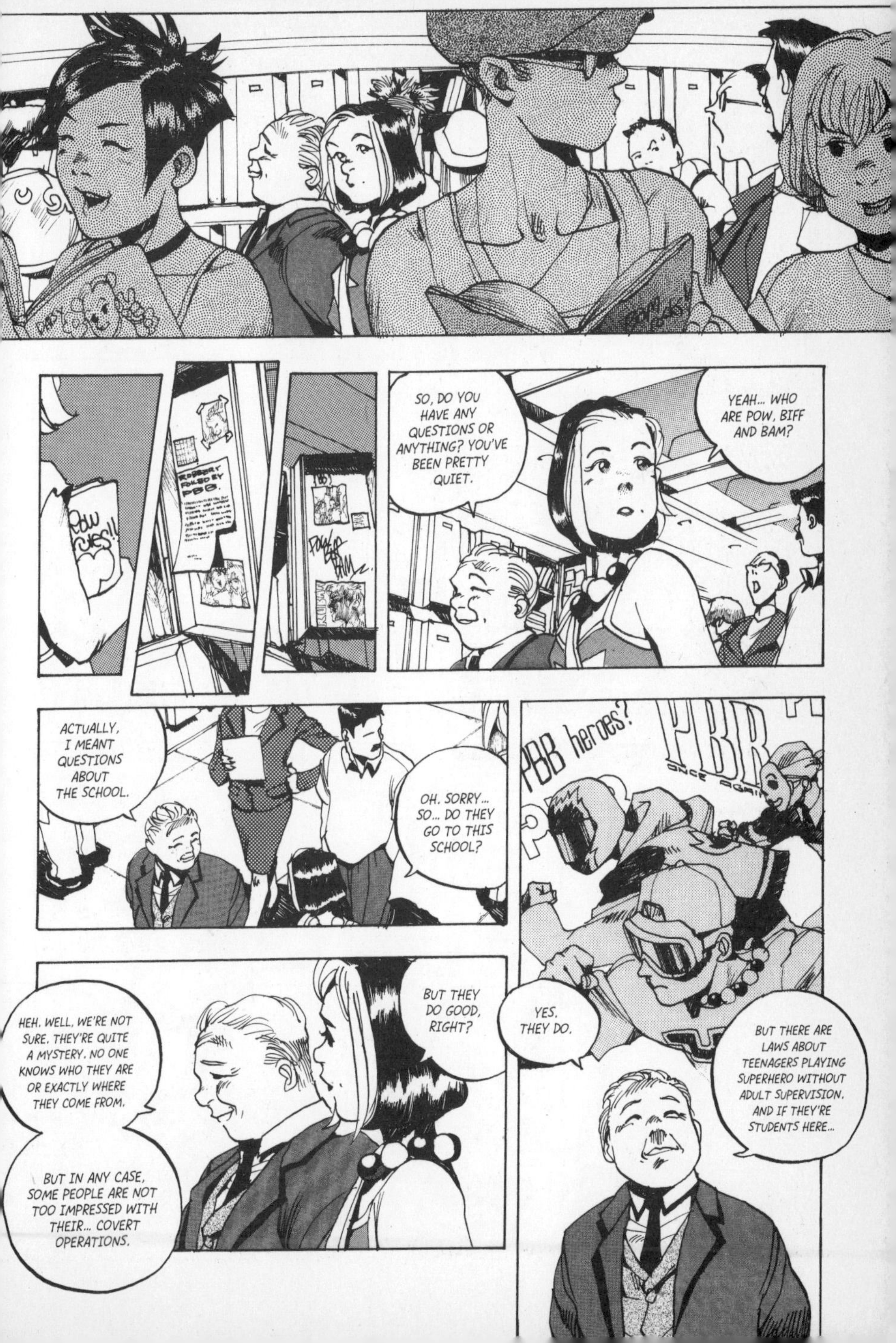

POW rules!!
ROBBERY FOILED BY PBB.
POW BIFF BAM
SO, DO YOU HAVE ANY QUESTIONS OR ANYTHING? YOU'VE BEEN PRETTY QUIET.
YEAH... WHO ARE POW, BIFF AND BAM?
ACTUALLY, I MEANT QUESTIONS ABOUT THE SCHOOL.
OH. SORRY... SO... DO THEY GO TO THIS SCHOOL?
PBB heroes?
PBB
HEH. WELL, WE'RE NOT SURE. THEY'RE QUITE A MYSTERY. NO ONE KNOWS WHO THEY ARE OR EXACTLY WHERE THEY COME FROM.
BUT IN ANY CASE, SOME PEOPLE ARE NOT TOO IMPRESSED WITH THEIR... COVERT OPERATIONS.
BUT THEY DO GOOD, RIGHT?
YES. THEY DO.
BUT THERE ARE LAWS ABOUT TEENAGERS PLAYING SUPERHERO WITHOUT ADULT SUPERVISION. AND IF THEY'RE STUDENTS HERE...

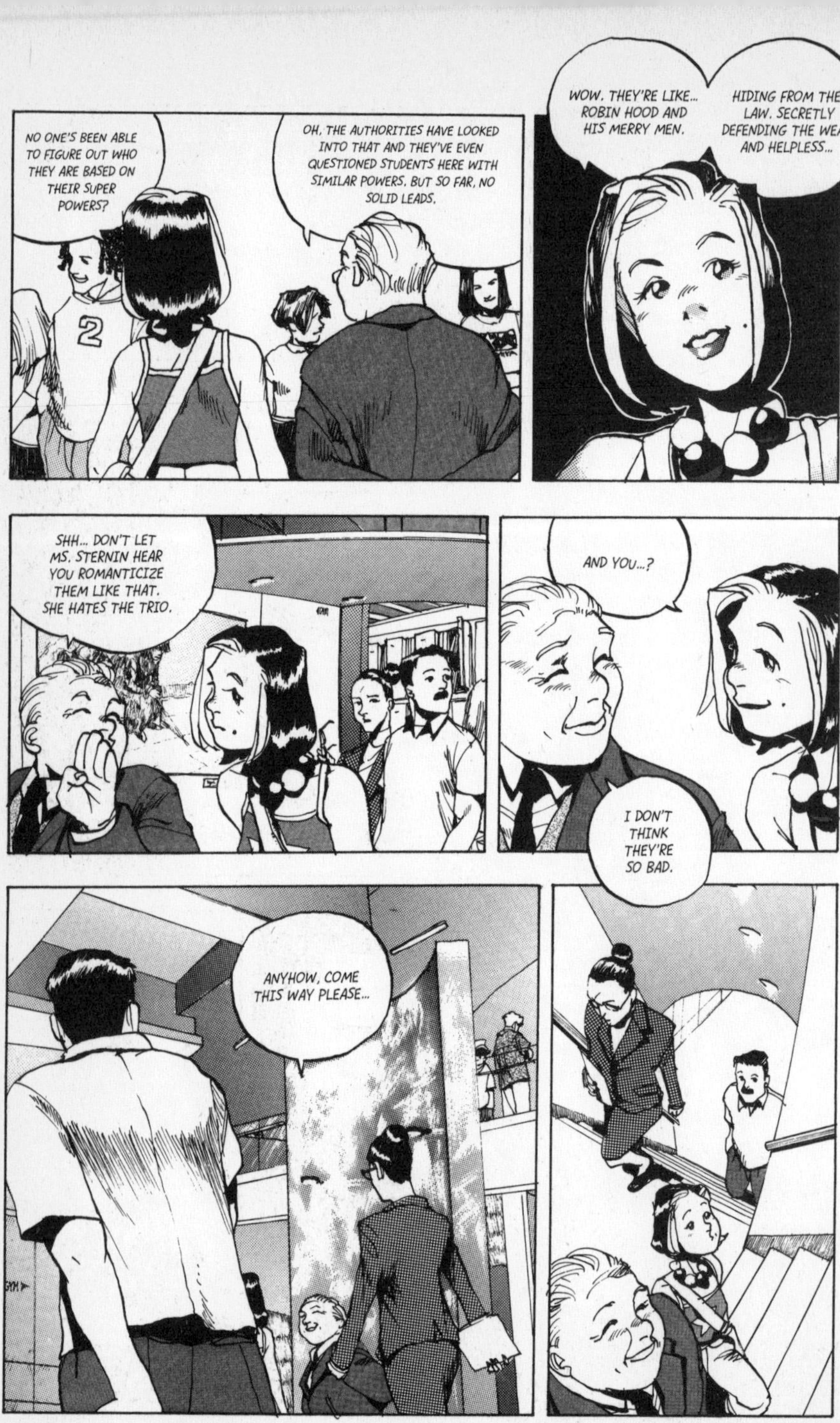
NO ONE'S BEEN ABLE TO FIGURE OUT WHO THEY ARE BASED ON THEIR SUPER POWERS?
OH, THE AUTHORITIES HAVE LOOKED INTO THAT AND THEY'VE EVEN QUESTIONED STUDENTS HERE WITH SIMILAR POWERS. BUT SO FAR, NO SOLID LEADS.
WOW. THEY'RE LIKE... ROBIN HOOD AND HIS MERRY MEN.
HIDING FROM THE LAW. SECRETLY DEFENDING THE WEAK AND HELPLESS...
SHH... DON'T LET MS. STERNIN HEAR YOU ROMANTICIZE THEM LIKE THAT. SHE HATES THE TRIO.
AND YOU...?
I DON'T THINK THEY'RE SO BAD.
ANYHOW, COME THIS WAY PLEASE...
GYM

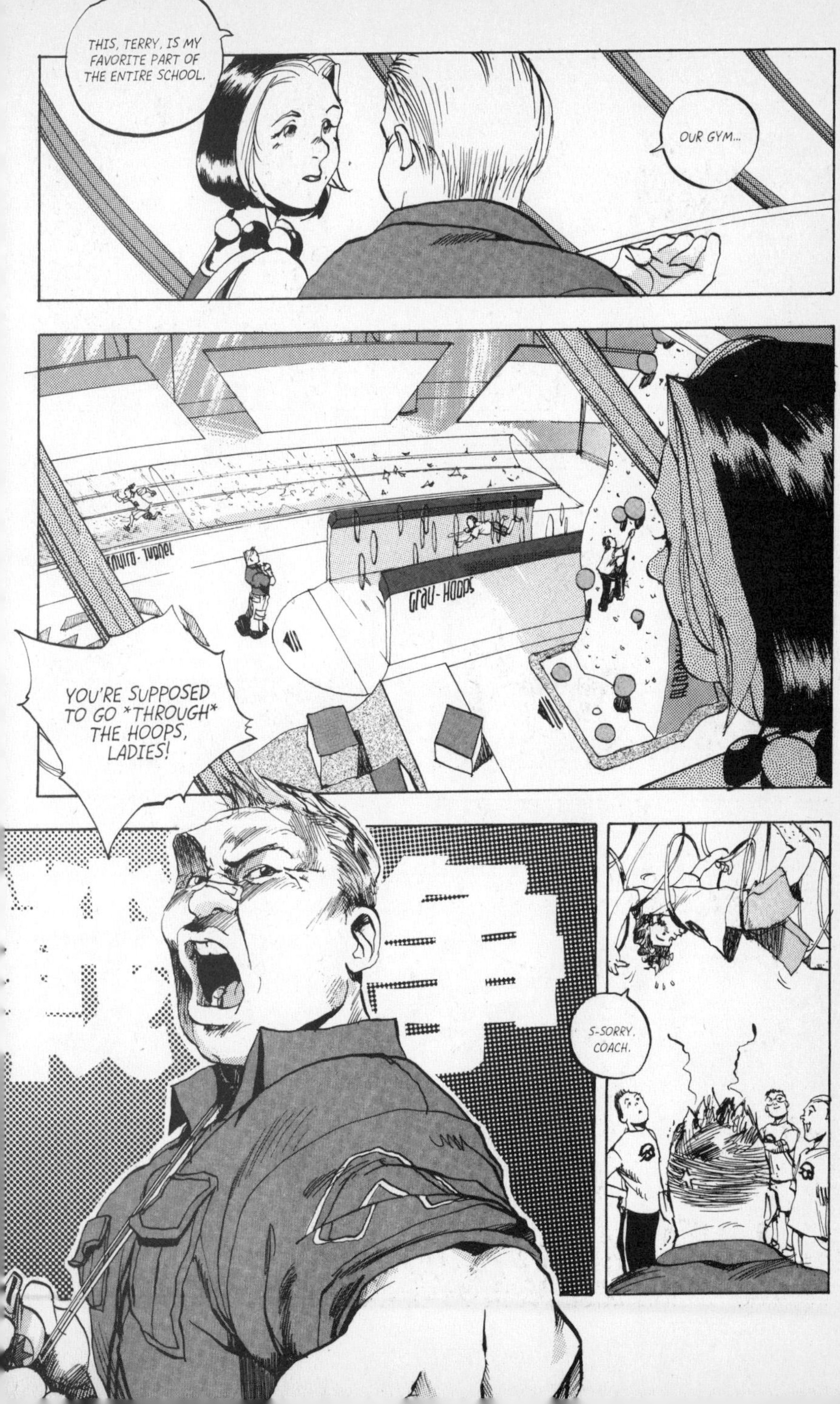
THIS, TERRY, IS MY FAVORITE PART OF THE ENTIRE SCHOOL.
OUR GYM...
GRAV-TUNNEL
GRAV-HOOPS
YOU'RE SUPPOSED TO GO *THROUGH* THE HOOPS, LADIES!
S-SORRY, COACH.

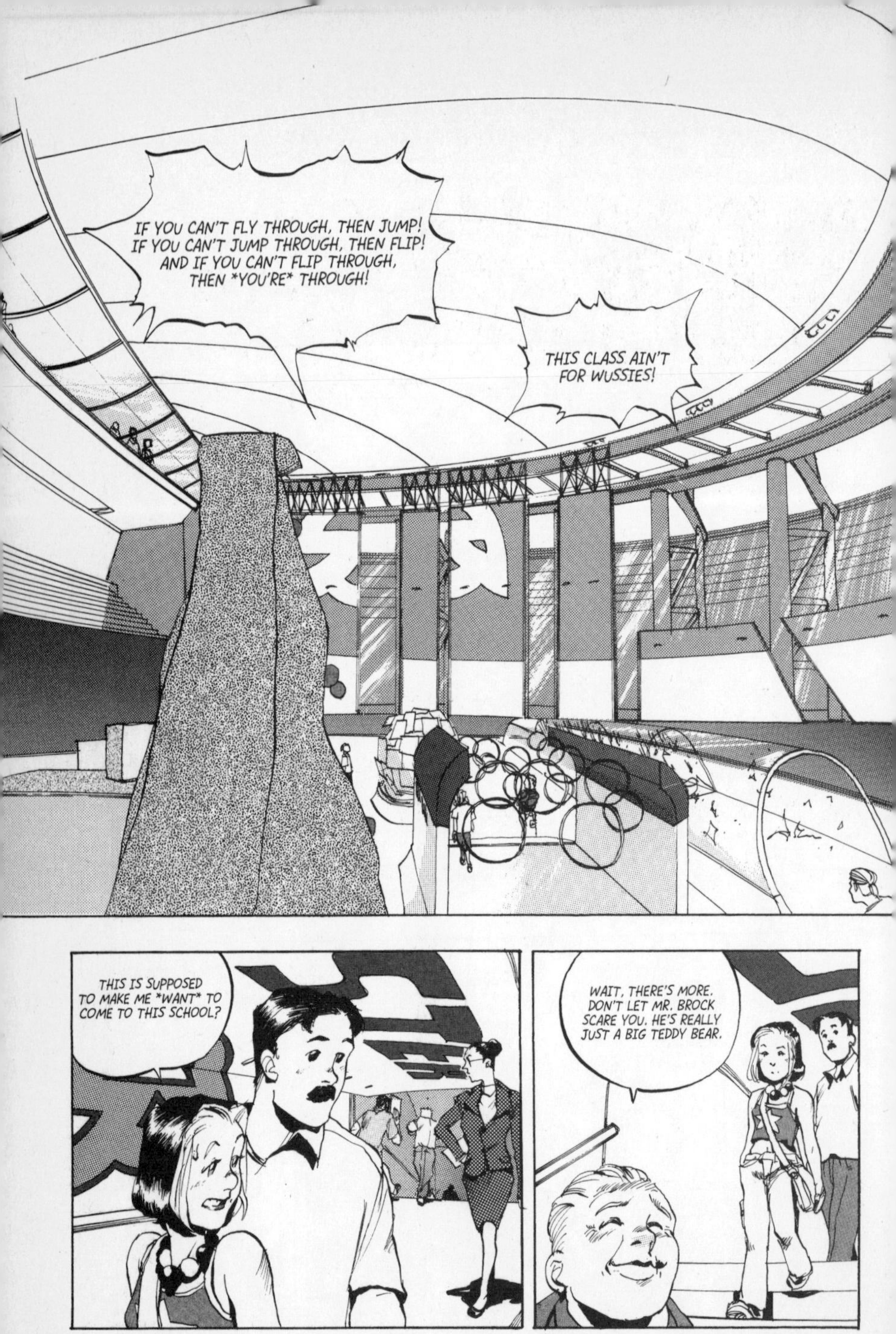
IF YOU CAN'T FLY THROUGH, THEN JUMP! IF YOU CAN'T JUMP THROUGH, THEN FLIP! AND IF YOU CAN'T FLIP THROUGH, THEN *YOU'RE* THROUGH!
THIS CLASS AIN'T FOR WUSSIES!
THIS IS SUPPOSED TO MAKE ME *WANT* TO COME TO THIS SCHOOL?
WAIT, THERE'S MORE. DON'T LET MR. BROCK SCARE YOU. HE'S REALLY JUST A BIG TEDDY BEAR.

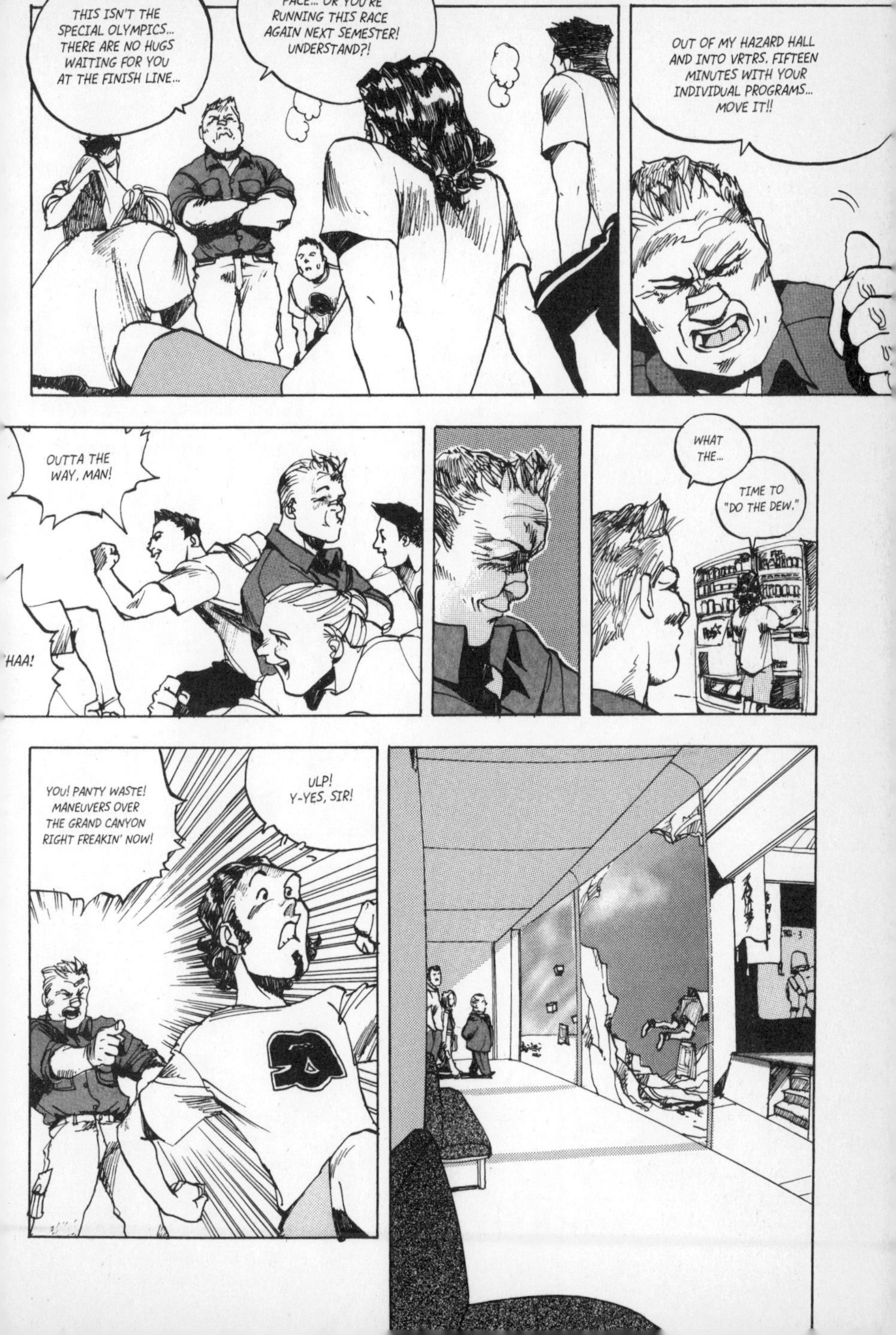
THIS ISN'T THE SPECIAL OLYMPICS... THERE ARE NO HUGS WAITING FOR YOU AT THE FINISH LINE...
YOU MAMA'S BOYS BETTER PICK UP THE PACE... OR YOU'RE RUNNING THIS RACE AGAIN NEXT SEMESTER! UNDERSTAND?!
OUT OF MY HAZARD HALL AND INTO VRTRS. FIFTEEN MINUTES WITH YOUR INDIVIDUAL PROGRAMS... MOVE IT!!
OUTTA THE WAY, MAN!
HAA!
WHAT THE...
TIME TO "DO THE DEW."
YOU! PANTY WASTE! MANEUVERS OVER THE GRAND CANYON RIGHT FREAKIN' NOW!
ULP! Y-YES, SIR!

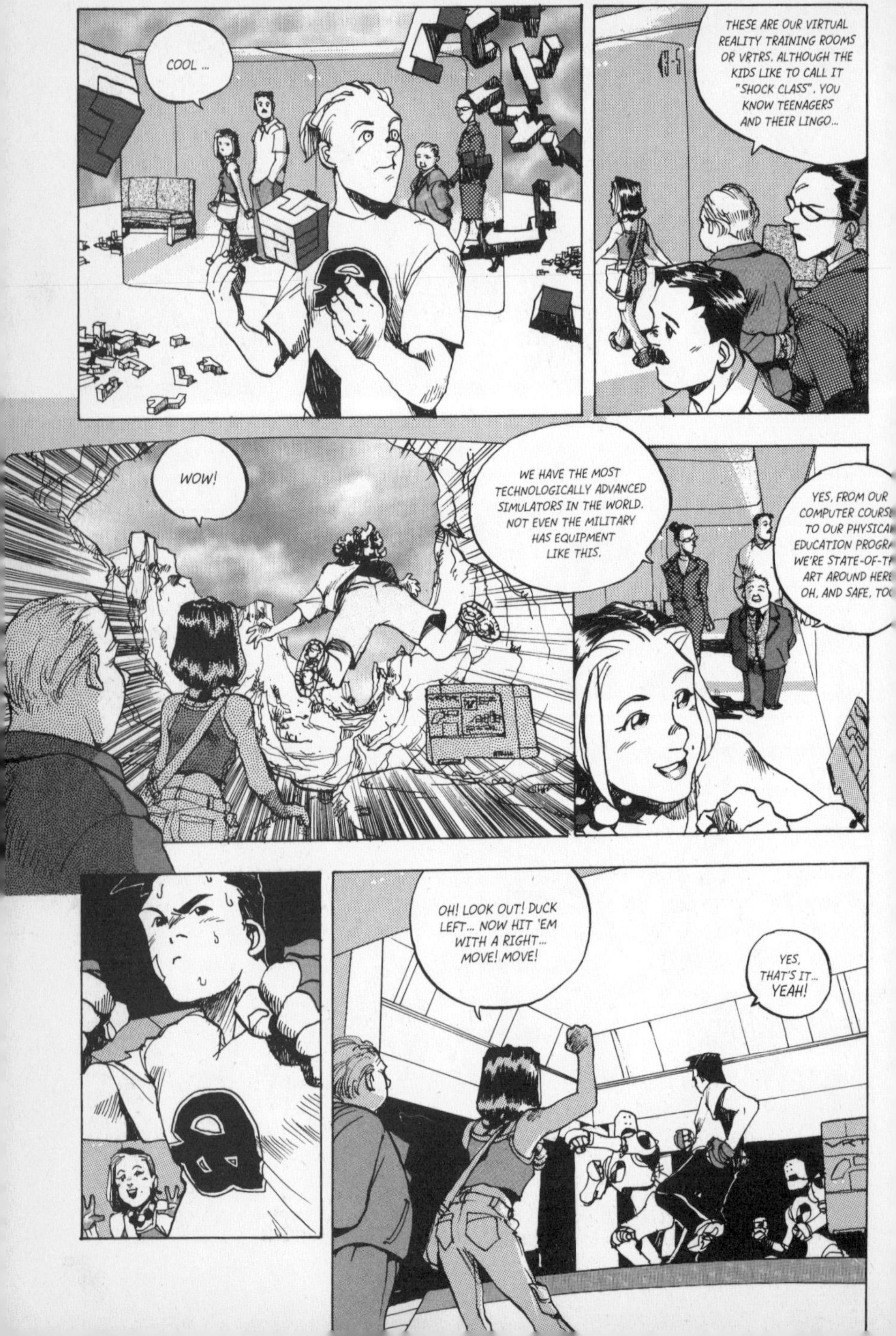
COOL ...
THESE ARE OUR VIRTUAL REALITY TRAINING ROOMS OR VRTRS. ALTHOUGH THE KIDS LIKE TO CALL IT "SHOCK CLASS". YOU KNOW TEENAGERS AND THEIR LINGO...
WOW!
WE HAVE THE MOST TECHNOLOGICALLY ADVANCED SIMULATORS IN THE WORLD. NOT EVEN THE MILITARY HAS EQUIPMENT LIKE THIS.
YES, FROM OUR COMPUTER COURS TO OUR PHYSICA EDUCATION PROGRA WE'RE STATE-OF-T ART AROUND HERE OH, AND SAFE, TO
OH! LOOK OUT! DUCK LEFT... NOW HIT 'EM WITH A RIGHT... MOVE! MOVE!
YES, THAT'S IT... YEAH!

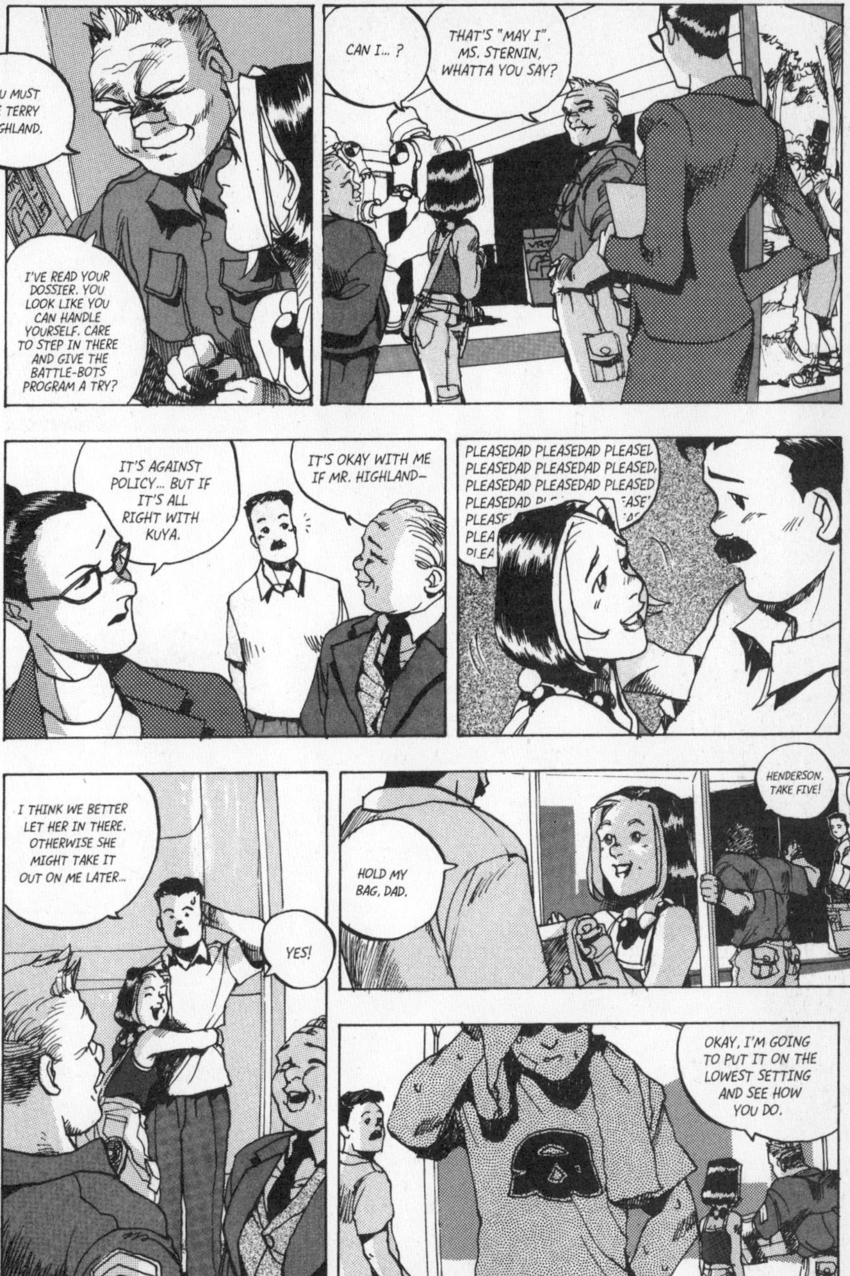

YOU MUST BE TERRY HIGHLAND.
I'VE READ YOUR DOSSIER. YOU LOOK LIKE YOU CAN HANDLE YOURSELF. CARE TO STEP IN THERE AND GIVE THE BATTLE-BOTS PROGRAM A TRY?
CAN I... ?
THAT'S "MAY I". MS. STERNIN, WHATTA YOU SAY?
IT'S AGAINST POLICY... BUT IF IT'S ALL RIGHT WITH KUYA.
IT'S OKAY WITH ME IF MR. HIGHLAND–
PLEASEDAD PLEASEDAD PLEASEL
PLEASEDAD PLEASEDAD PLEASED,
PLEASEDAD PLEASEDAD PLEASED
I THINK WE BETTER LET HER IN THERE. OTHERWISE SHE MIGHT TAKE IT OUT ON ME LATER...
YES!
HOLD MY BAG, DAD.
HENDERSON, TAKE FIVE!
SURE, MR. B.
OKAY, I'M GOING TO PUT IT ON THE LOWEST SETTING AND SEE HOW YOU DO.

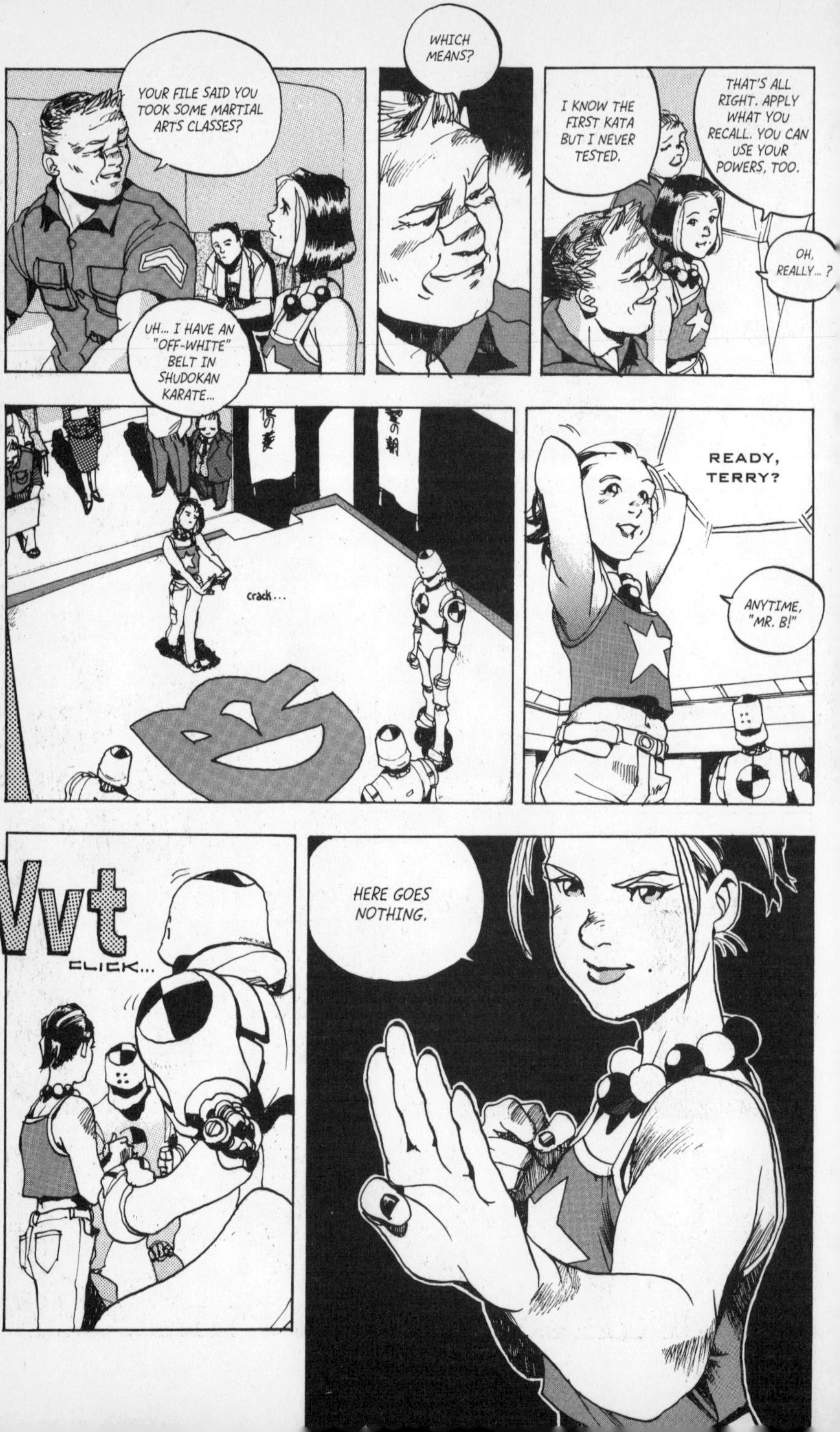
YOUR FILE SAID YOU TOOK SOME MARTIAL ARTS CLASSES?
UH... I HAVE AN "OFF-WHITE" BELT IN SHUDOKAN KARATE...
WHICH MEANS?
I KNOW THE FIRST KATA BUT I NEVER TESTED.
THAT'S ALL RIGHT. APPLY WHAT YOU RECALL. YOU CAN USE YOUR POWERS, TOO.
OH, REALLY... ?
crack...
READY, TERRY?
ANYTIME, "MR. B!"
Vvt
CLICK...
HERE GOES NOTHING.

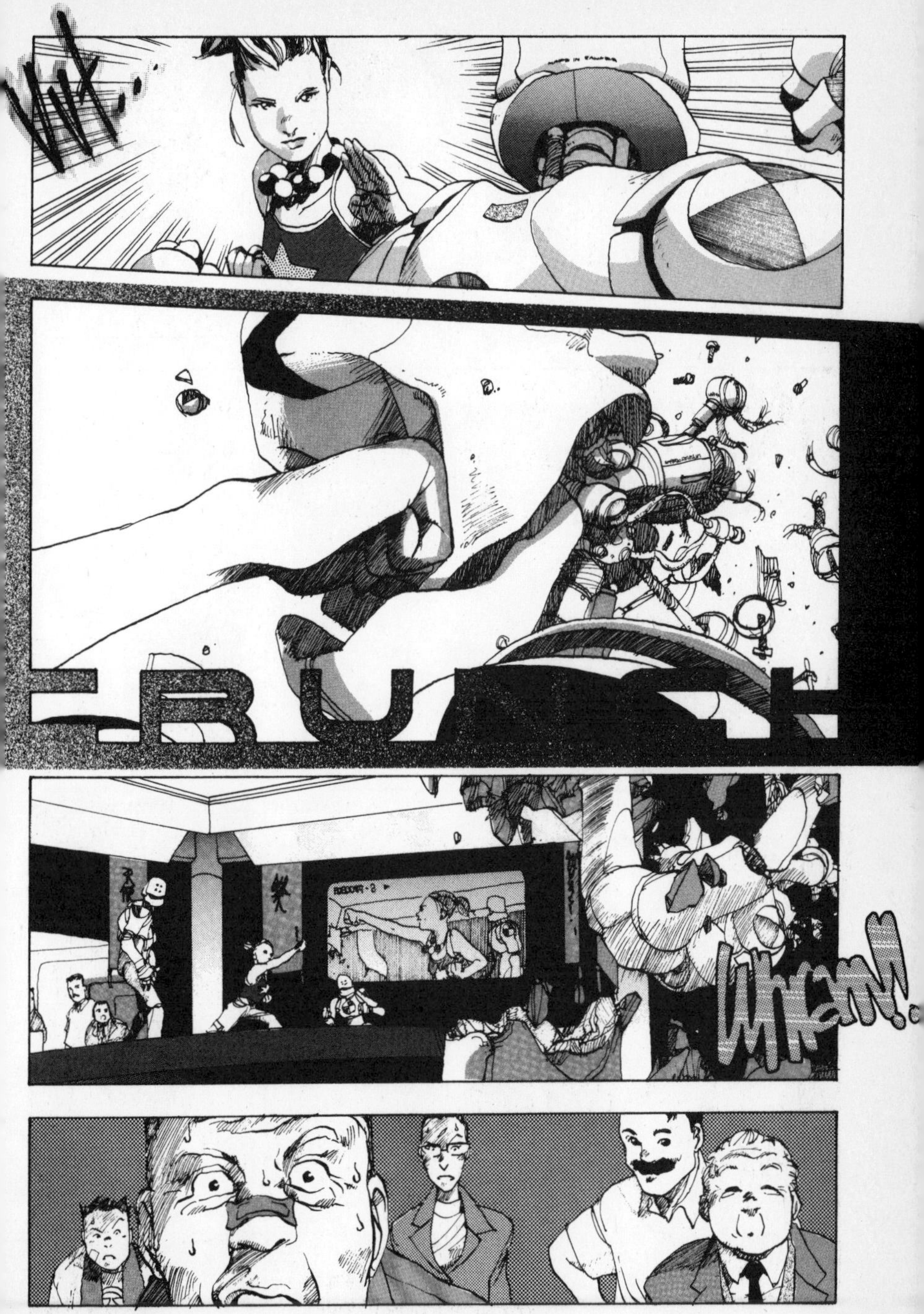
Wham!!

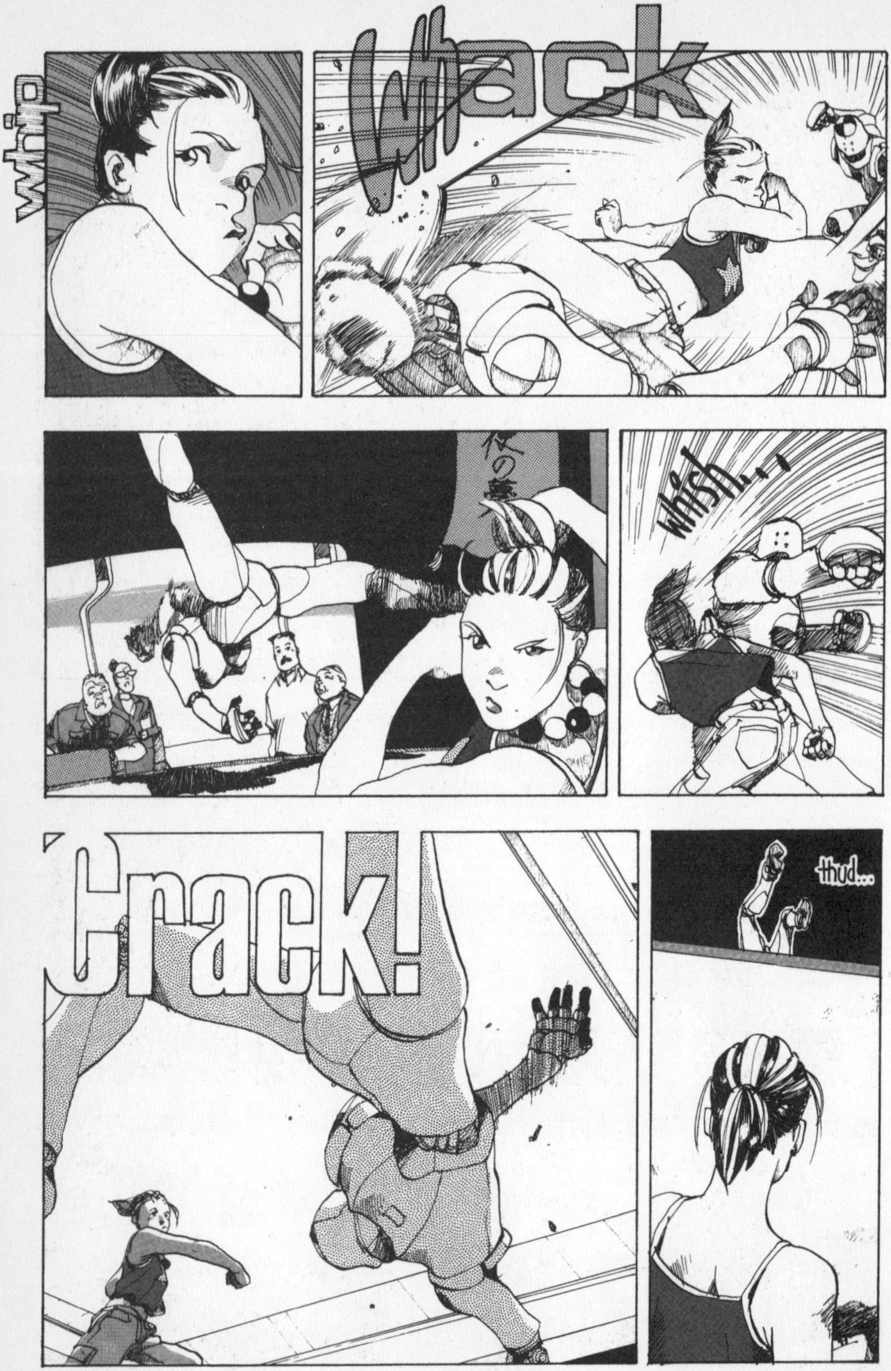
whip
Whack
whish...
Crack!
thud...

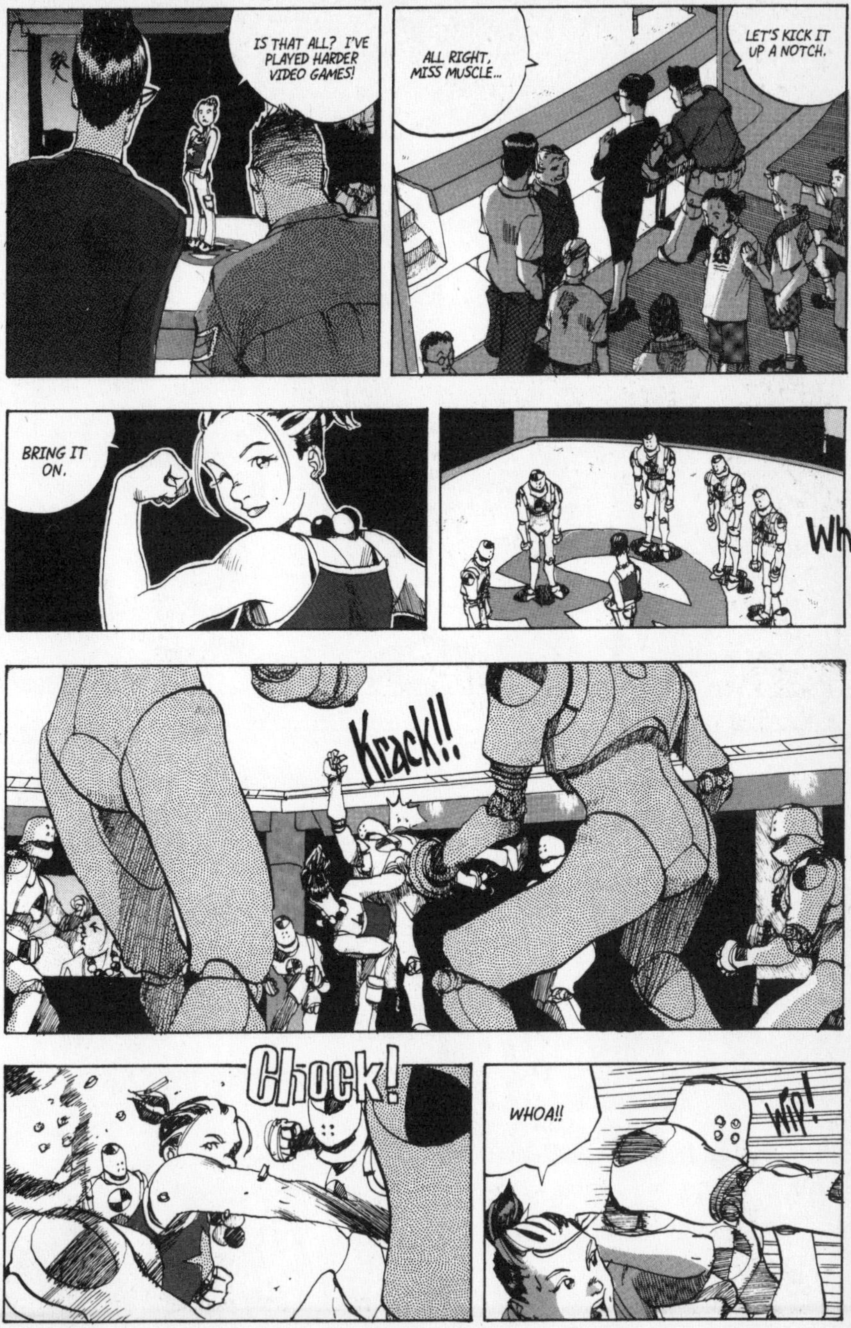
IS THAT ALL? I'VE PLAYED HARDER VIDEO GAMES!
ALL RIGHT, MISS MUSCLE...
LET'S KICK IT UP A NOTCH.
BRING IT ON.
Whom...
Krack!!
Chock!
WHOA!!
Wip!

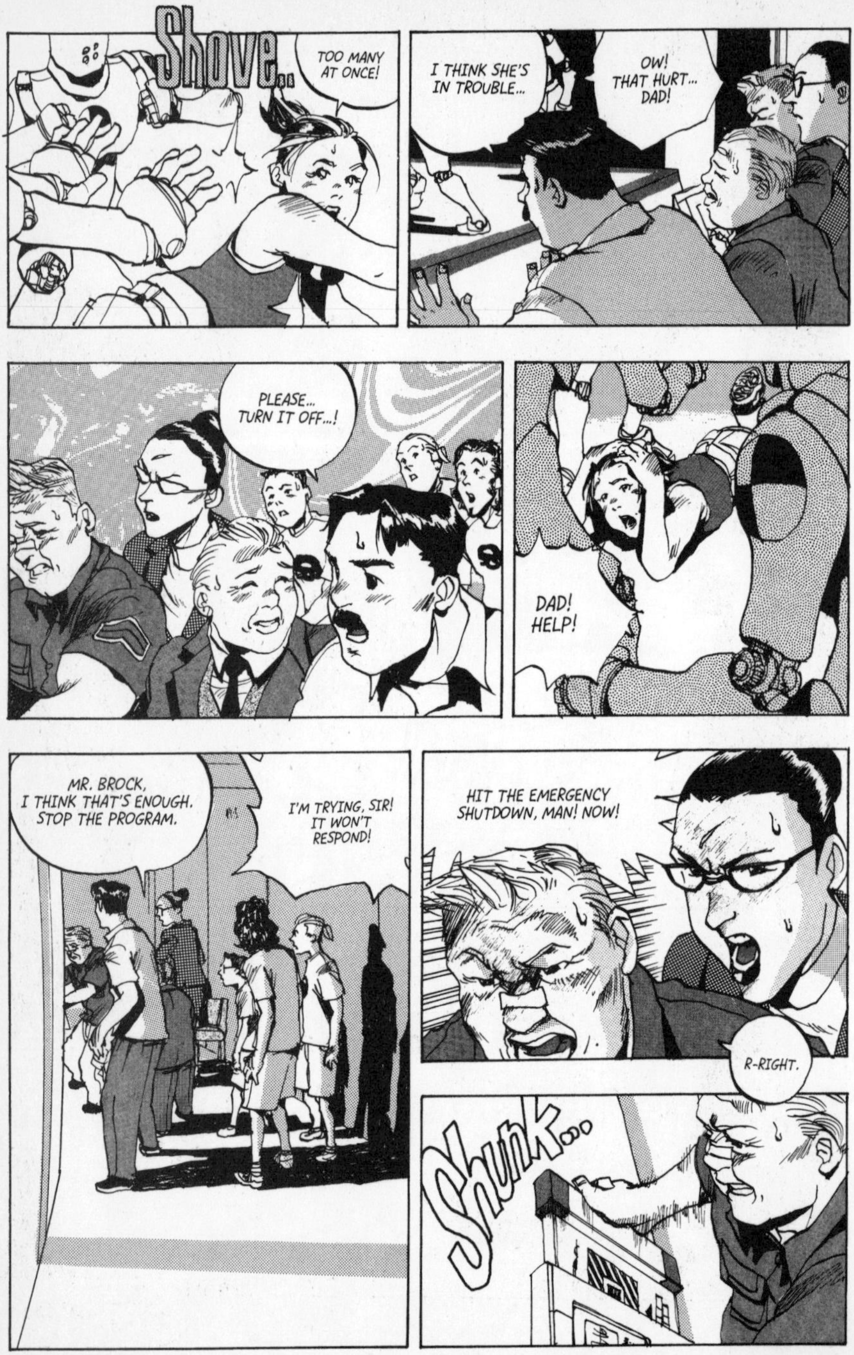
Shove..
TOO MANY AT ONCE!
I THINK SHE'S IN TROUBLE...
OW! THAT HURT... DAD!
PLEASE... TURN IT OFF...!
DAD! HELP!
MR. BROCK, I THINK THAT'S ENOUGH. STOP THE PROGRAM.
I'M TRYING, SIR! IT WON'T RESPOND!
HIT THE EMERGENCY SHUTDOWN, MAN! NOW!
R-RIGHT.
Shunk...

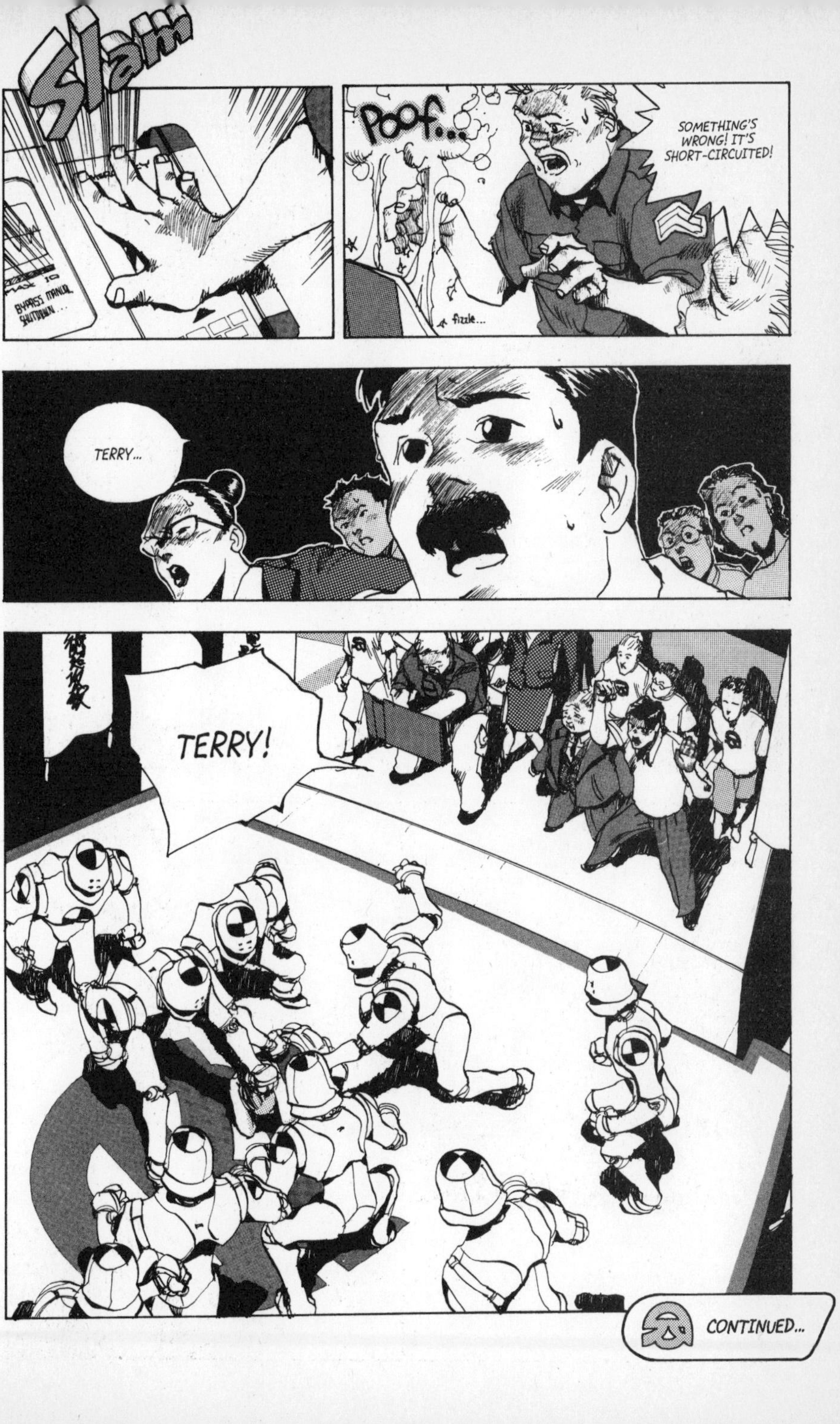

Slam
BYPASS MANUAL SHUTDOWN...
POOF...
SOMETHING'S WRONG! IT'S SHORT-CIRCUITED!
fizzle...
TERRY...
TERRY!
CONTINUED...

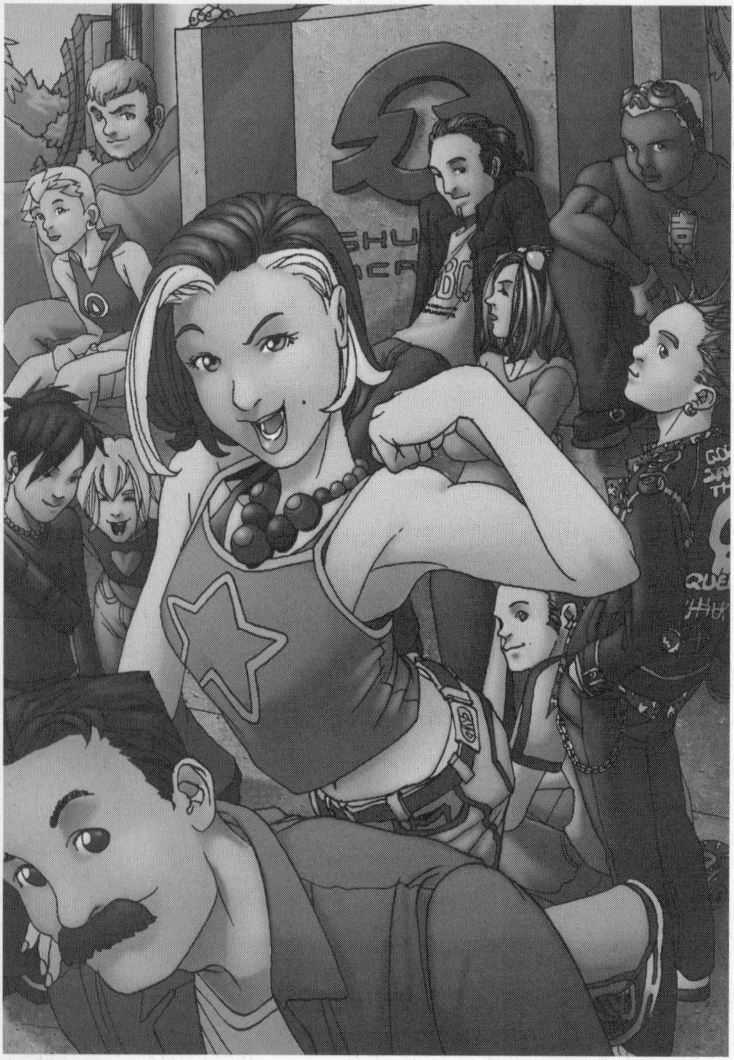

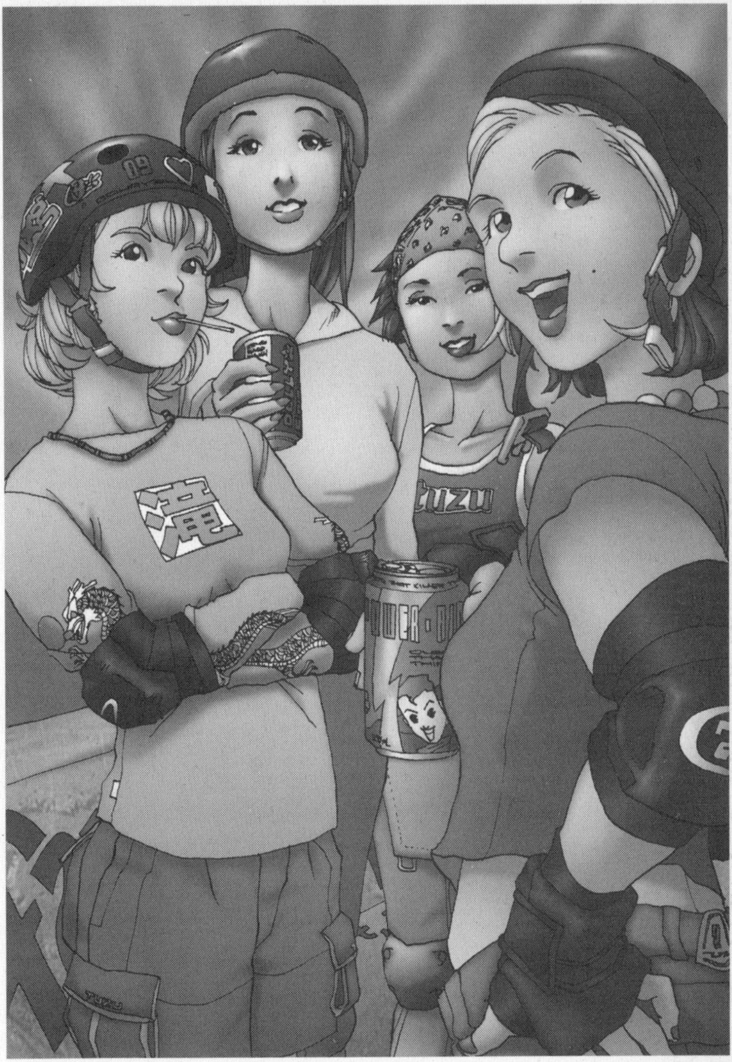
09

Chapter two

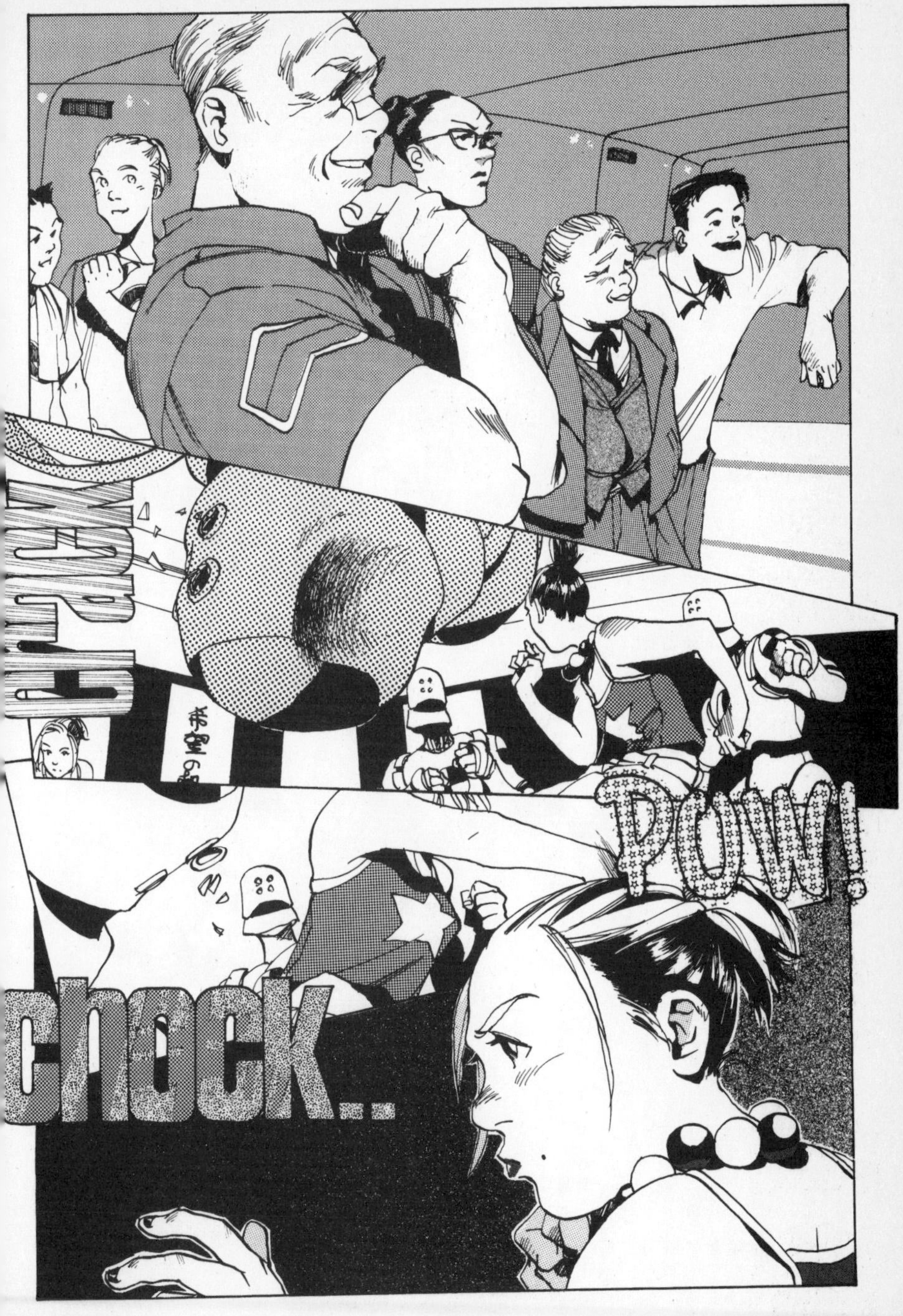
希望の
POW!
chock...

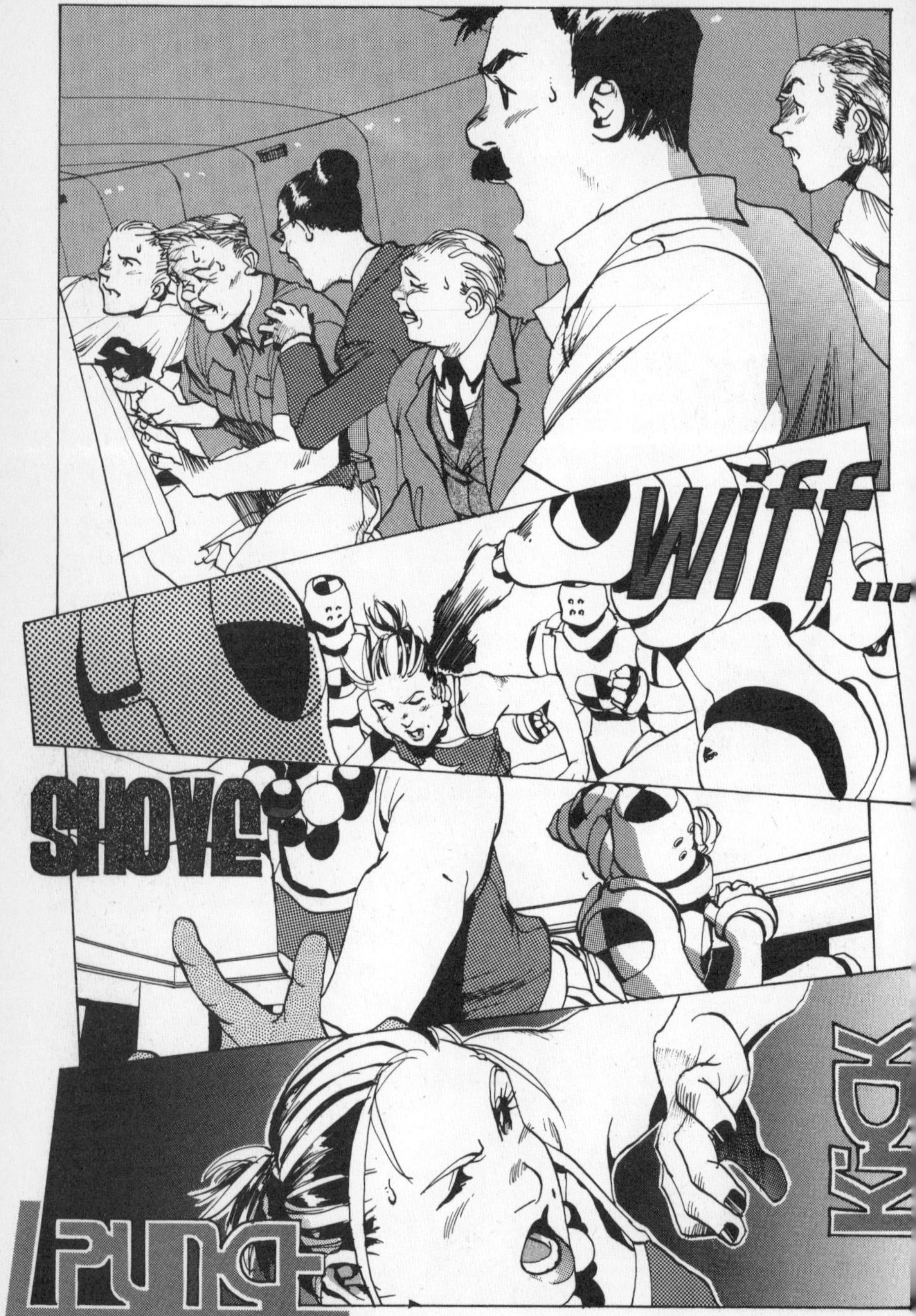
wiff...
SHOVE
KICK
PUNCH

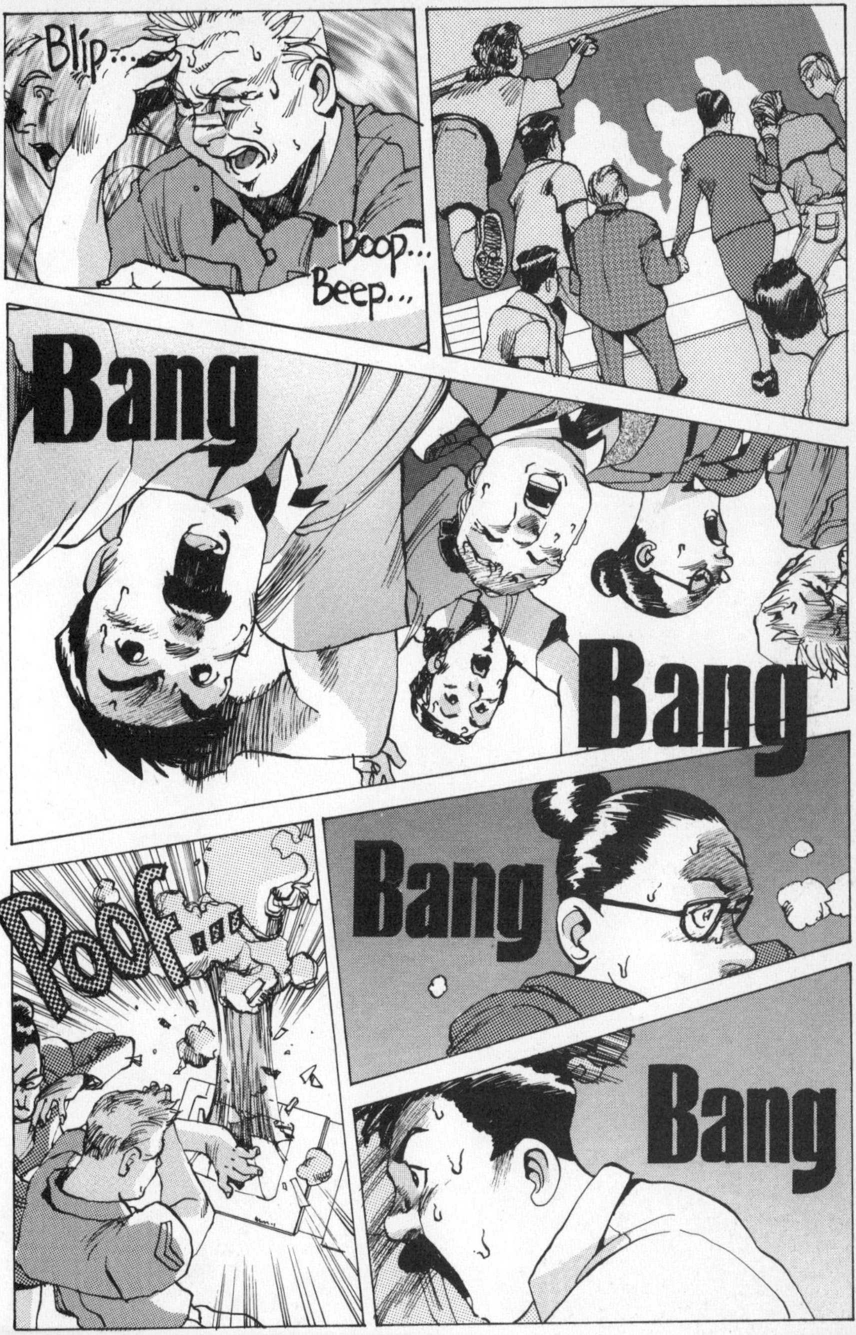
Blip...
Boop...
Beep...
Bang
Bang
Poof...
Bang
Bang

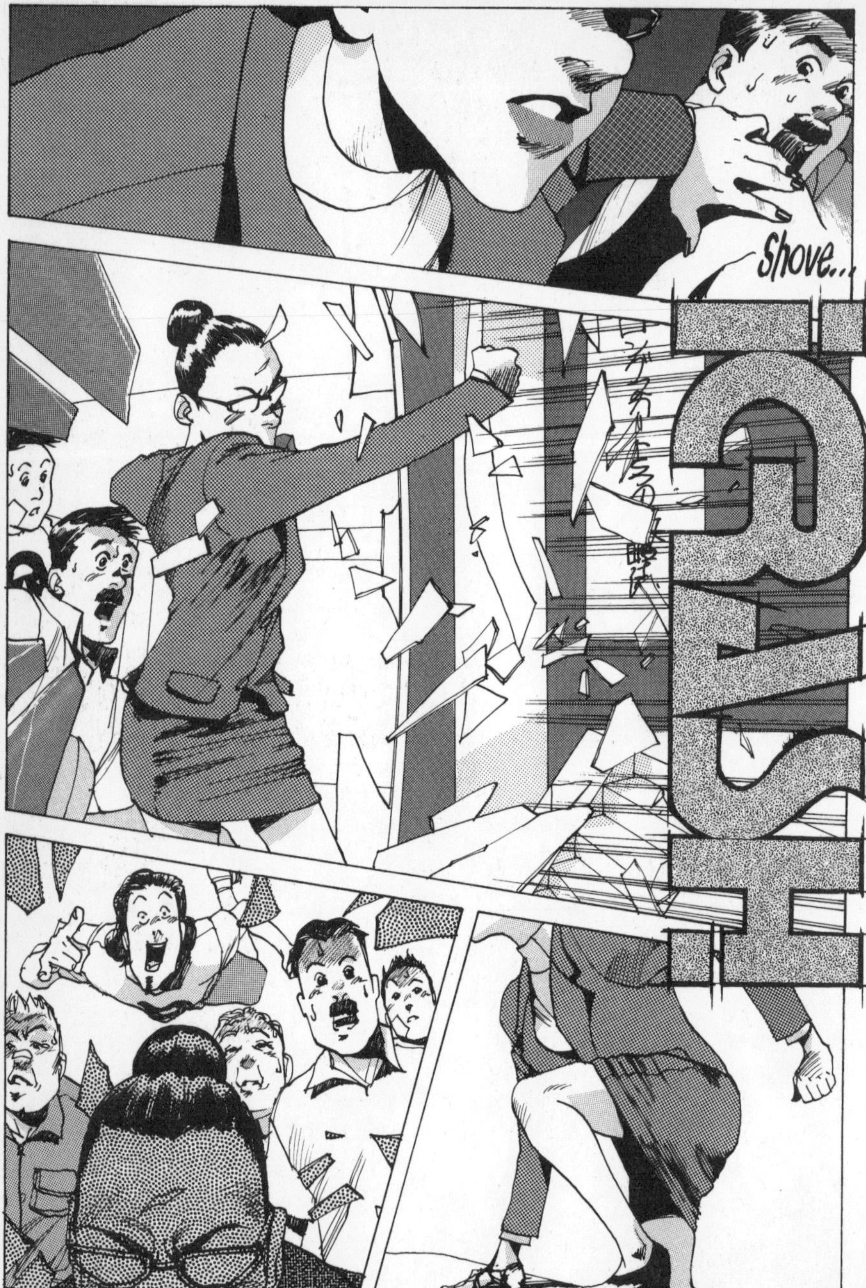
Shove...
CRASH

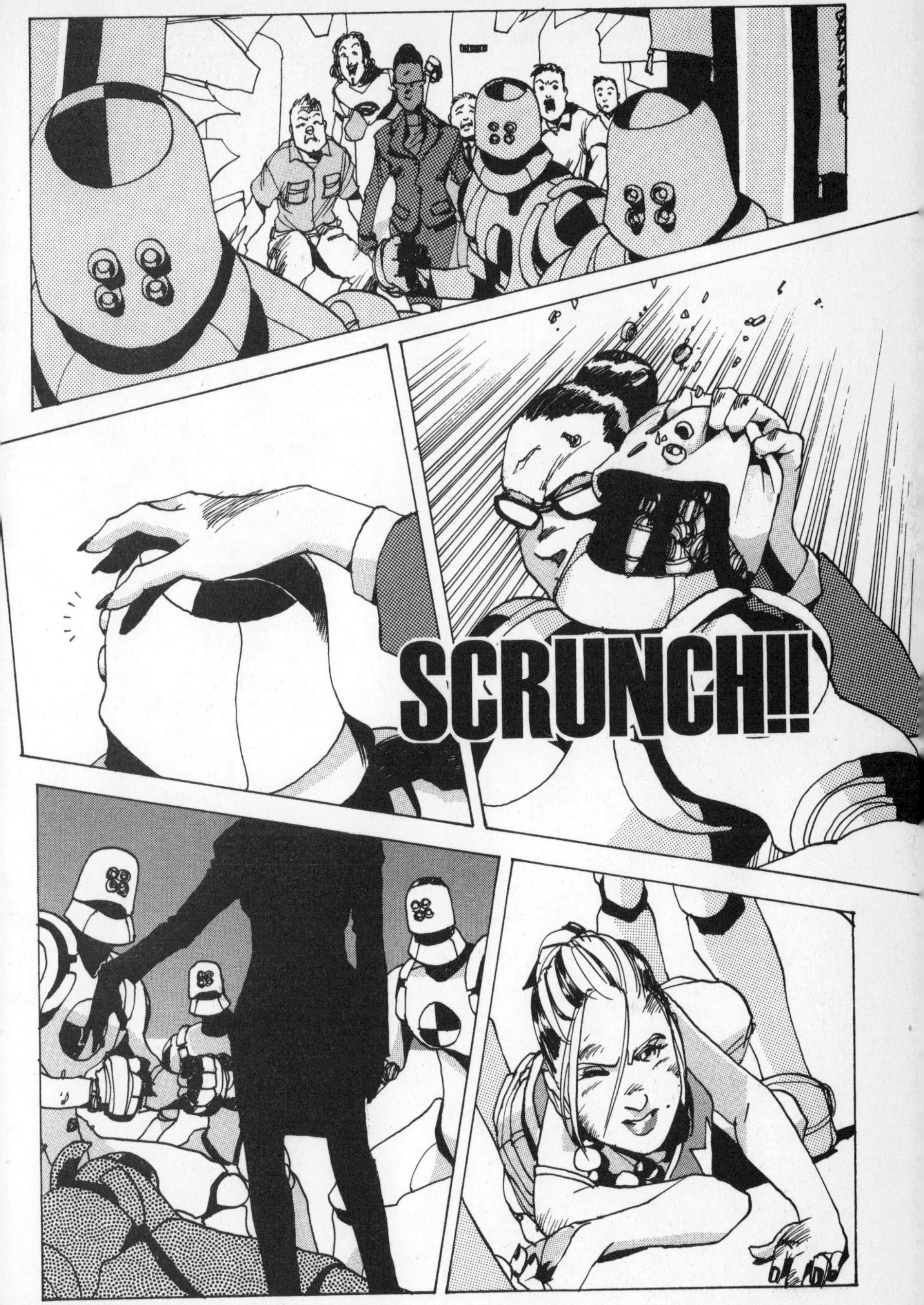
SCRUNCH!!

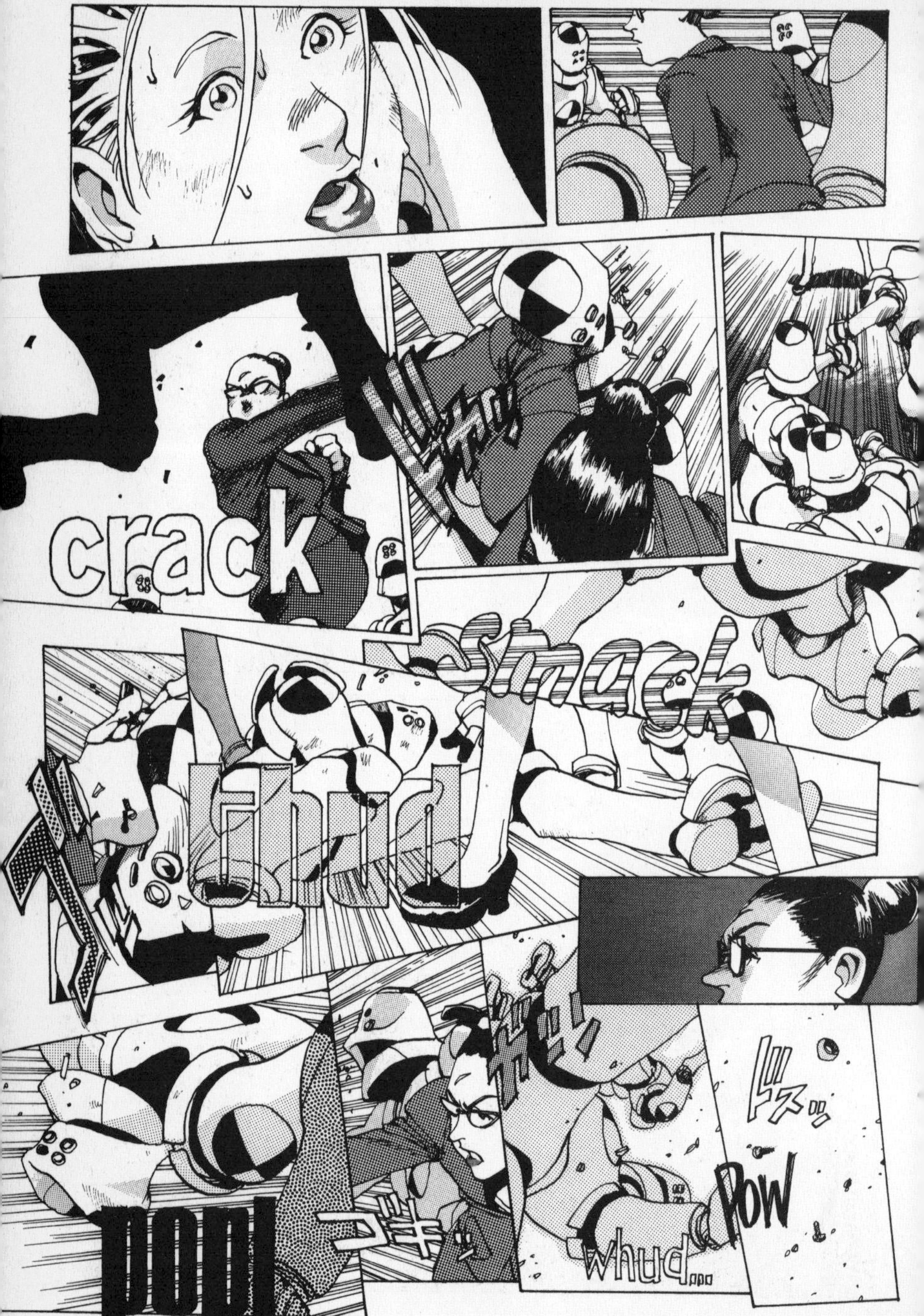
crack
Smack
thud
ドスッ
POW
whud...
ゴキッ
pop!

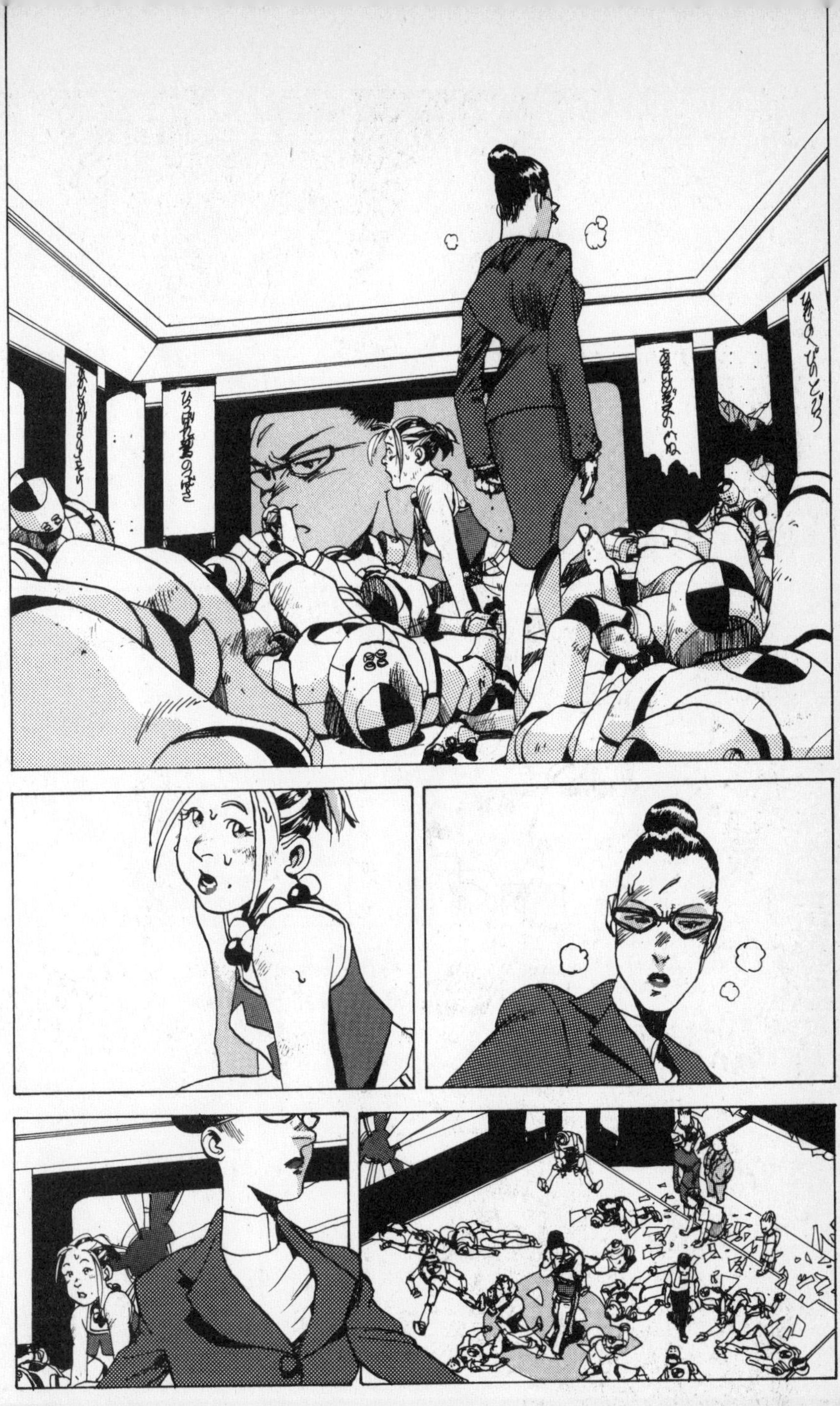

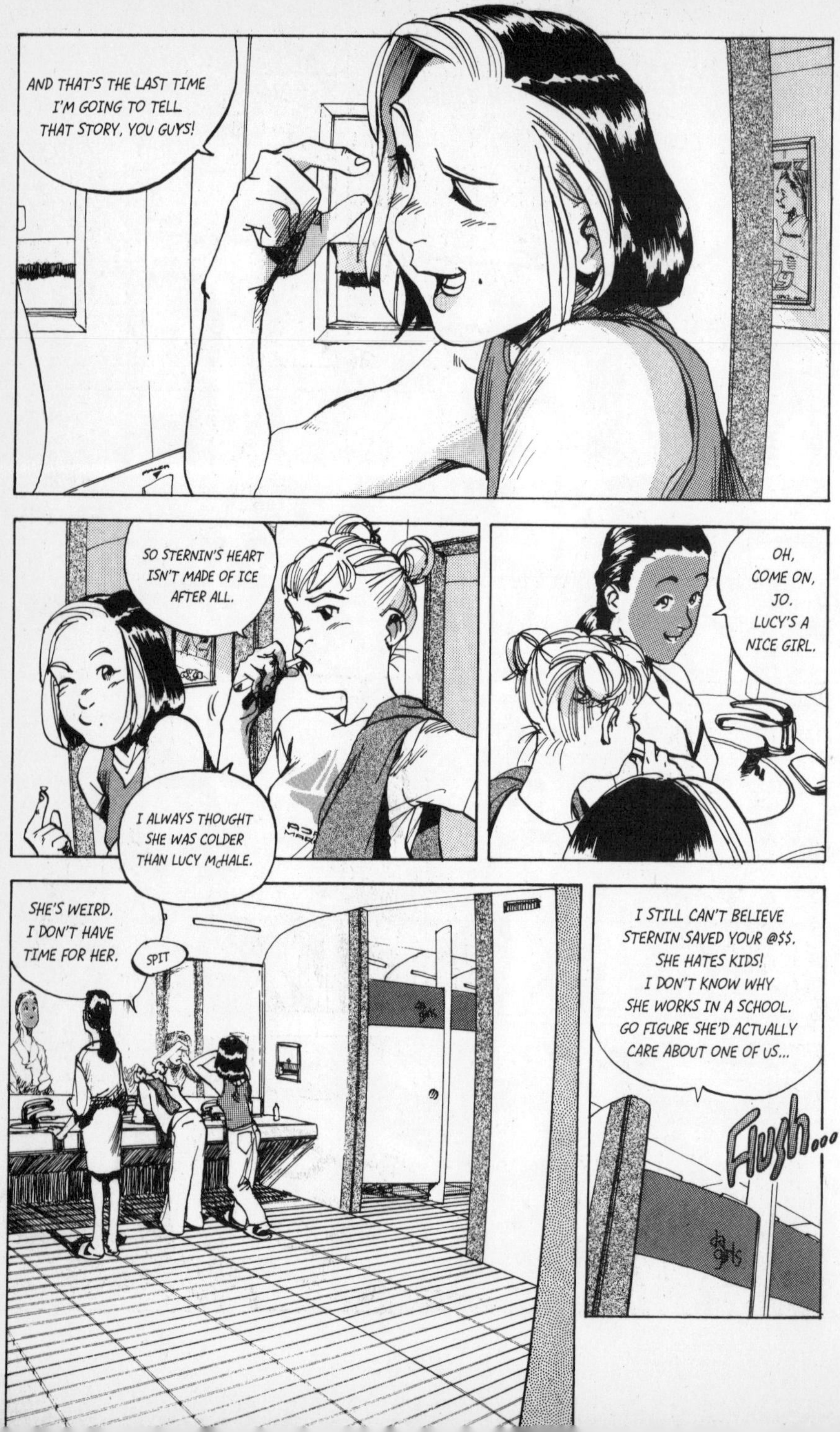
AND THAT'S THE LAST TIME I'M GOING TO TELL THAT STORY, YOU GUYS!
SO STERNIN'S HEART ISN'T MADE OF ICE AFTER ALL.
I ALWAYS THOUGHT SHE WAS COLDER THAN LUCY McHALE.
OH, COME ON, JO. LUCY'S A NICE GIRL.
SHE'S WEIRD. I DON'T HAVE TIME FOR HER.
SPIT
I STILL CAN'T BELIEVE STERNIN SAVED YOUR @$$. SHE HATES KIDS! I DON'T KNOW WHY SHE WORKS IN A SCHOOL. GO FIGURE SHE'D ACTUALLY CARE ABOUT ONE OF US...
Flush...

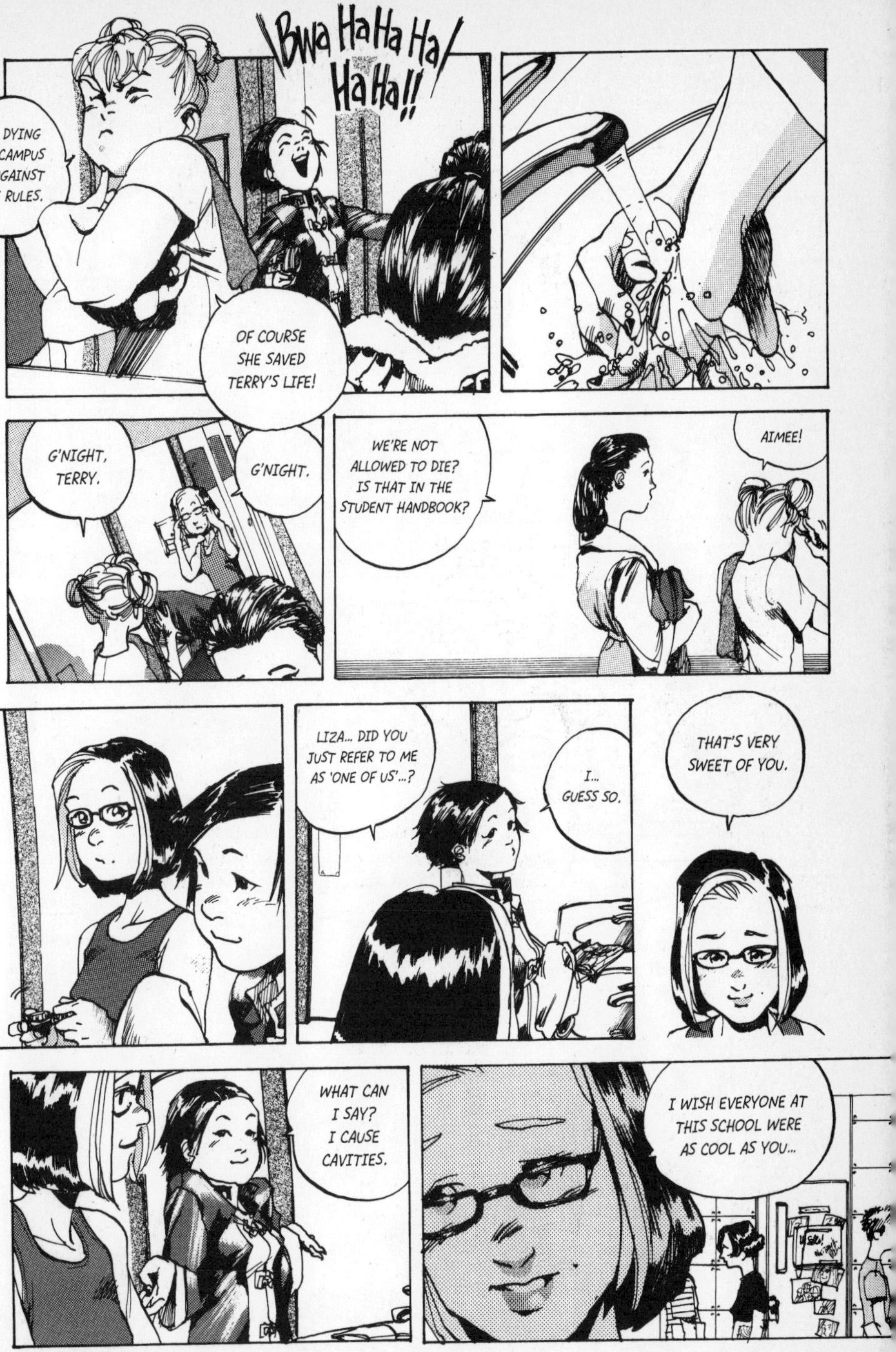
UH, DYING ON CAMPUS IS AGAINST THE RULES.
Bwa Ha Ha Ha Ha Ha!!
OF COURSE SHE SAVED TERRY'S LIFE!
G'NIGHT, TERRY.
G'NIGHT.
WE'RE NOT ALLOWED TO DIE? IS THAT IN THE STUDENT HANDBOOK?
AIMEE!
LIZA... DID YOU JUST REFER TO ME AS 'ONE OF US'...?
I... GUESS SO.
THAT'S VERY SWEET OF YOU.
WHAT CAN I SAY? I CAUSE CAVITIES.
I WISH EVERYONE AT THIS SCHOOL WERE AS COOL AS YOU...

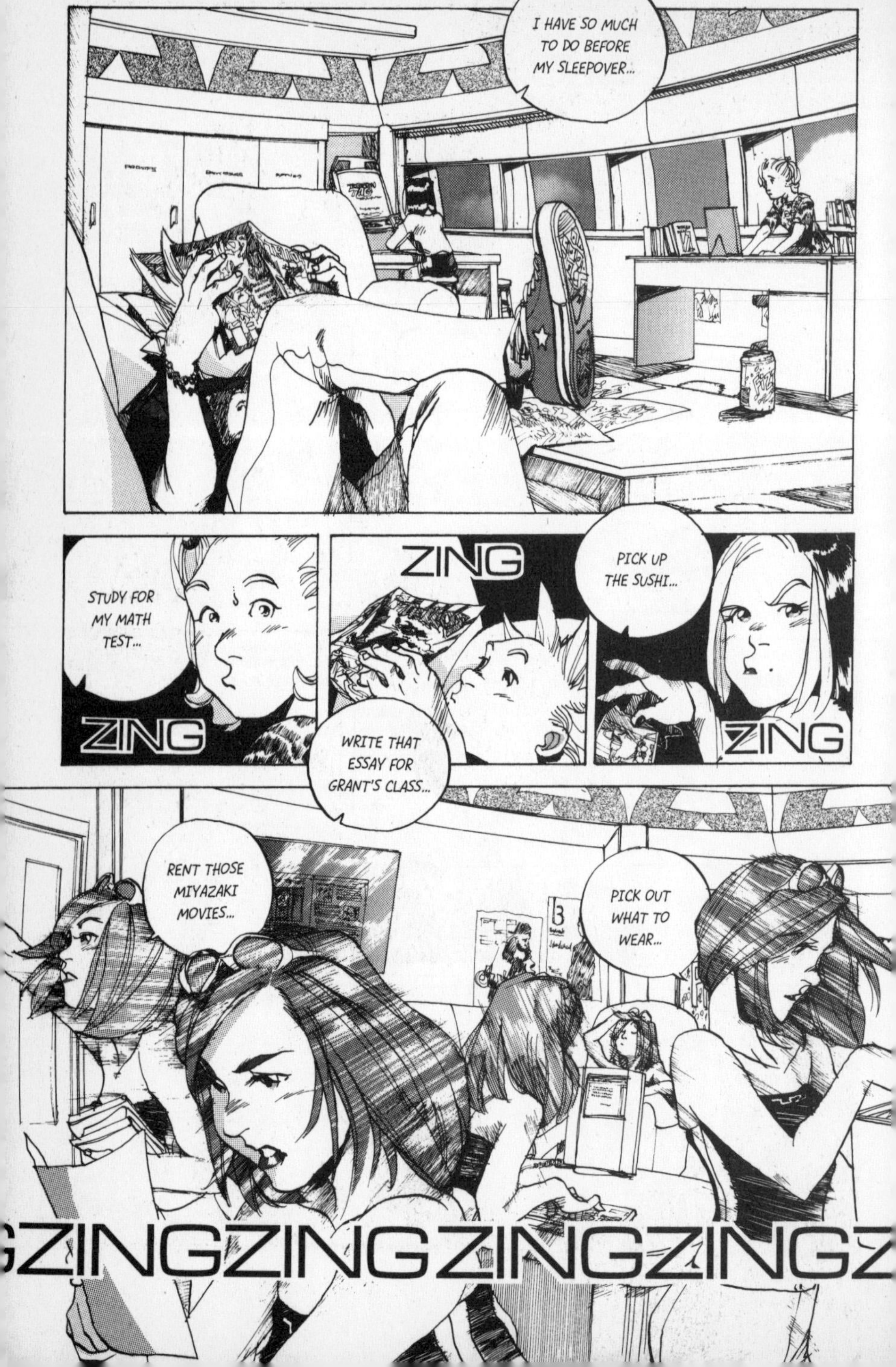
I HAVE SO MUCH TO DO BEFORE MY SLEEPOVER...
STUDY FOR MY MATH TEST...
ZING
ZING
PICK UP THE SUSHI...
ZING
WRITE THAT ESSAY FOR GRANT'S CLASS...
RENT THOSE MIYAZAKI MOVIES...
PICK OUT WHAT TO WEAR...
GZINGZINGZINGZINGZ

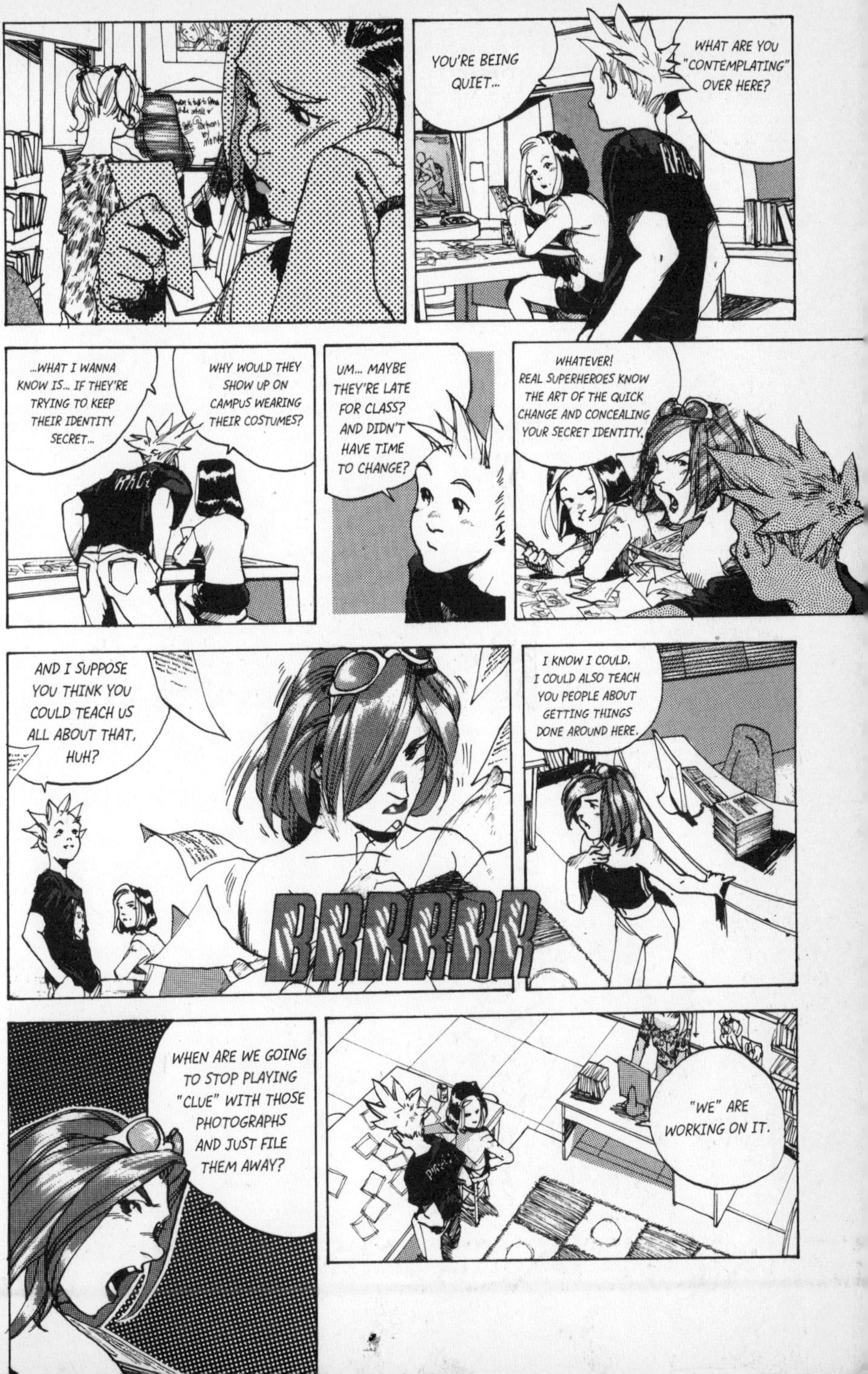
YOU'RE BEING QUIET...
WHAT ARE YOU "CONTEMPLATING" OVER HERE?
...WHAT I WANNA KNOW IS... IF THEY'RE TRYING TO KEEP THEIR IDENTITY SECRET...
WHY WOULD THEY SHOW UP ON CAMPUS WEARING THEIR COSTUMES?
UM... MAYBE THEY'RE LATE FOR CLASS? AND DIDN'T HAVE TIME TO CHANGE?
WHATEVER! REAL SUPERHEROES KNOW THE ART OF THE QUICK CHANGE AND CONCEALING YOUR SECRET IDENTITY.
AND I SUPPOSE YOU THINK YOU COULD TEACH US ALL ABOUT THAT, HUH?
I KNOW I COULD. I COULD ALSO TEACH YOU PEOPLE ABOUT GETTING THINGS DONE AROUND HERE.
BRRRRR
WHEN ARE WE GOING TO STOP PLAYING "CLUE" WITH THOSE PHOTOGRAPHS AND JUST FILE THEM AWAY?
"WE" ARE WORKING ON IT.

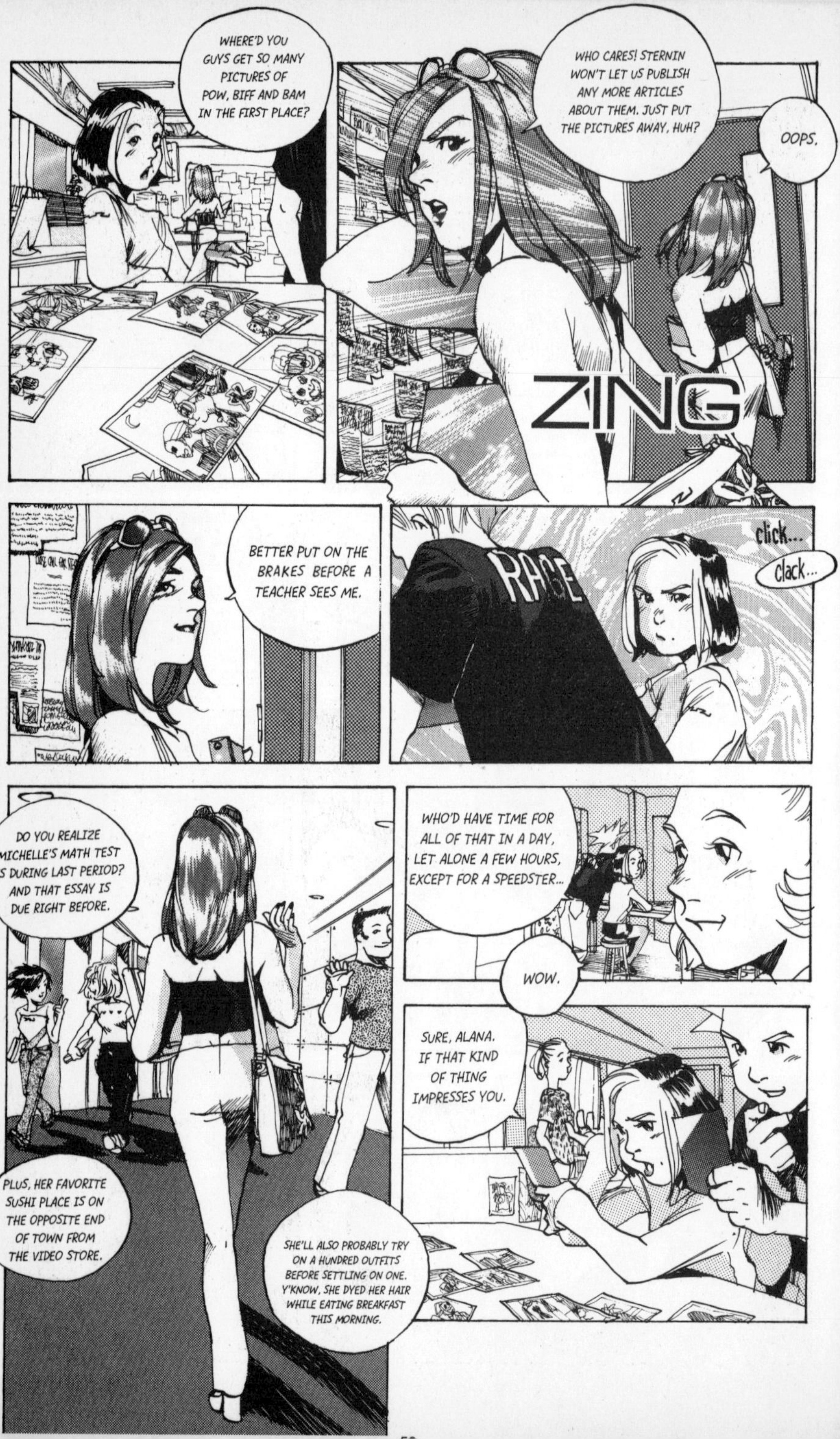
WHERE'D YOU GUYS GET SO MANY PICTURES OF POW, BIFF AND BAM IN THE FIRST PLACE?
WHO CARES! STERNIN WON'T LET US PUBLISH ANY MORE ARTICLES ABOUT THEM. JUST PUT THE PICTURES AWAY, HUH?
OOPS.
ZING
BETTER PUT ON THE BRAKES BEFORE A TEACHER SEES ME.
RAGE
click...
clack...
DO YOU REALIZE MICHELLE'S MATH TEST IS DURING LAST PERIOD? AND THAT ESSAY IS DUE RIGHT BEFORE.
PLUS, HER FAVORITE SUSHI PLACE IS ON THE OPPOSITE END OF TOWN FROM THE VIDEO STORE.
SHE'LL ALSO PROBABLY TRY ON A HUNDRED OUTFITS BEFORE SETTLING ON ONE. Y'KNOW, SHE DYED HER HAIR WHILE EATING BREAKFAST THIS MORNING.
WHO'D HAVE TIME FOR ALL OF THAT IN A DAY, LET ALONE A FEW HOURS, EXCEPT FOR A SPEEDSTER...
WOW.
SURE, ALANA. IF THAT KIND OF THING IMPRESSES YOU.

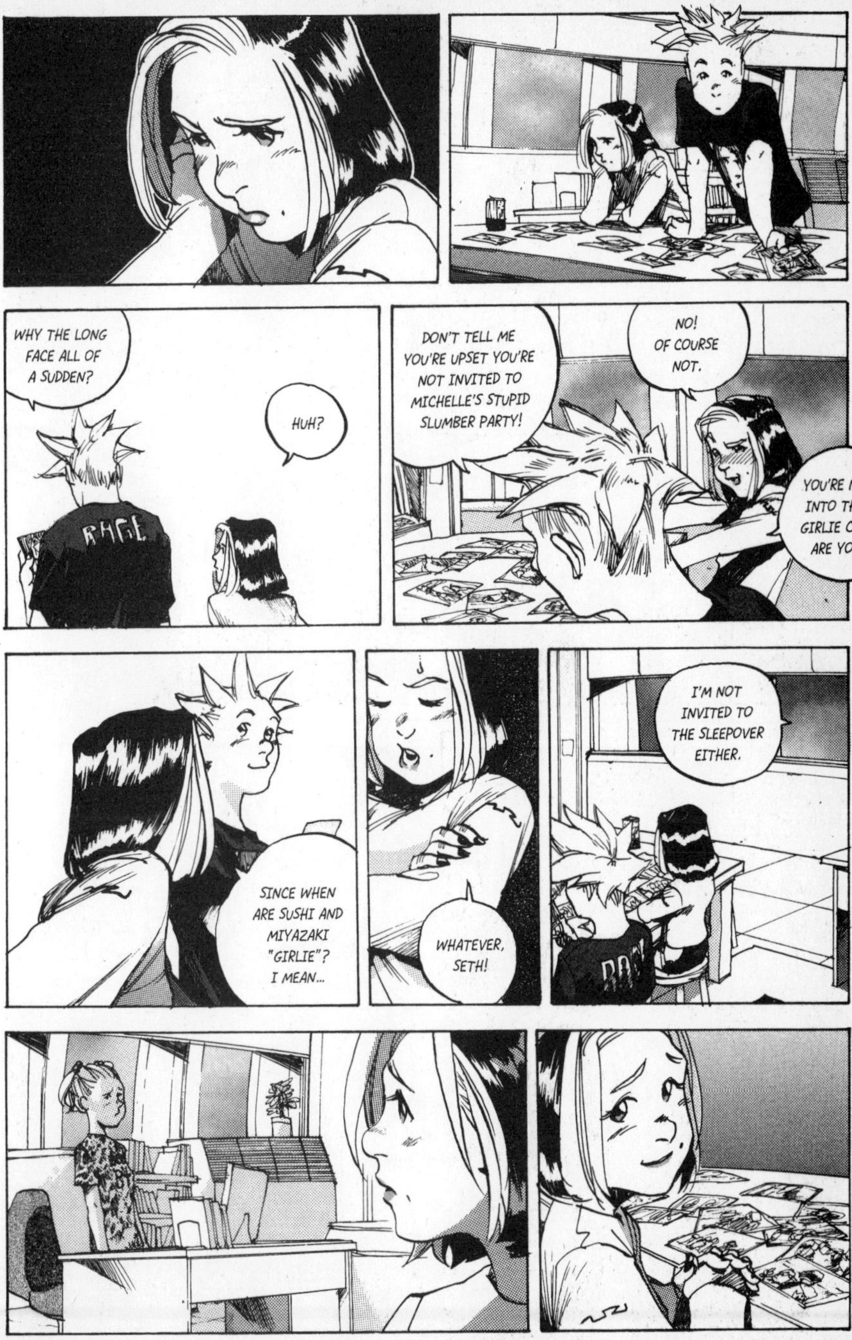
WHY THE LONG FACE ALL OF A SUDDEN?
HUH?
DON'T TELL ME YOU'RE UPSET YOU'RE NOT INVITED TO MICHELLE'S STUPID SLUMBER PARTY!
NO! OF COURSE NOT.
YOU'RE NOT INTO THAT GIRLIE CRAP, ARE YOU?
SINCE WHEN ARE SUSHI AND MIYAZAKI "GIRLIE"? I MEAN...
WHATEVER, SETH!
I'M NOT INVITED TO THE SLEEPOVER EITHER.

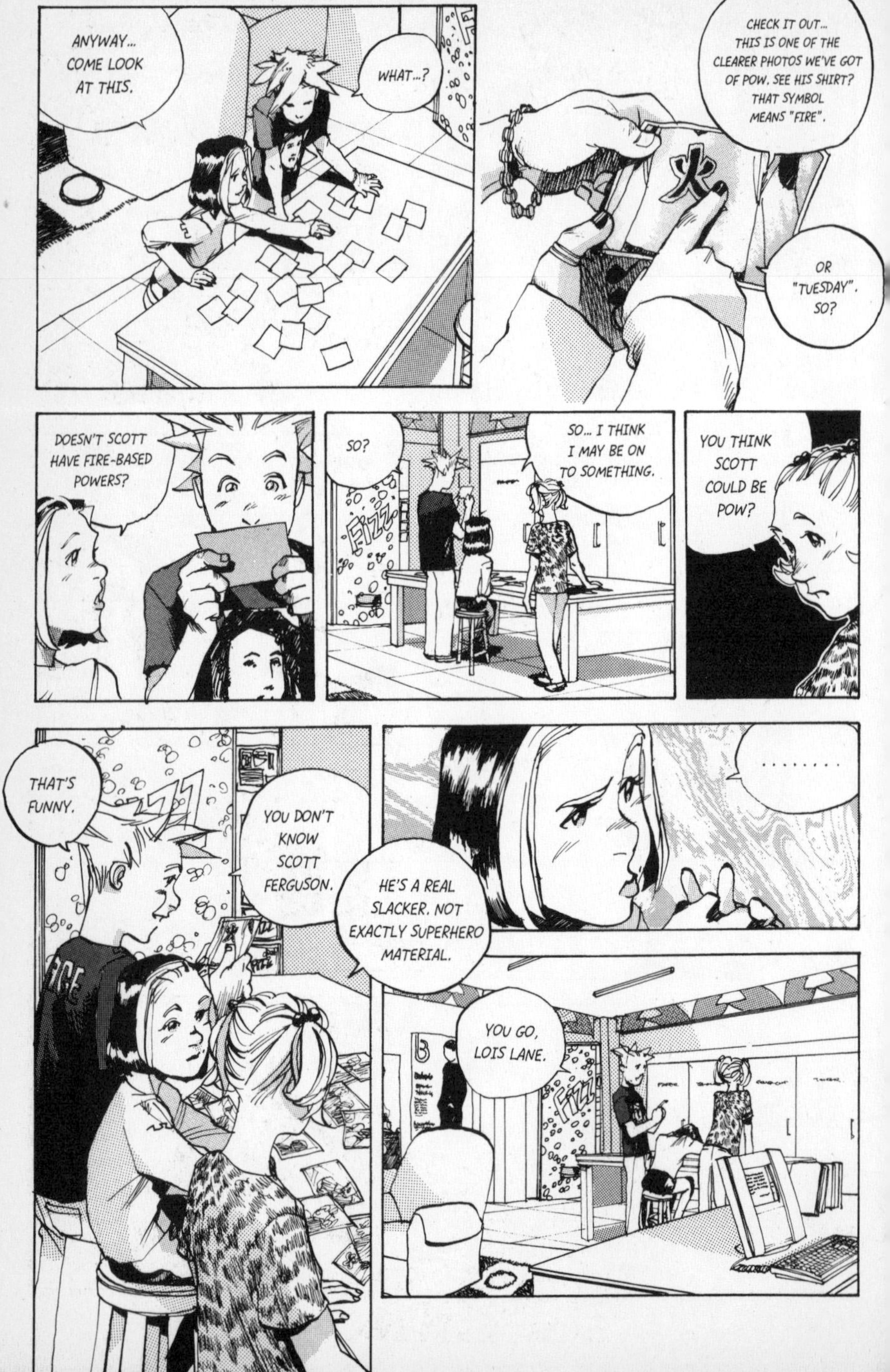
ANYWAY... COME LOOK AT THIS.
WHAT...?
CHECK IT OUT... THIS IS ONE OF THE CLEARER PHOTOS WE'VE GOT OF POW. SEE HIS SHIRT? THAT SYMBOL MEANS "FIRE".
火
OR "TUESDAY". SO?
DOESN'T SCOTT HAVE FIRE-BASED POWERS?
SO?
SO... I THINK I MAY BE ON TO SOMETHING.
FIZZ
YOU THINK SCOTT COULD BE POW?
THAT'S FUNNY.
YOU DON'T KNOW SCOTT FERGUSON.
HE'S A REAL SLACKER. NOT EXACTLY SUPERHERO MATERIAL.
....
YOU GO, LOIS LANE.
FIZZ

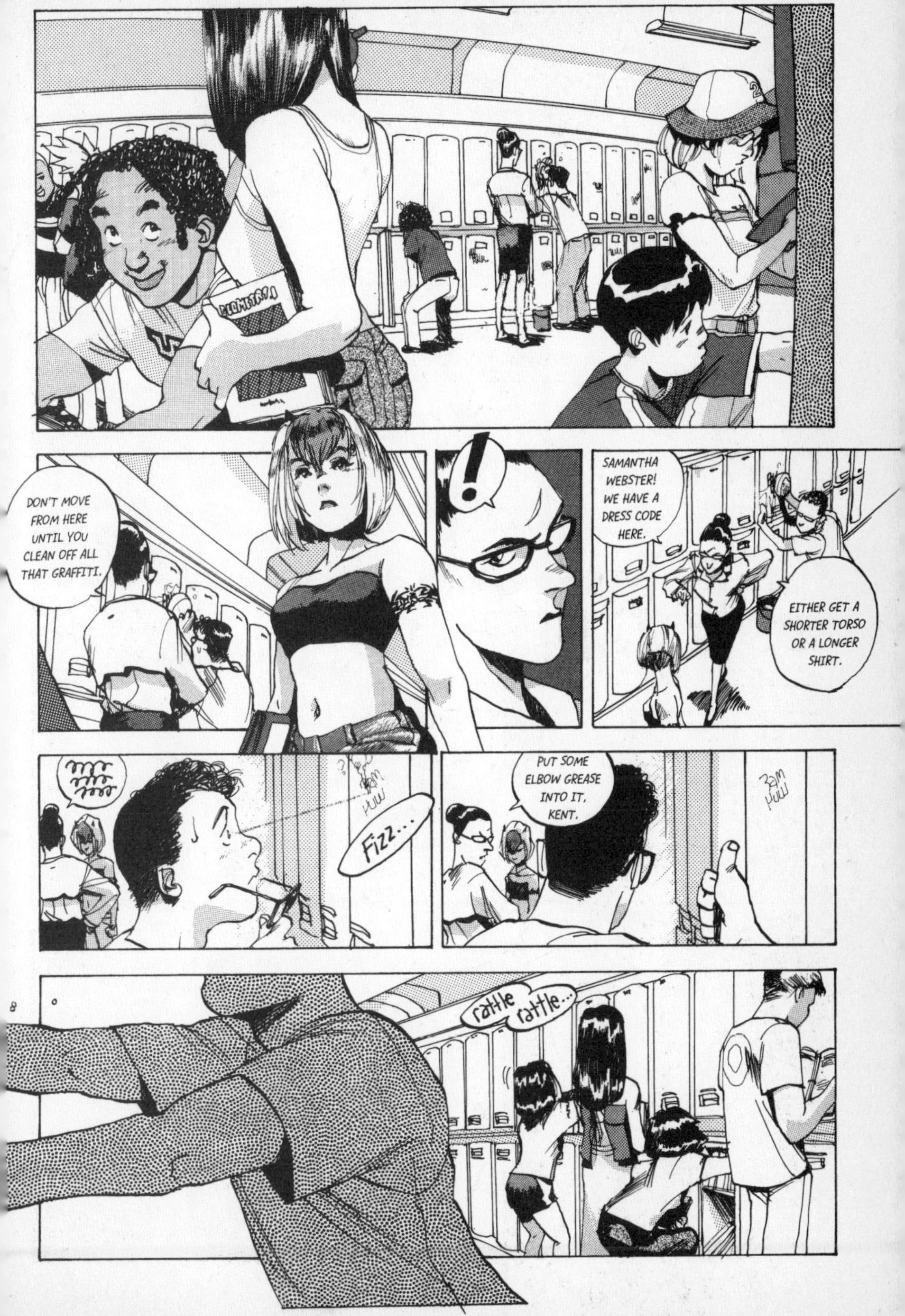
DON'T MOVE FROM HERE UNTIL YOU CLEAN OFF ALL THAT GRAFFITI.
!
SAMANTHA WEBSTER! WE HAVE A DRESS CODE HERE.
EITHER GET A SHORTER TORSO OR A LONGER SHIRT.
Fizz...
PUT SOME ELBOW GREASE INTO IT, KENT.
rattle rattle...

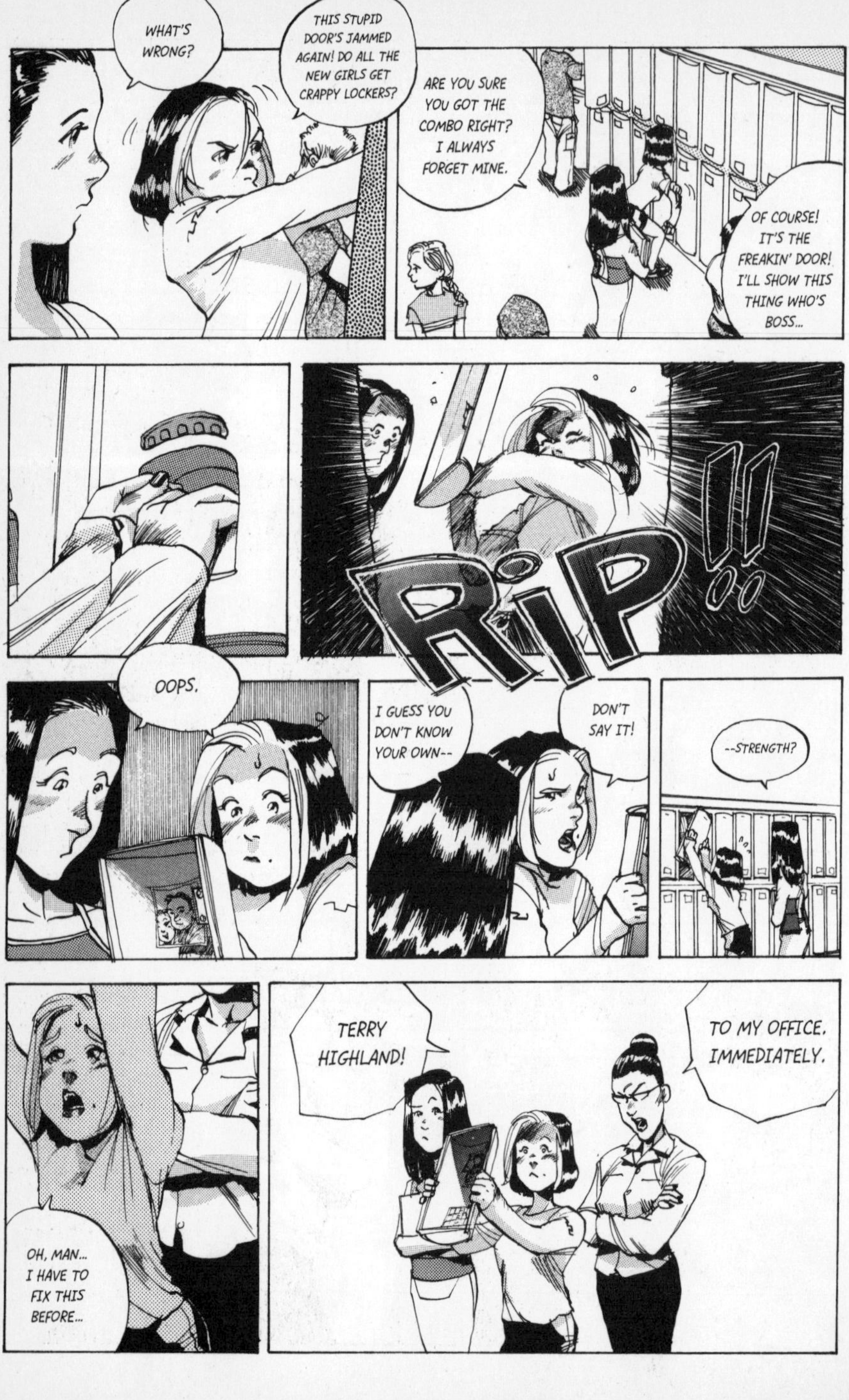
WHAT'S WRONG?
THIS STUPID DOOR'S JAMMED AGAIN! DO ALL THE NEW GIRLS GET CRAPPY LOCKERS?
ARE YOU SURE YOU GOT THE COMBO RIGHT? I ALWAYS FORGET MINE.
OF COURSE! IT'S THE FREAKIN' DOOR! I'LL SHOW THIS THING WHO'S BOSS...
RIP!!
OOPS.
I GUESS YOU DON'T KNOW YOUR OWN--
DON'T SAY IT!
--STRENGTH?
OH, MAN... I HAVE TO FIX THIS BEFORE...
TERRY HIGHLAND!
TO MY OFFICE. IMMEDIATELY.

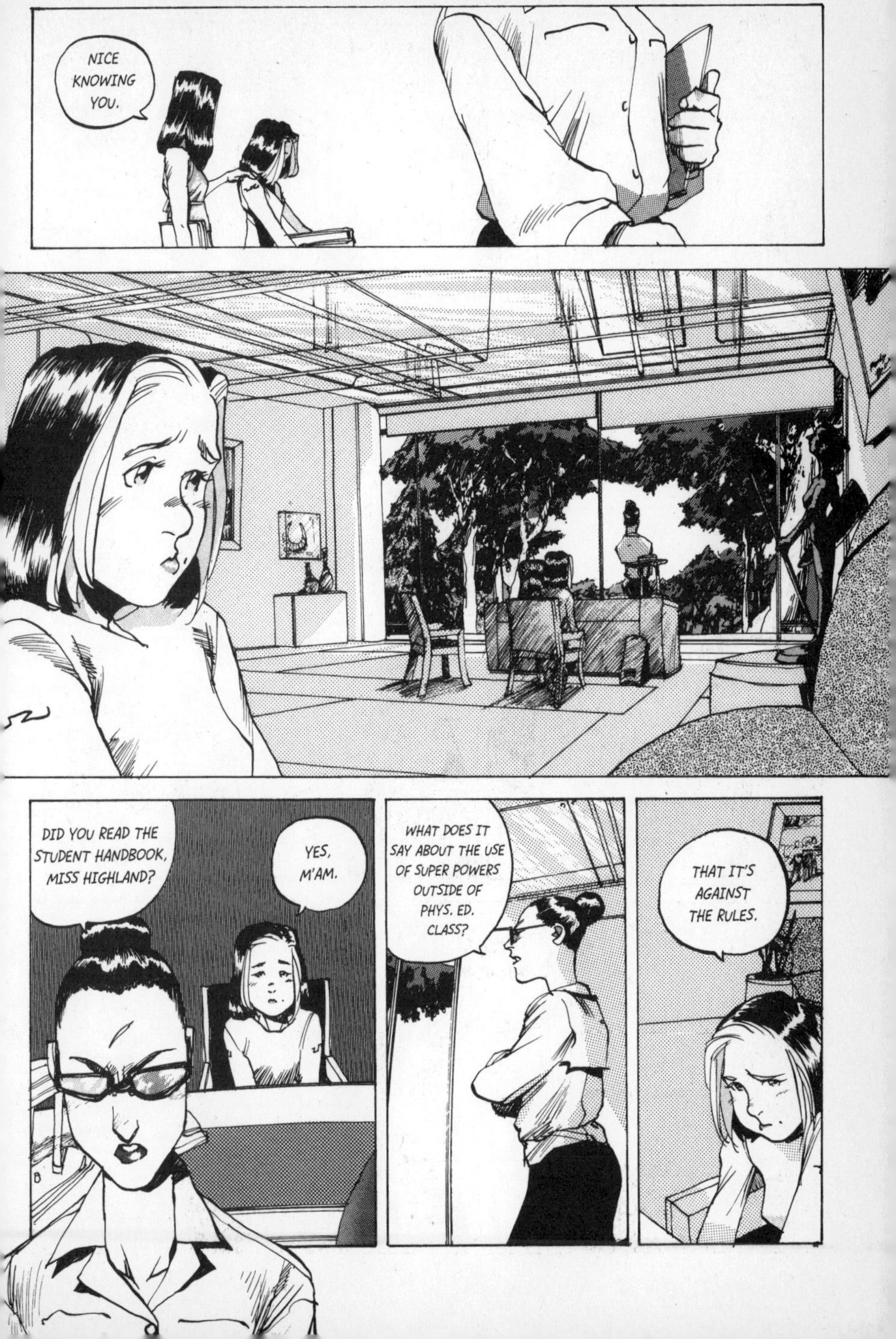
NICE KNOWING YOU.
DID YOU READ THE STUDENT HANDBOOK, MISS HIGHLAND?
YES, M'AM.
WHAT DOES IT SAY ABOUT THE USE OF SUPER POWERS OUTSIDE OF PHYS. ED. CLASS?
THAT IT'S AGAINST THE RULES.

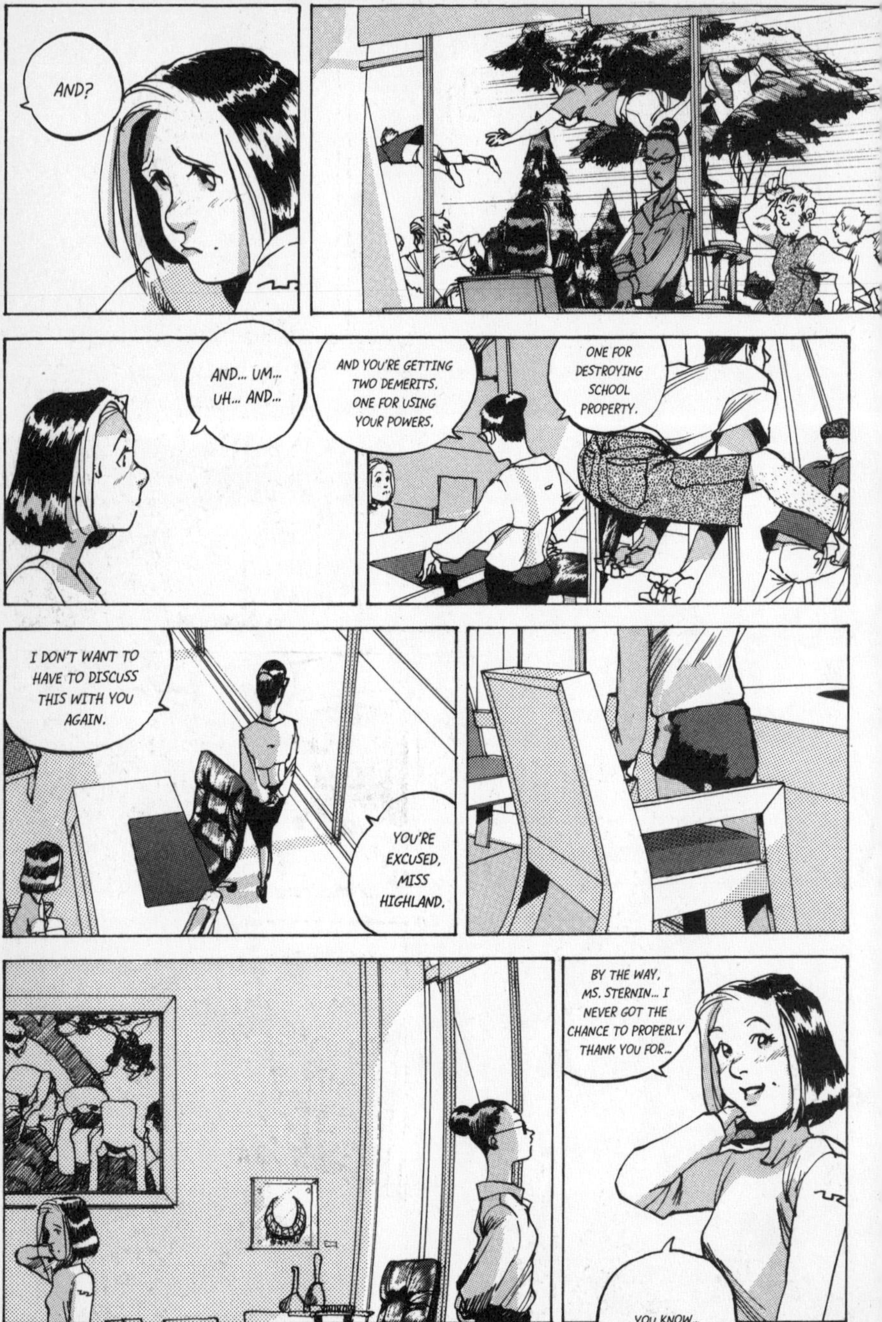
AND?
AND... UM... UH... AND...
AND YOU'RE GETTING TWO DEMERITS. ONE FOR USING YOUR POWERS.
ONE FOR DESTROYING SCHOOL PROPERTY.
I DON'T WANT TO HAVE TO DISCUSS THIS WITH YOU AGAIN.
YOU'RE EXCUSED, MISS HIGHLAND.
BY THE WAY, MS. STERNIN... I NEVER GOT THE CHANCE TO PROPERLY THANK YOU FOR...
YOU KNOW...

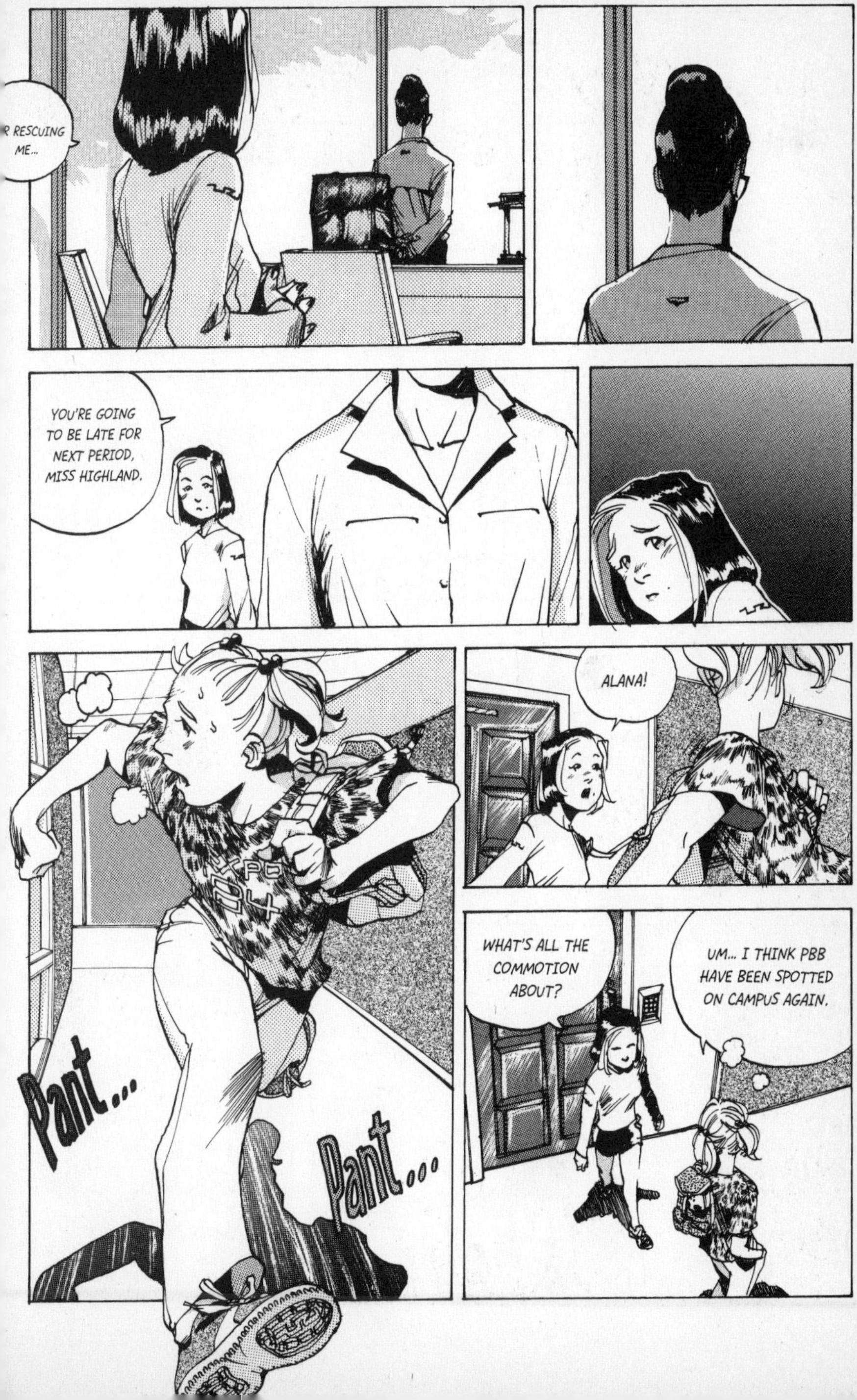
R RESCUING ME...
YOU'RE GOING TO BE LATE FOR NEXT PERIOD, MISS HIGHLAND.
Pant...
Pant...
ALANA!
WHAT'S ALL THE COMMOTION ABOUT?
UM... I THINK PBB HAVE BEEN SPOTTED ON CAMPUS AGAIN.

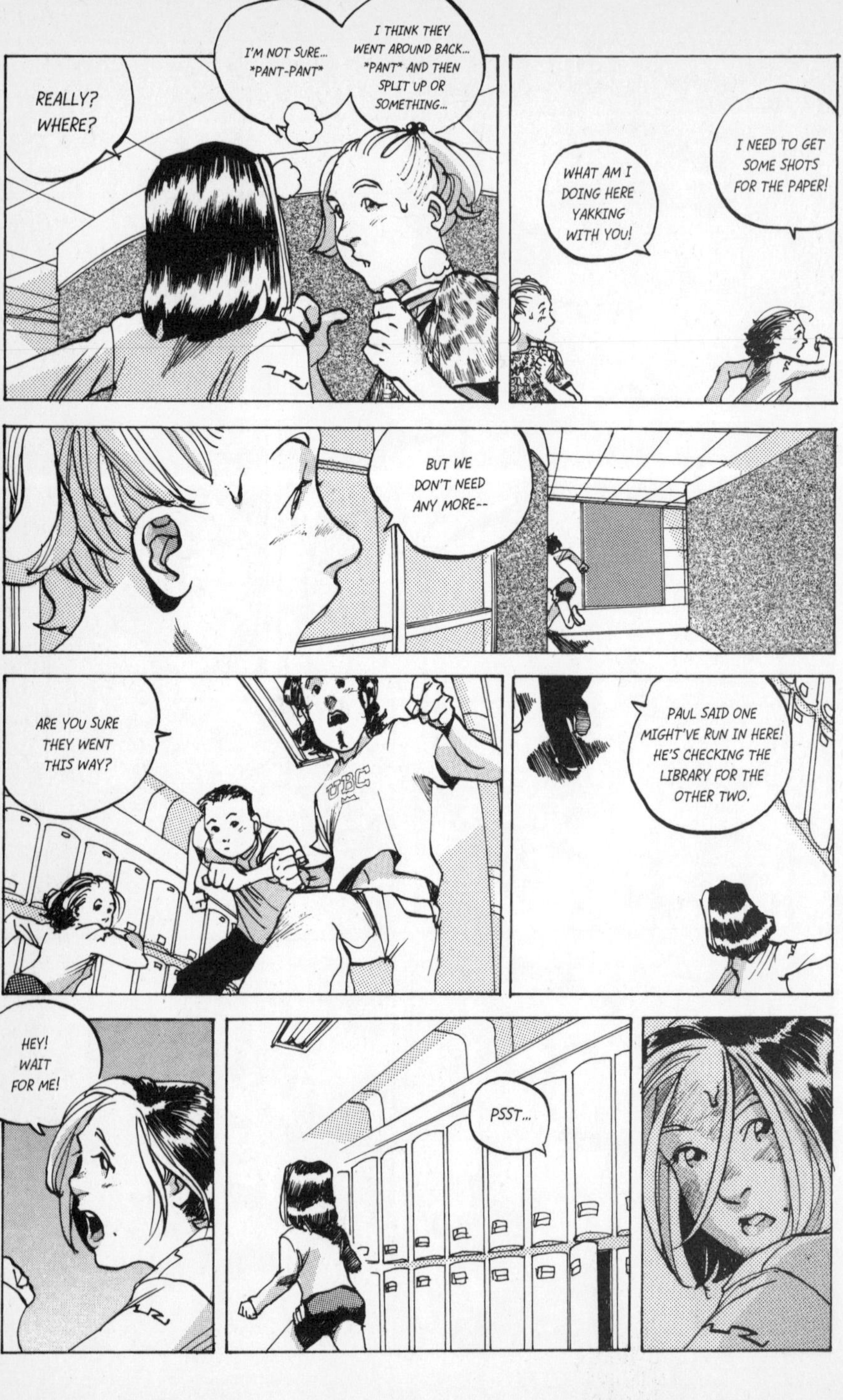
REALLY? WHERE?
I'M NOT SURE... *PANT-PANT*
I THINK THEY WENT AROUND BACK... *PANT* AND THEN SPLIT UP OR SOMETHING...
I NEED TO GET SOME SHOTS FOR THE PAPER!
WHAT AM I DOING HERE YAKKING WITH YOU!
BUT WE DON'T NEED ANY MORE--
ARE YOU SURE THEY WENT THIS WAY?
PAUL SAID ONE MIGHT'VE RUN IN HERE! HE'S CHECKING THE LIBRARY FOR THE OTHER TWO.
HEY! WAIT FOR ME!
PSST...

...IN HERE...

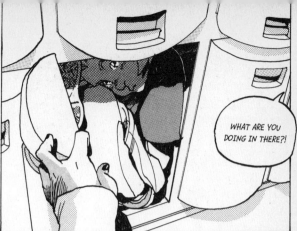

WHAT ARE YOU DOING IN THERE?!

ROLLERBLADING. WHAT'S IT LOOK LIKE? I'M, UH, HIDING FROM STERNIN.

WHY?

I, UH, SKIPPED MY MORNING CLASSES TO, UH, GO TO THE COMIC SHOP.

DO YOU EVER GO TO CLASS?

YES, MOM.

HEY! DID YOU HEAR? PBB WERE SPOTTED ON CAMPUS. I WONDER WHERE SCOTT WAS THE WHOLE TIME...

YEAH, YEAH, WHATEVER.

NOW CLOSE THE DOOR. IT'S COLD.

SORRY.

S'ALRIGHT.

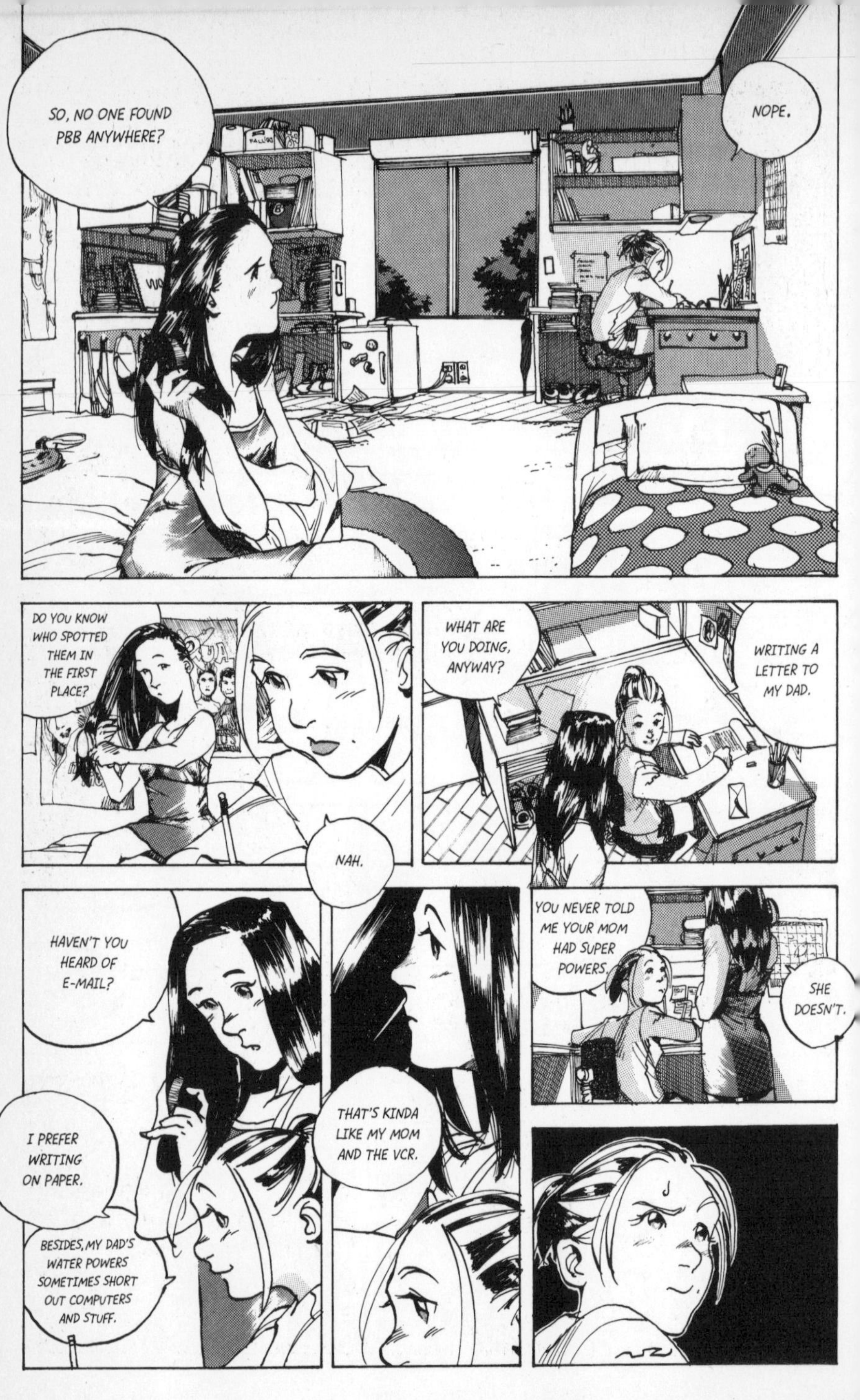
SO, NO ONE FOUND PBB ANYWHERE?
NOPE.
DO YOU KNOW WHO SPOTTED THEM IN THE FIRST PLACE?
NAH.
WHAT ARE YOU DOING, ANYWAY?
WRITING A LETTER TO MY DAD.
HAVEN'T YOU HEARD OF E-MAIL?
I PREFER WRITING ON PAPER.
BESIDES, MY DAD'S WATER POWERS SOMETIMES SHORT OUT COMPUTERS AND STUFF.
THAT'S KINDA LIKE MY MOM AND THE VCR.
YOU NEVER TOLD ME YOUR MOM HAD SUPER POWERS.
SHE DOESN'T.

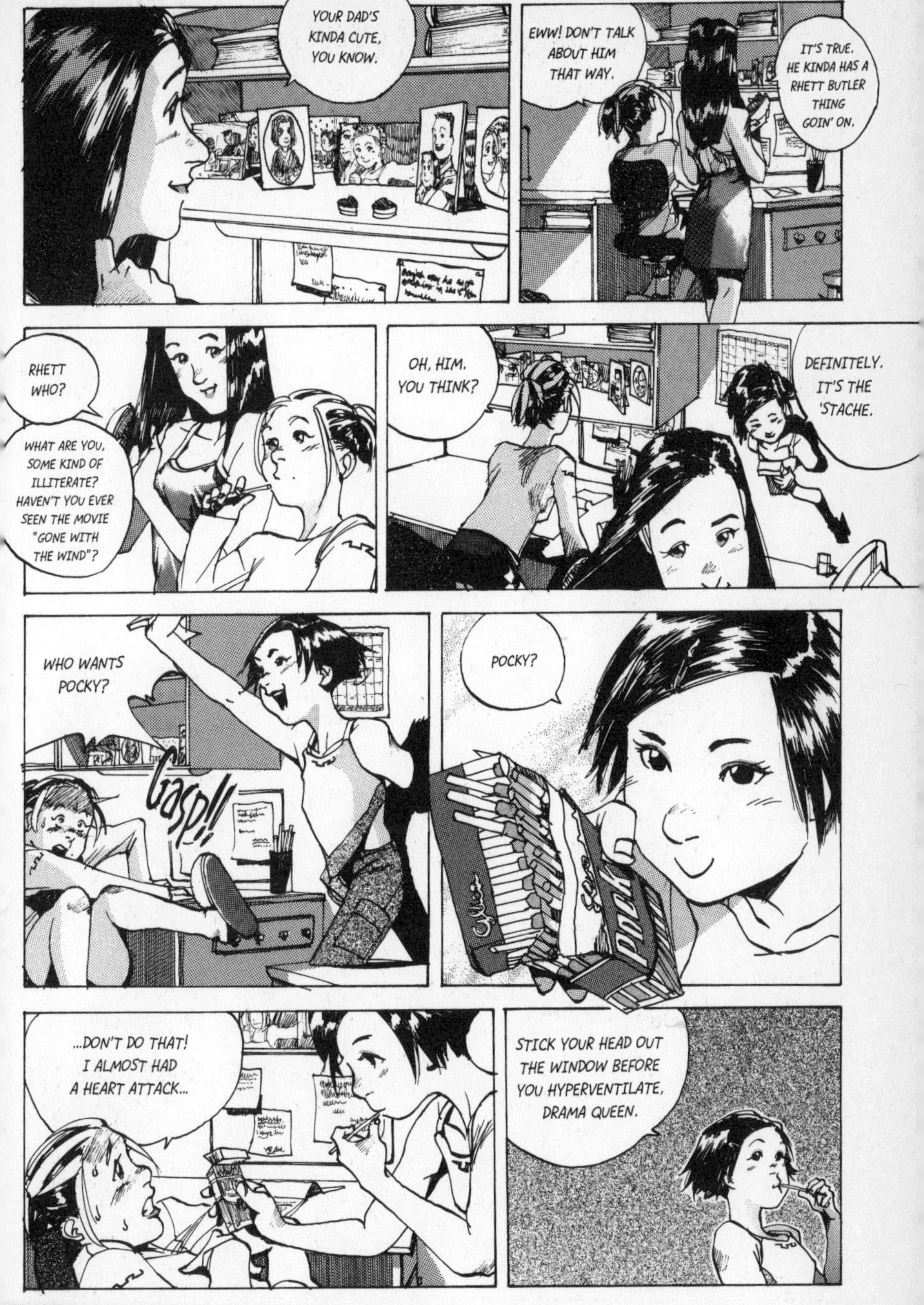
YOUR DAD'S KINDA CUTE, YOU KNOW.
EWW! DON'T TALK ABOUT HIM THAT WAY.
IT'S TRUE. HE KINDA HAS A RHETT BUTLER THING GOIN' ON.
RHETT WHO?
WHAT ARE YOU, SOME KIND OF ILLITERATE? HAVEN'T YOU EVER SEEN THE MOVIE "GONE WITH THE WIND"?
OH, HIM. YOU THINK?
DEFINITELY. IT'S THE 'STACHE.
WHO WANTS POCKY?
Gasp!!
POCKY?
...DON'T DO THAT! I ALMOST HAD A HEART ATTACK...
STICK YOUR HEAD OUT THE WINDOW BEFORE YOU HYPERVENTILATE, DRAMA QUEEN.

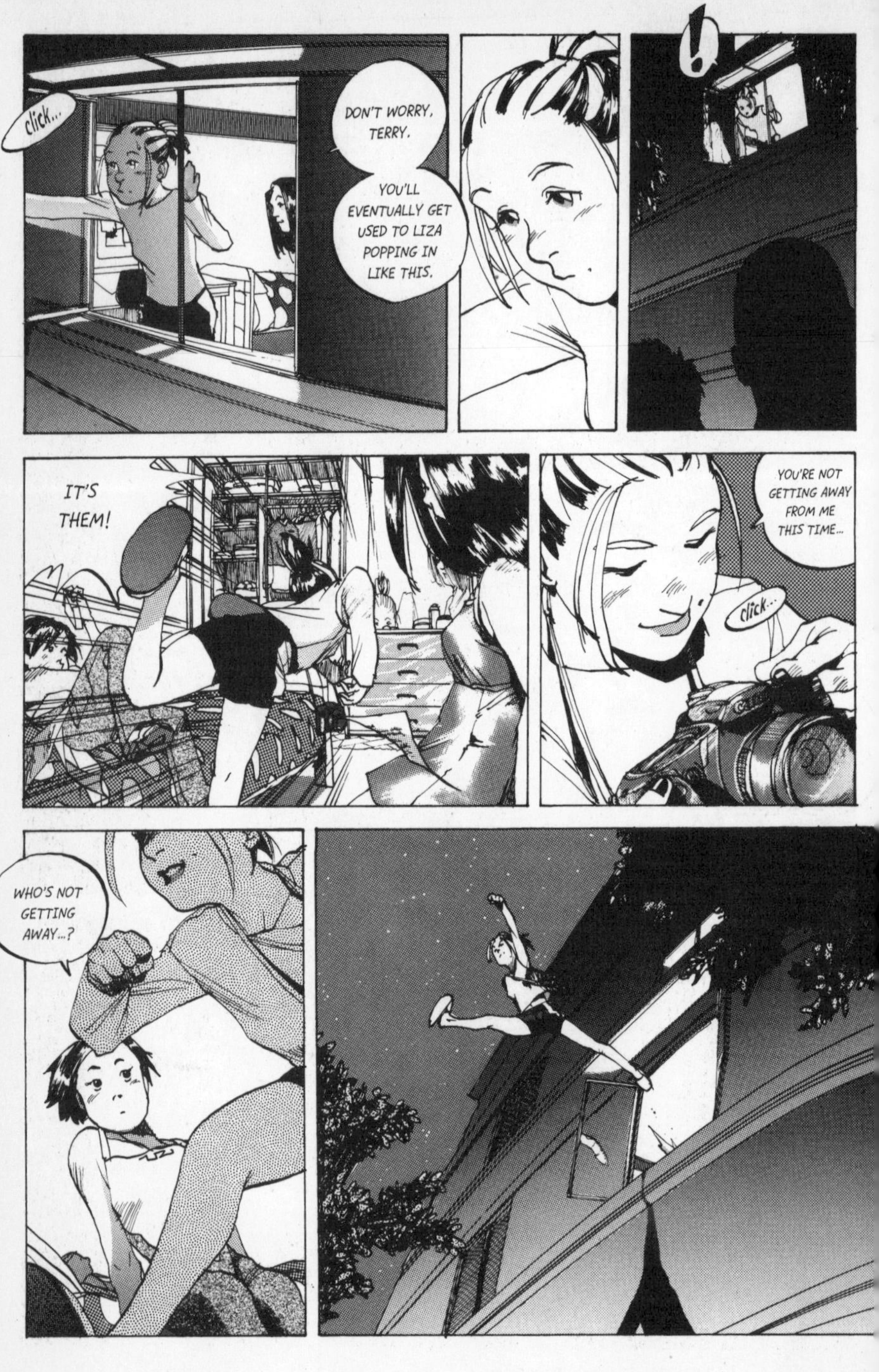
click...
DON'T WORRY, TERRY.
YOU'LL EVENTUALLY GET USED TO LIZA POPPING IN LIKE THIS.
!
IT'S THEM!
YOU'RE NOT GETTING AWAY FROM ME THIS TIME...
click...
WHO'S NOT GETTING AWAY...?

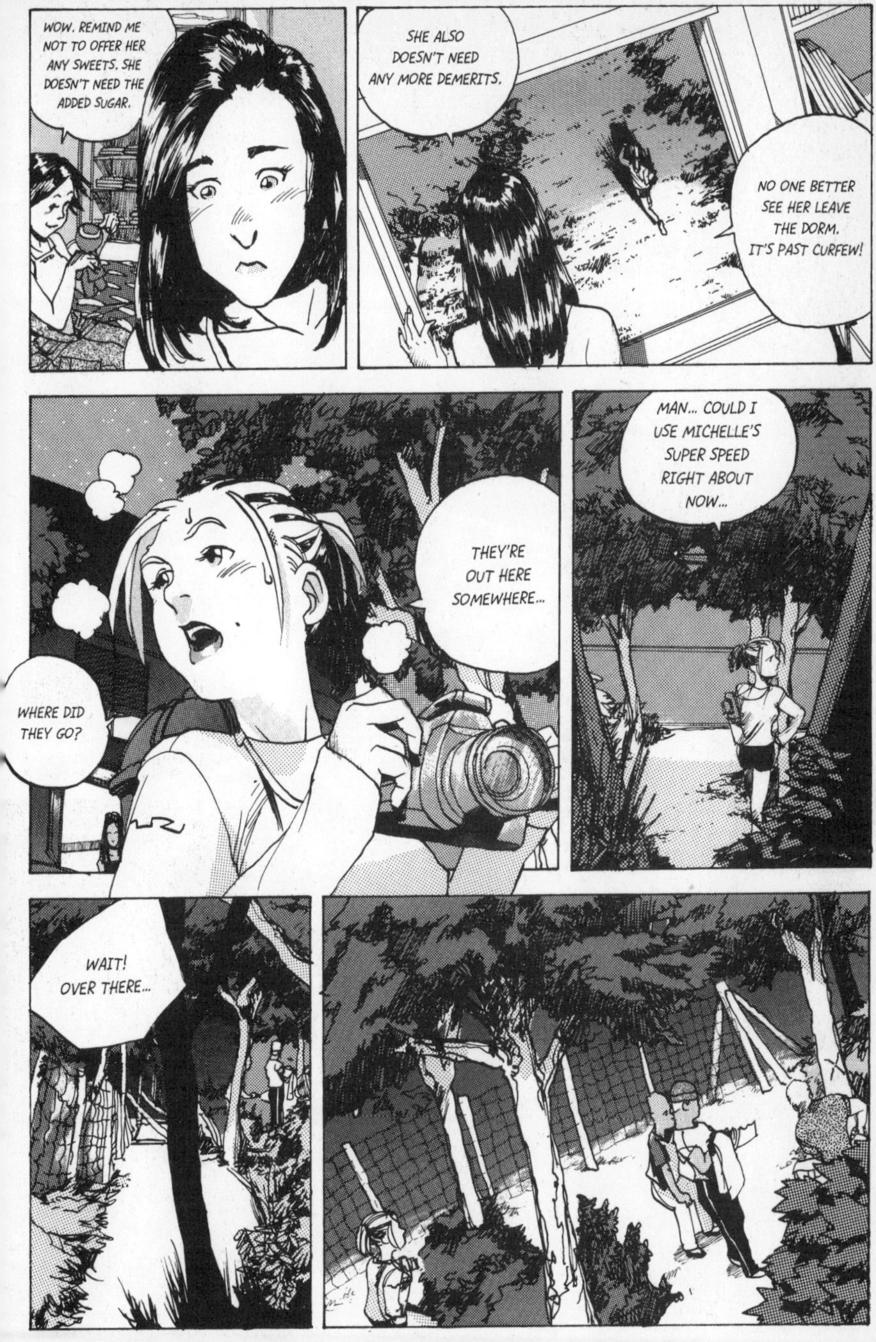

WOW. REMIND ME NOT TO OFFER HER ANY SWEETS. SHE DOESN'T NEED THE ADDED SUGAR.
SHE ALSO DOESN'T NEED ANY MORE DEMERITS.
NO ONE BETTER SEE HER LEAVE THE DORM. IT'S PAST CURFEW!
WHERE DID THEY GO?
THEY'RE OUT HERE SOMEWHERE...
MAN... COULD I USE MICHELLE'S SUPER SPEED RIGHT ABOUT NOW...
WAIT! OVER THERE...

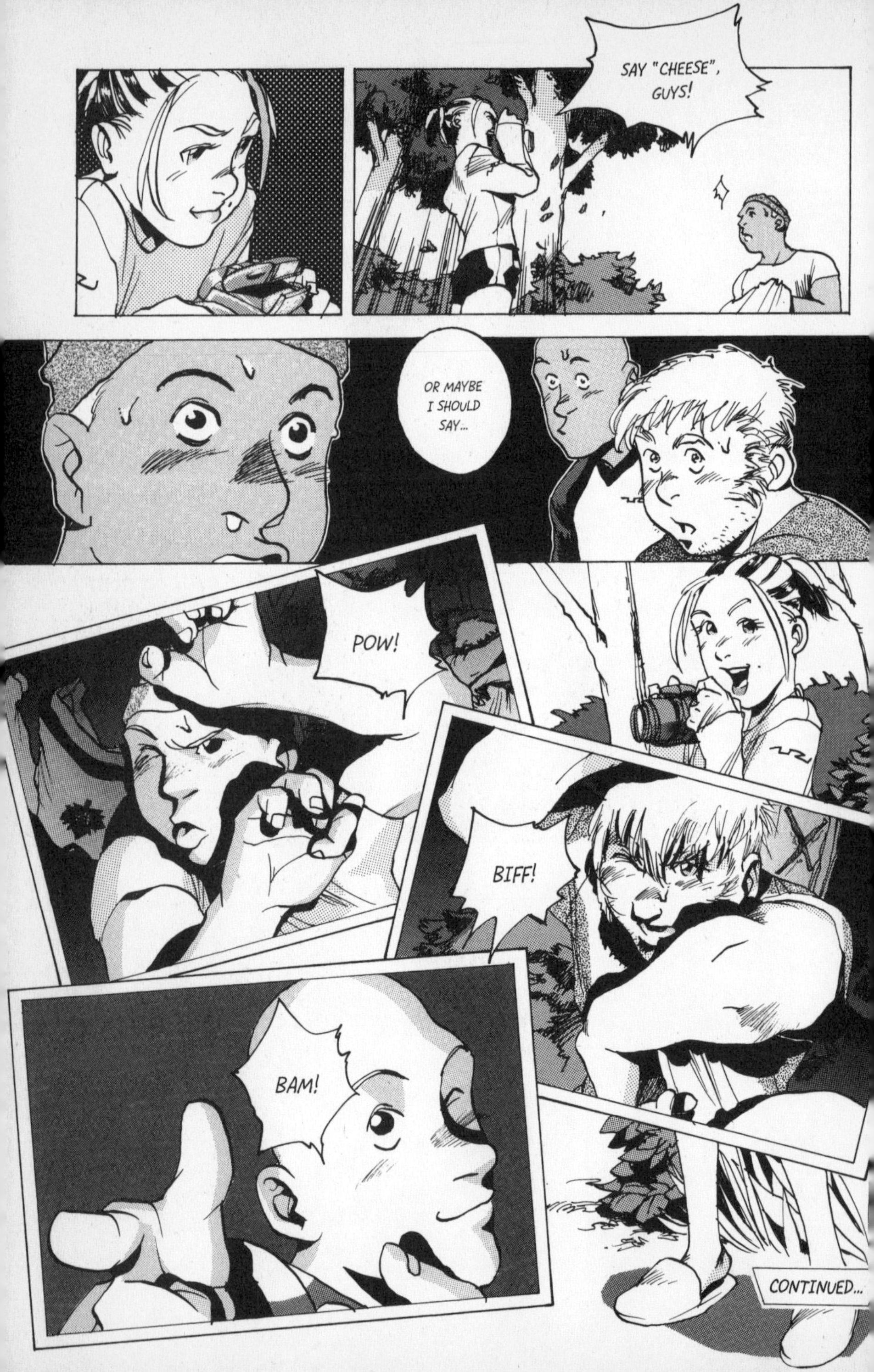
SAY "CHEESE", GUYS!
OR MAYBE I SHOULD SAY...
POW!
BIFF!
BAM!
CONTINUED...

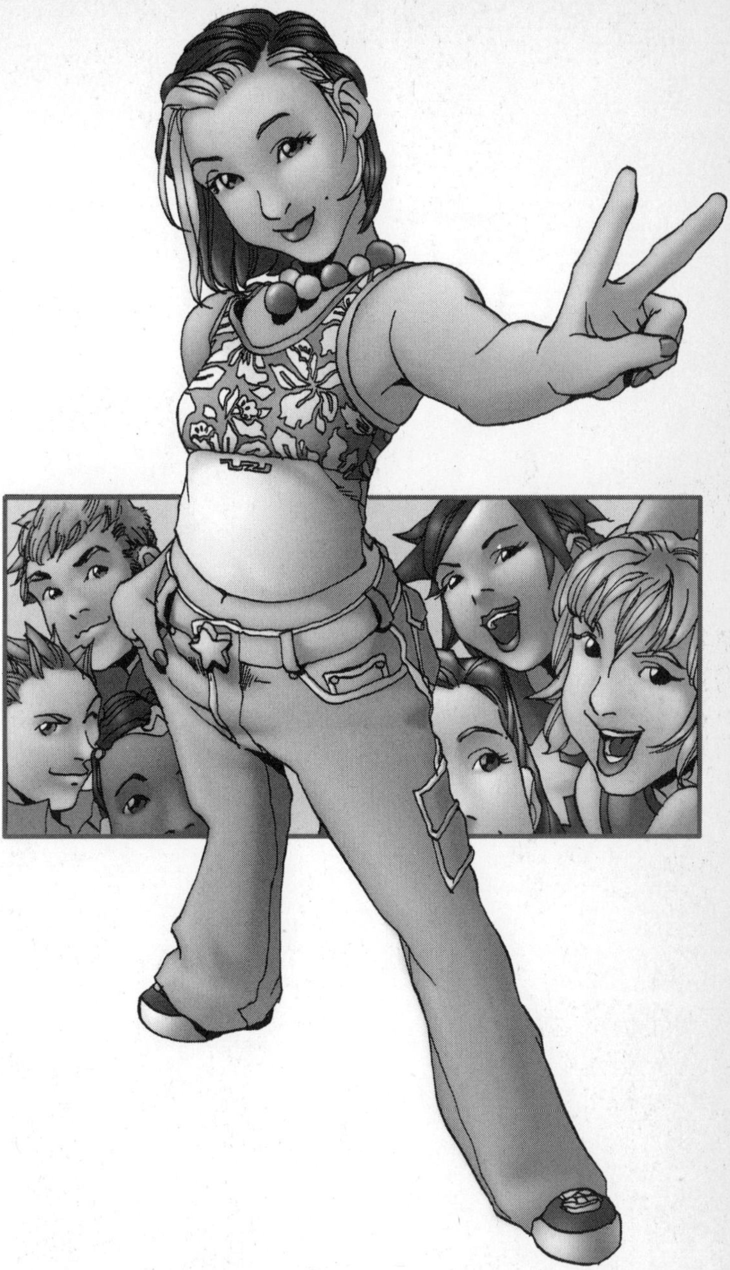

Chapter three

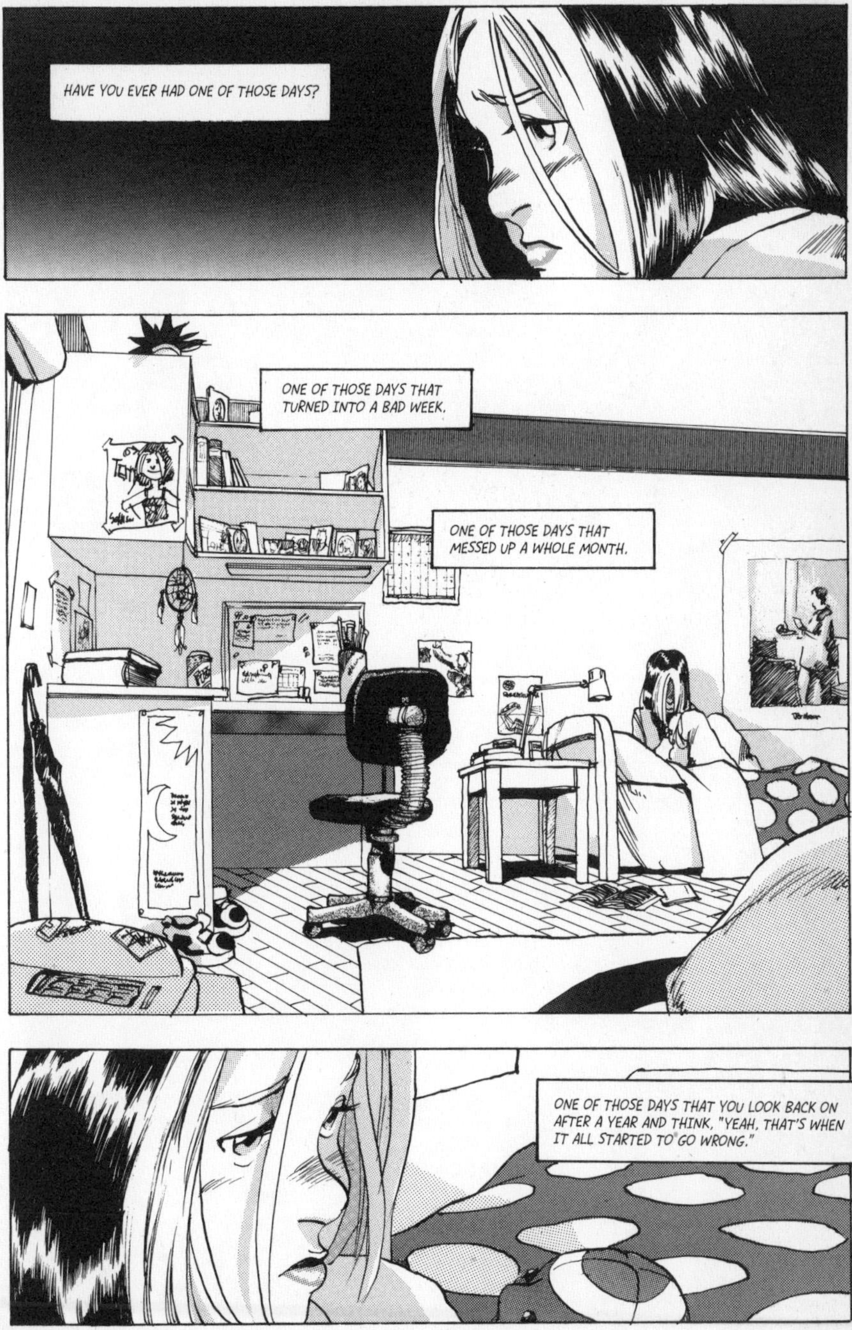
HAVE YOU EVER HAD ONE OF THOSE DAYS?
ONE OF THOSE DAYS THAT TURNED INTO A BAD WEEK.
ONE OF THOSE DAYS THAT MESSED UP A WHOLE MONTH.
ONE OF THOSE DAYS THAT YOU LOOK BACK ON AFTER A YEAR AND THINK, "YEAH, THAT'S WHEN IT ALL STARTED TO GO WRONG."

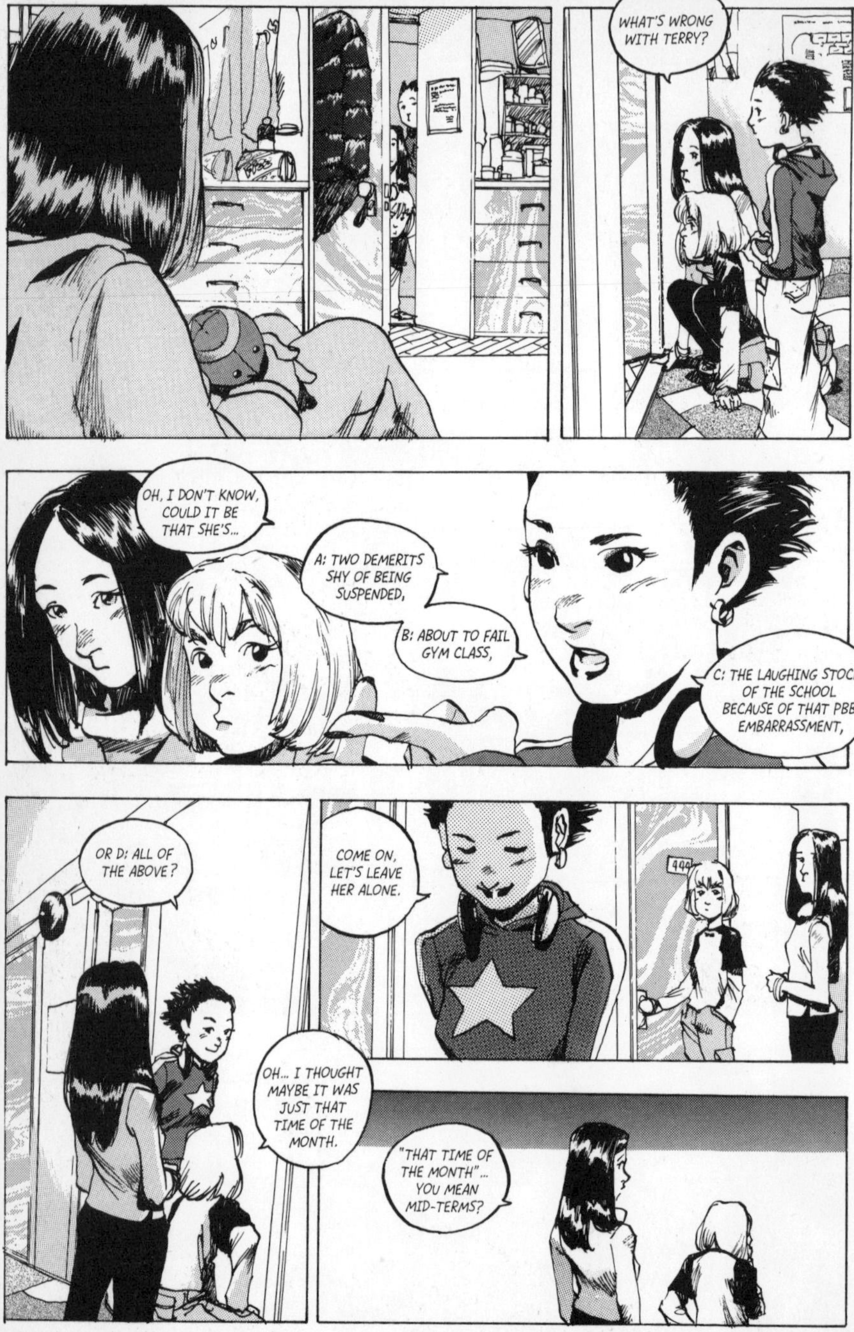
WHAT'S WRONG WITH TERRY?
OH, I DON'T KNOW, COULD IT BE THAT SHE'S...
A: TWO DEMERITS SHY OF BEING SUSPENDED,
B: ABOUT TO FAIL GYM CLASS,
C: THE LAUGHING STOCK OF THE SCHOOL BECAUSE OF THAT PBB EMBARRASSMENT,
OR D: ALL OF THE ABOVE?
COME ON, LET'S LEAVE HER ALONE.
OH... I THOUGHT MAYBE IT WAS JUST THAT TIME OF THE MONTH.
"THAT TIME OF THE MONTH"... YOU MEAN MID-TERMS?

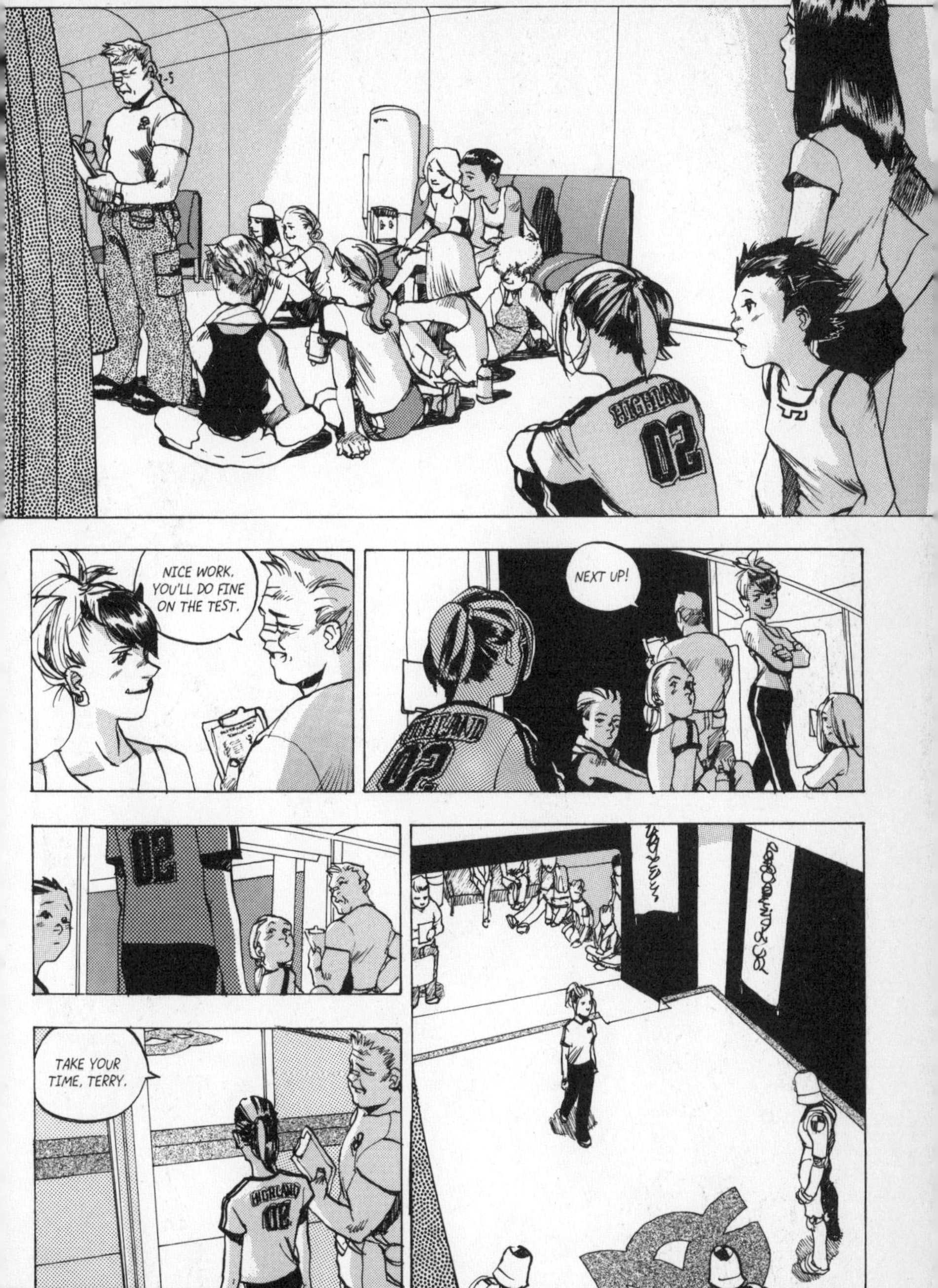
NICE WORK. YOU'LL DO FINE ON THE TEST.
NEXT UP!
TAKE YOUR TIME, TERRY.

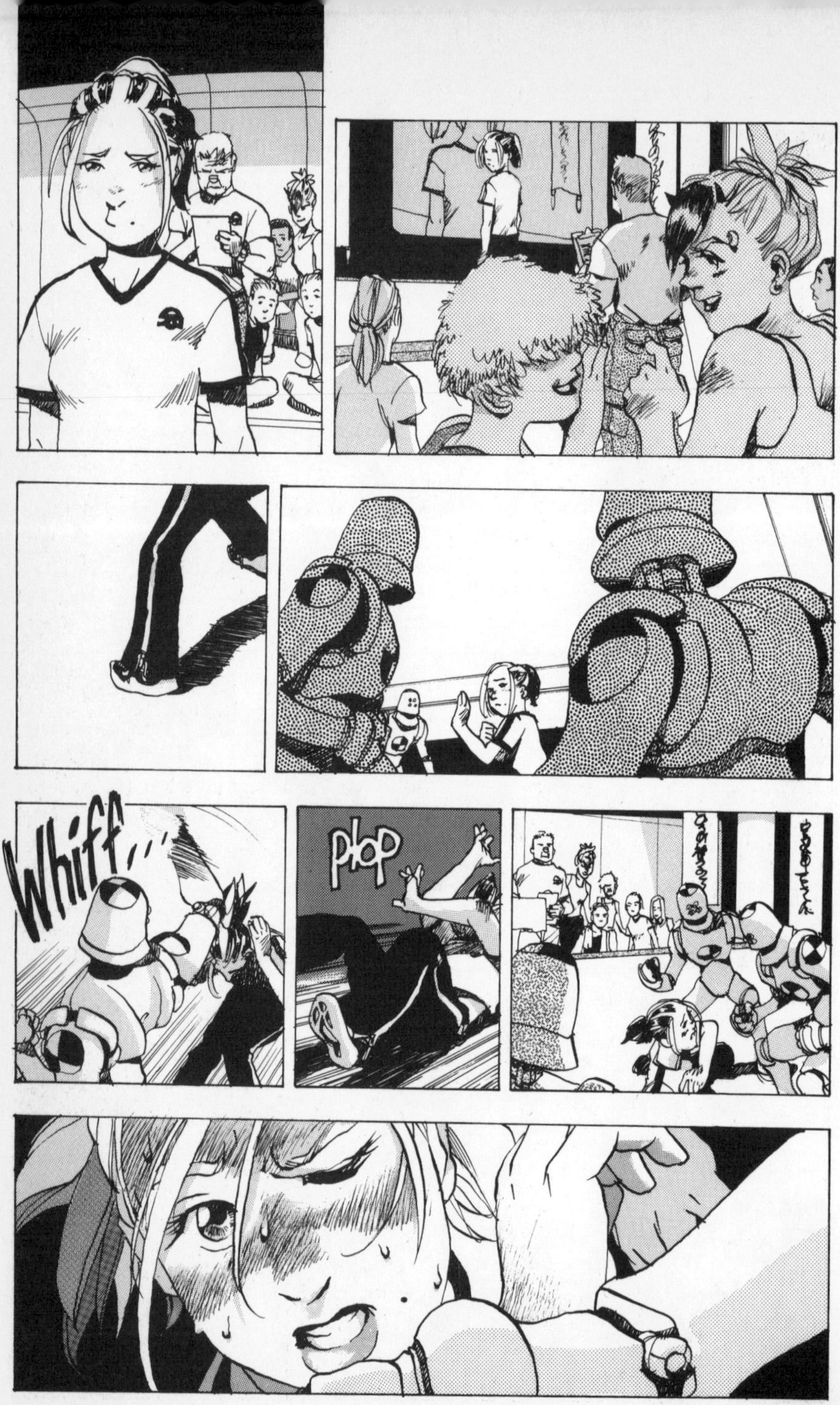
Whiff,,,
plop

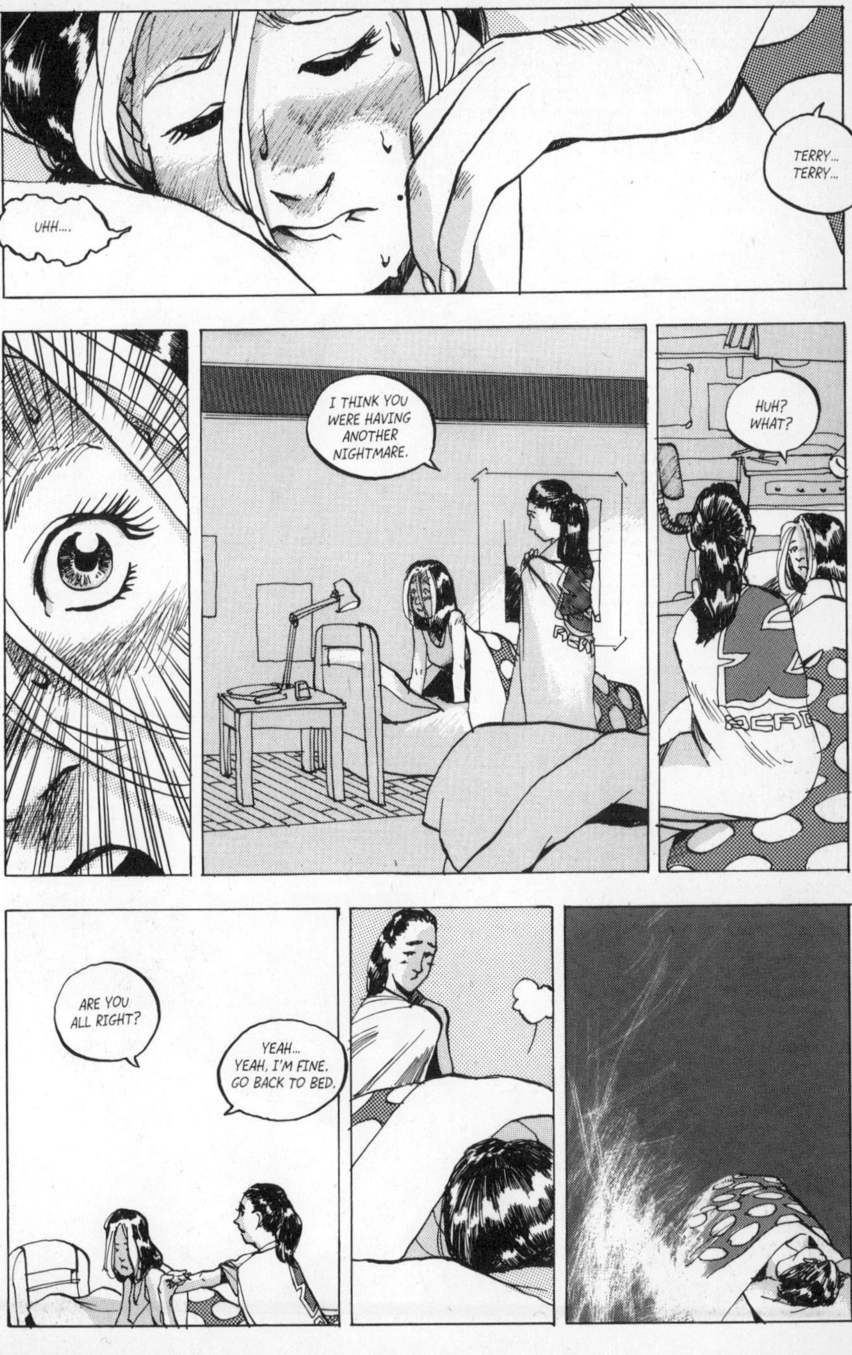
TERRY... TERRY...
UHH....
I THINK YOU WERE HAVING ANOTHER NIGHTMARE.
HUH? WHAT?
ARE YOU ALL RIGHT?
YEAH... YEAH, I'M FINE. GO BACK TO BED.

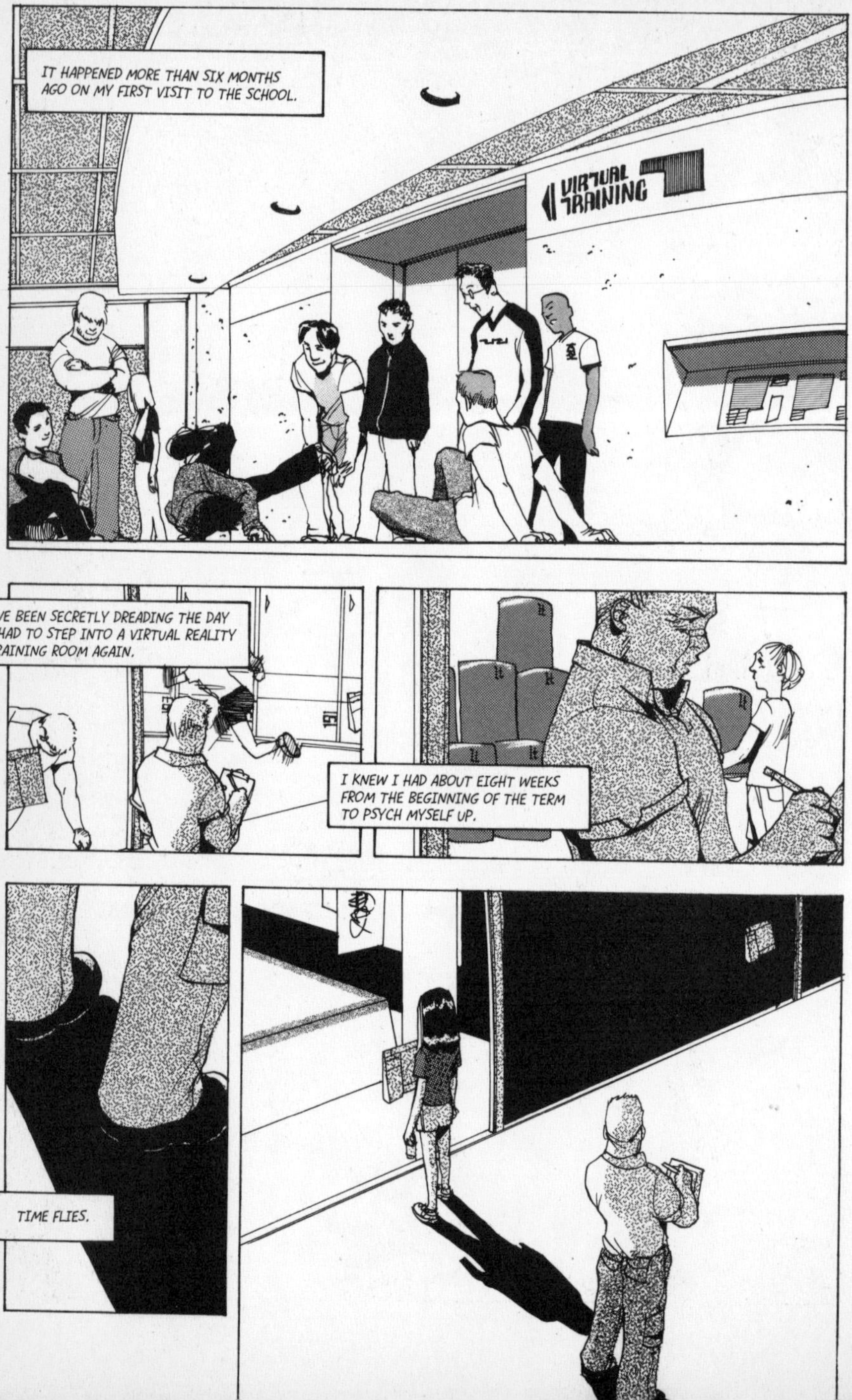

IT HAPPENED MORE THAN SIX MONTHS AGO ON MY FIRST VISIT TO THE SCHOOL.
VIRTUAL TRAINING
I'VE BEEN SECRETLY DREADING THE DAY I HAD TO STEP INTO A VIRTUAL REALITY TRAINING ROOM AGAIN.
I KNEW I HAD ABOUT EIGHT WEEKS FROM THE BEGINNING OF THE TERM TO PSYCH MYSELF UP.
TIME FLIES.

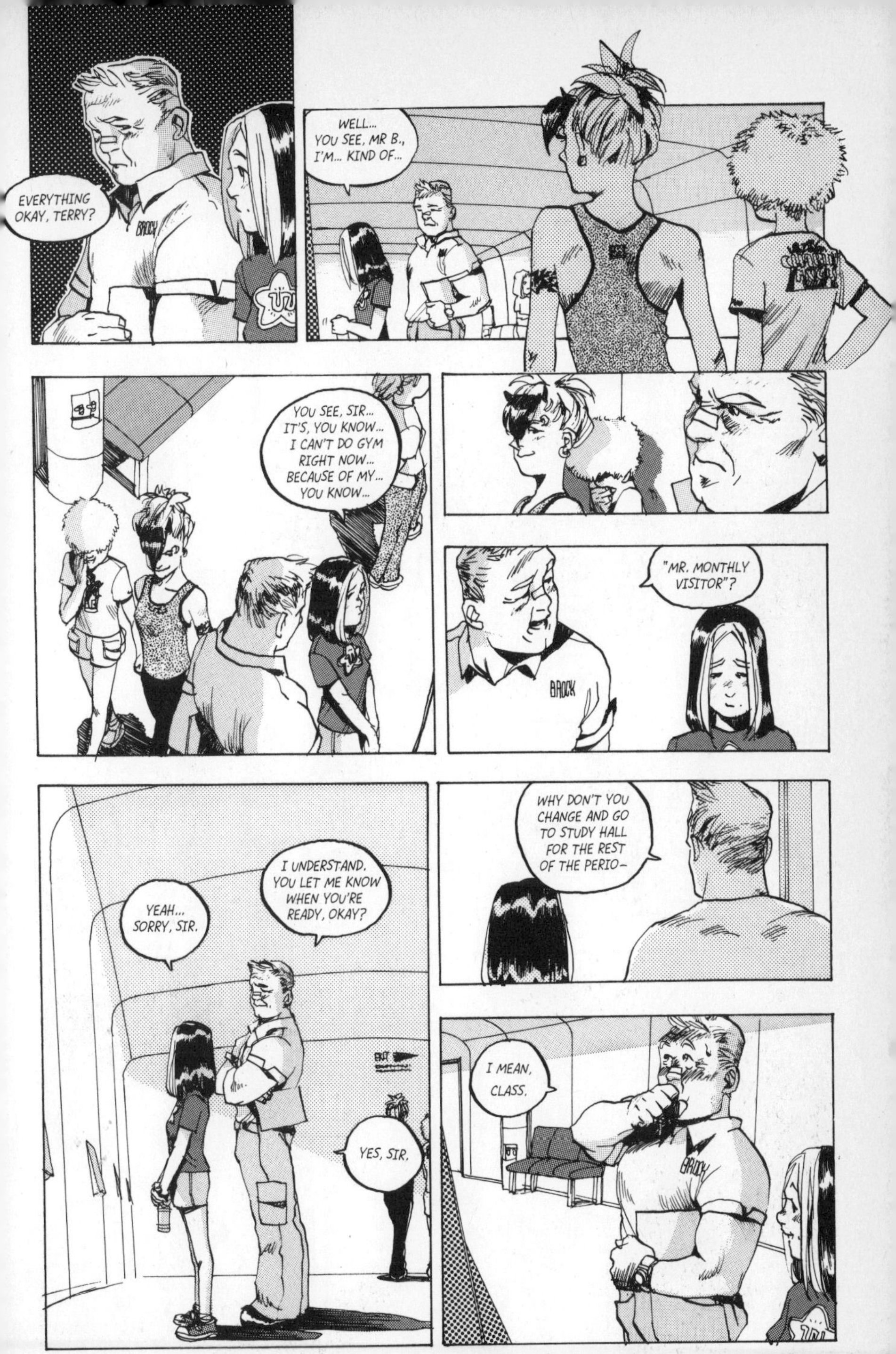
EVERYTHING OKAY, TERRY?
WELL... YOU SEE, MR B., I'M... KIND OF...
YOU SEE, SIR... IT'S, YOU KNOW... I CAN'T DO GYM RIGHT NOW... BECAUSE OF MY... YOU KNOW...
"MR. MONTHLY VISITOR"?
I UNDERSTAND. YOU LET ME KNOW WHEN YOU'RE READY, OKAY?
YEAH... SORRY, SIR.
YES, SIR.
WHY DON'T YOU CHANGE AND GO TO STUDY HALL FOR THE REST OF THE PERIO–
I MEAN, CLASS.

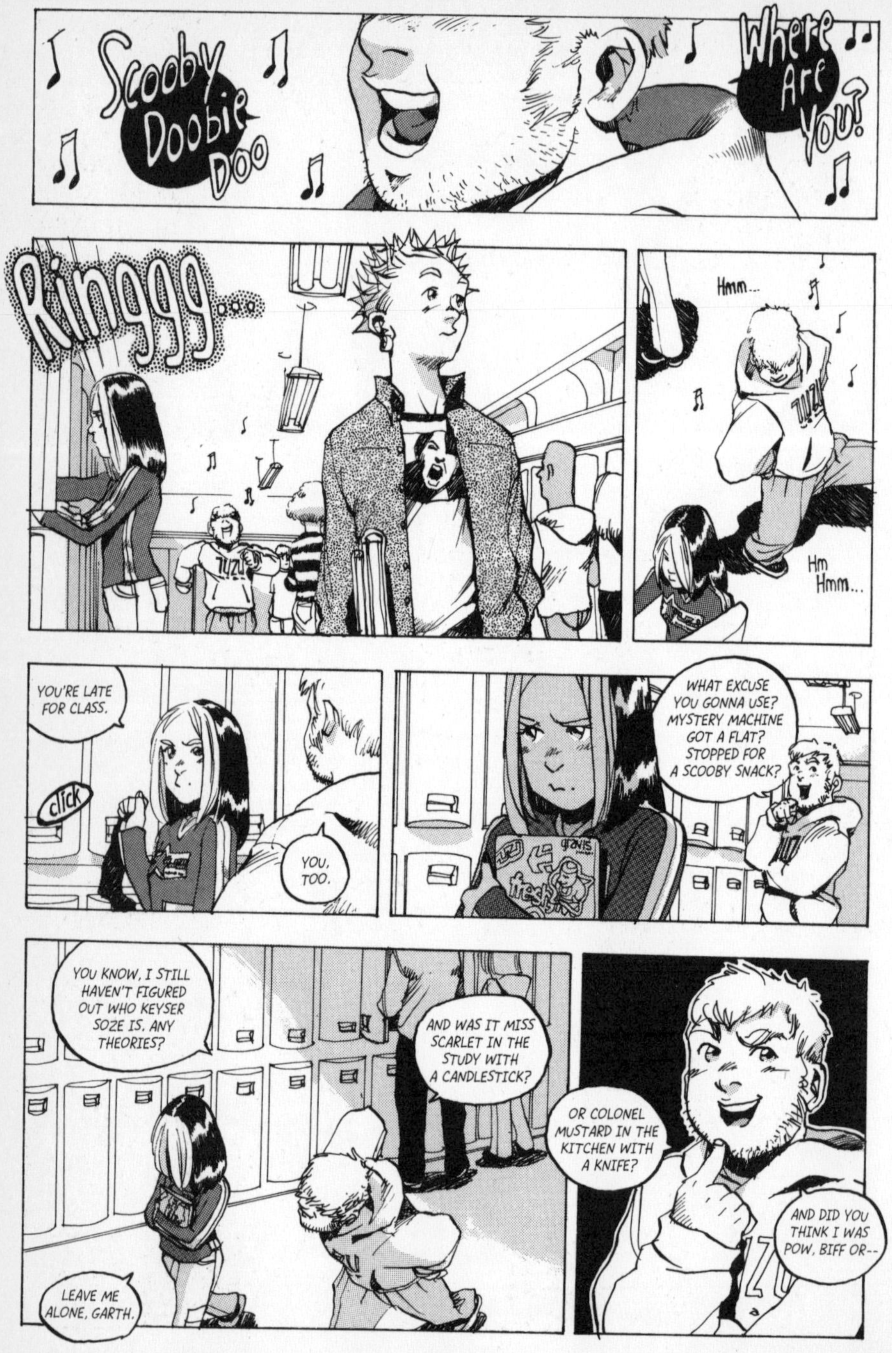
Scooby Doobie Doo
Where Are You?
Ringgg...
Hmm...
Hm Hmm...
YOU'RE LATE FOR CLASS.
click
YOU, TOO.
WHAT EXCUSE YOU GONNA USE? MYSTERY MACHINE GOT A FLAT? STOPPED FOR A SCOOBY SNACK?
YOU KNOW, I STILL HAVEN'T FIGURED OUT WHO KEYSER SOZE IS. ANY THEORIES?
AND WAS IT MISS SCARLET IN THE STUDY WITH A CANDLESTICK?
LEAVE ME ALONE, GARTH.
OR COLONEL MUSTARD IN THE KITCHEN WITH A KNIFE?
AND DID YOU THINK I WAS POW, BIFF OR--

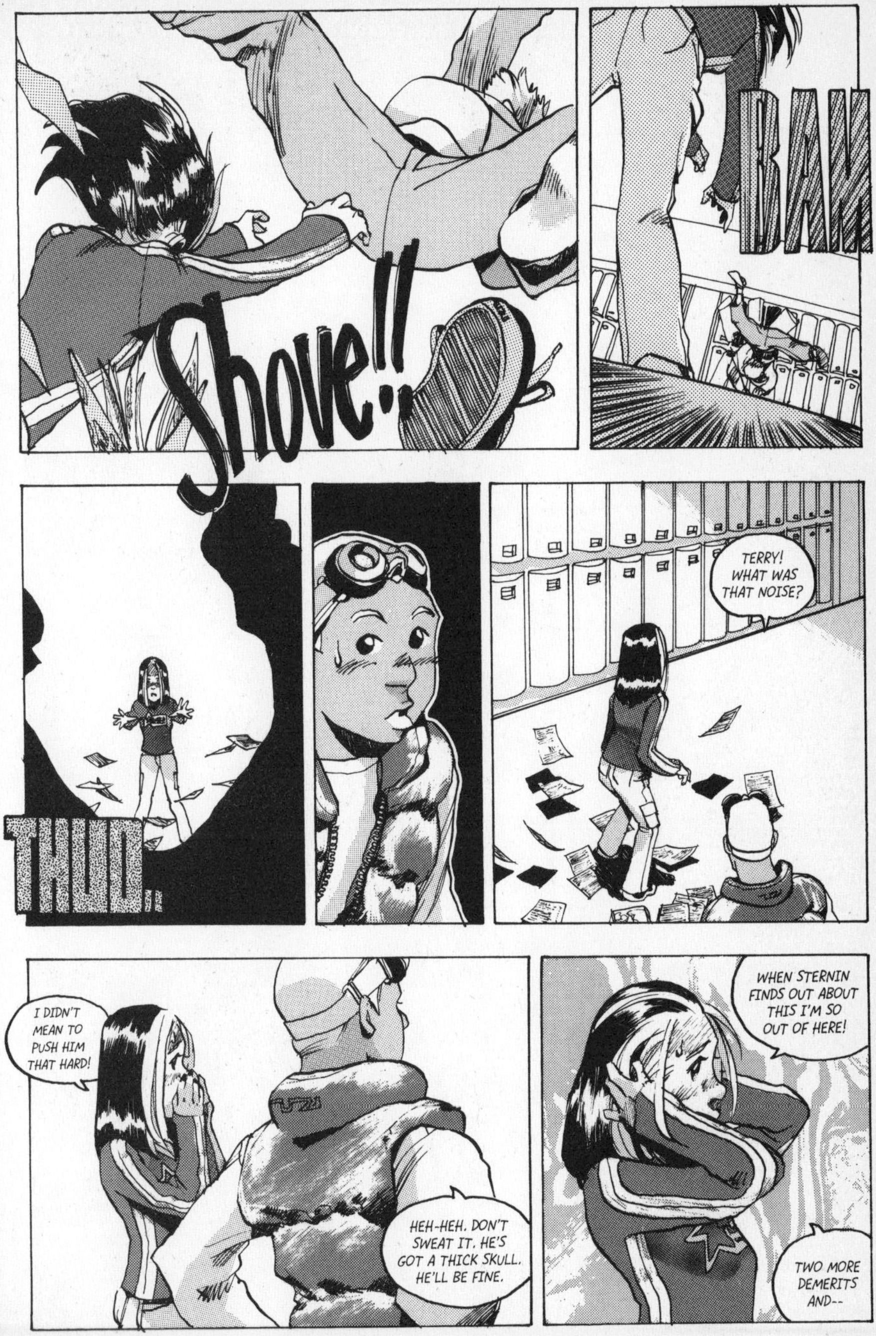
SHOVE!!
BAM
THUD..
TERRY! WHAT WAS THAT NOISE?
I DIDN'T MEAN TO PUSH HIM THAT HARD!
HEH-HEH. DON'T SWEAT IT. HE'S GOT A THICK SKULL. HE'LL BE FINE.
WHEN STERNIN FINDS OUT ABOUT THIS I'M SO OUT OF HERE!
TWO MORE DEMERITS AND--

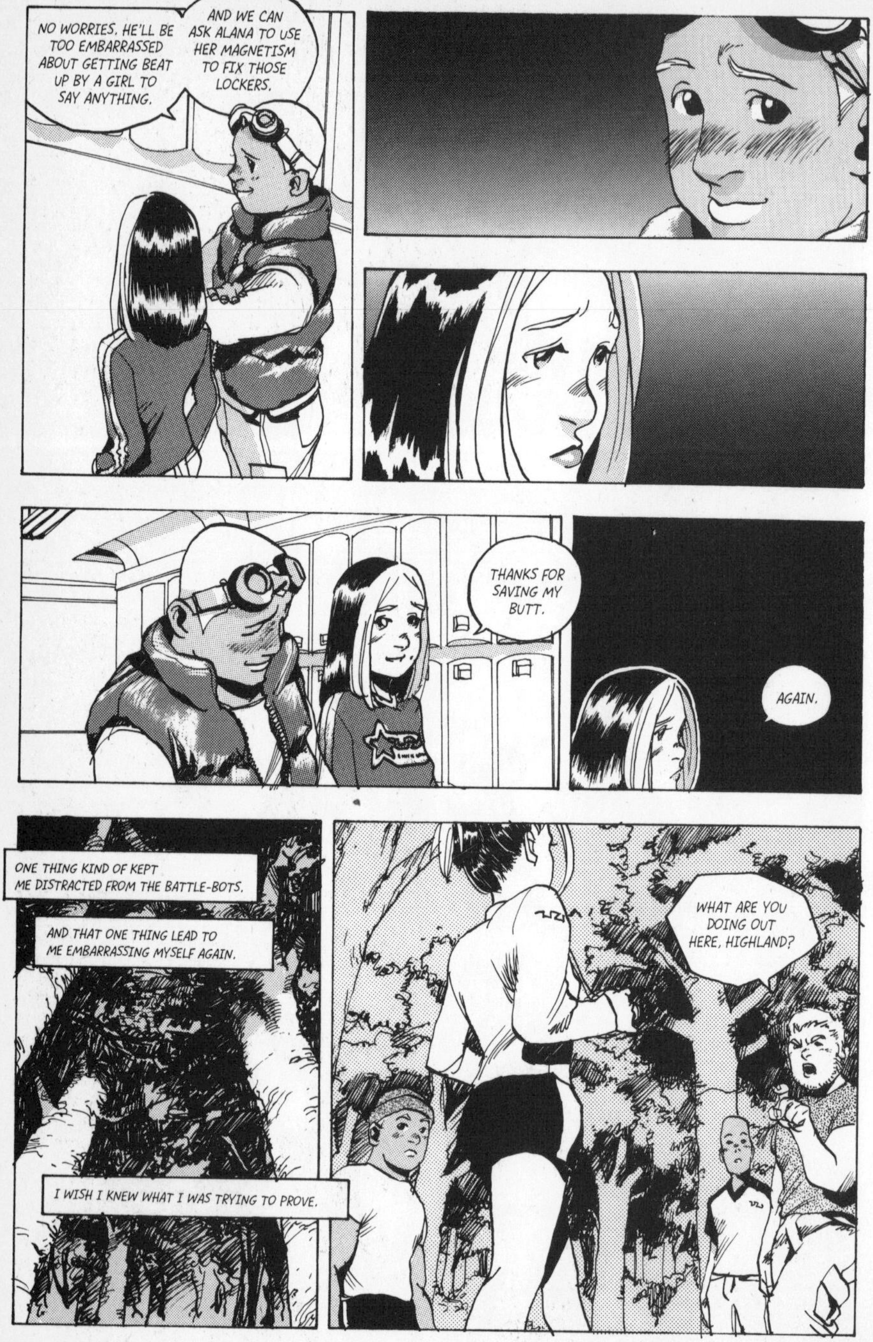
NO WORRIES. HE'LL BE TOO EMBARRASSED ABOUT GETTING BEAT UP BY A GIRL TO SAY ANYTHING.
AND WE CAN ASK ALANA TO USE HER MAGNETISM TO FIX THOSE LOCKERS.
THANKS FOR SAVING MY BUTT.
AGAIN.
ONE THING KIND OF KEPT ME DISTRACTED FROM THE BATTLE-BOTS.
AND THAT ONE THING LEAD TO ME EMBARRASSING MYSELF AGAIN.
I WISH I KNEW WHAT I WAS TRYING TO PROVE.
WHAT ARE YOU DOING OUT HERE, HIGHLAND?

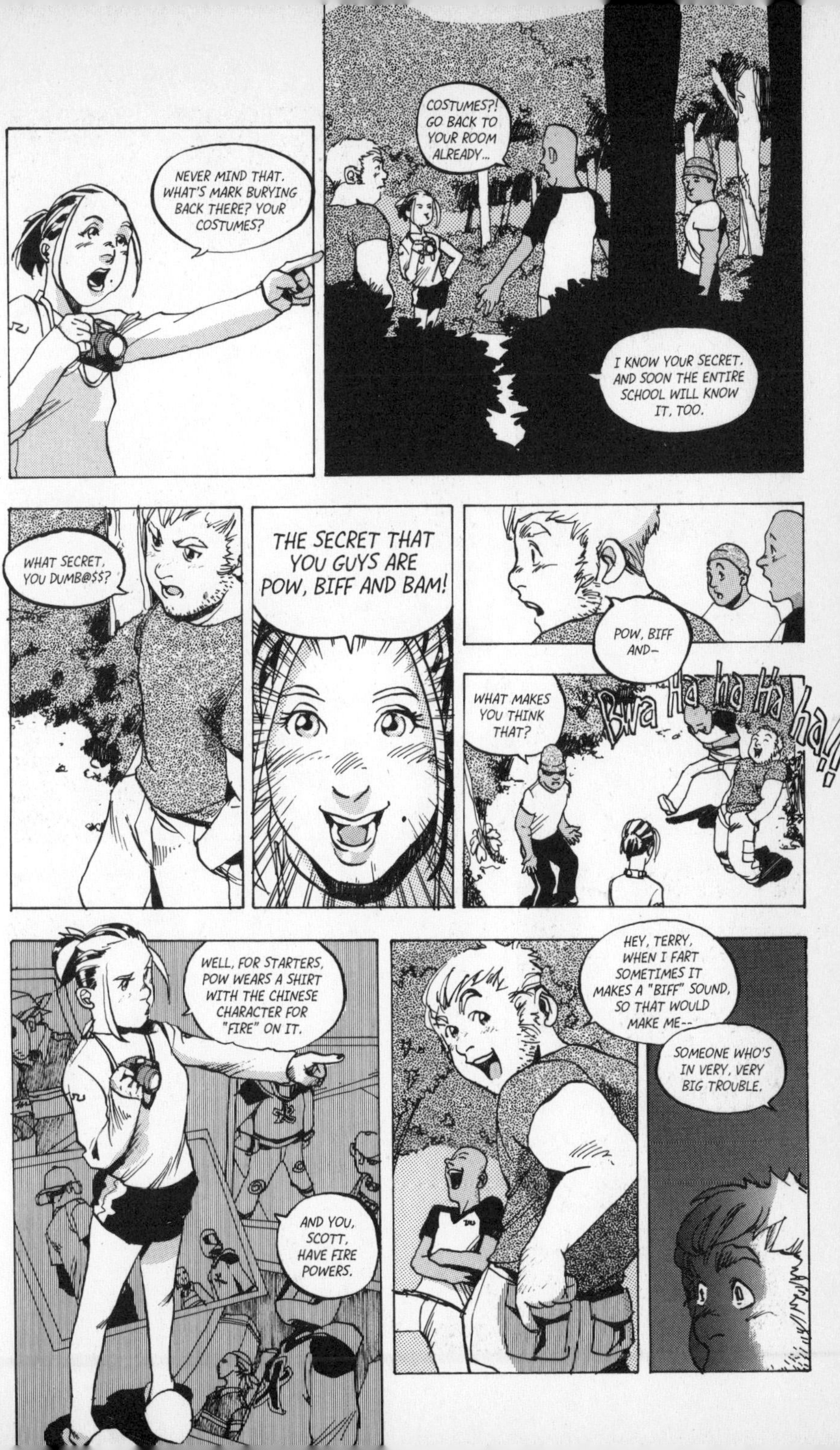
NEVER MIND THAT. WHAT'S MARK BURYING BACK THERE? YOUR COSTUMES?
COSTUMES?! GO BACK TO YOUR ROOM ALREADY...
I KNOW YOUR SECRET. AND SOON THE ENTIRE SCHOOL WILL KNOW IT, TOO.
WHAT SECRET, YOU DUMB@$$?
THE SECRET THAT YOU GUYS ARE POW, BIFF AND BAM!
POW, BIFF AND--
WHAT MAKES YOU THINK THAT?
Bwa Ha ha Ha ha!!
WELL, FOR STARTERS, POW WEARS A SHIRT WITH THE CHINESE CHARACTER FOR "FIRE" ON IT.
AND YOU, SCOTT, HAVE FIRE POWERS.
HEY, TERRY, WHEN I FART SOMETIMES IT MAKES A "BIFF" SOUND, SO THAT WOULD MAKE ME--
SOMEONE WHO'S IN VERY, VERY BIG TROUBLE.

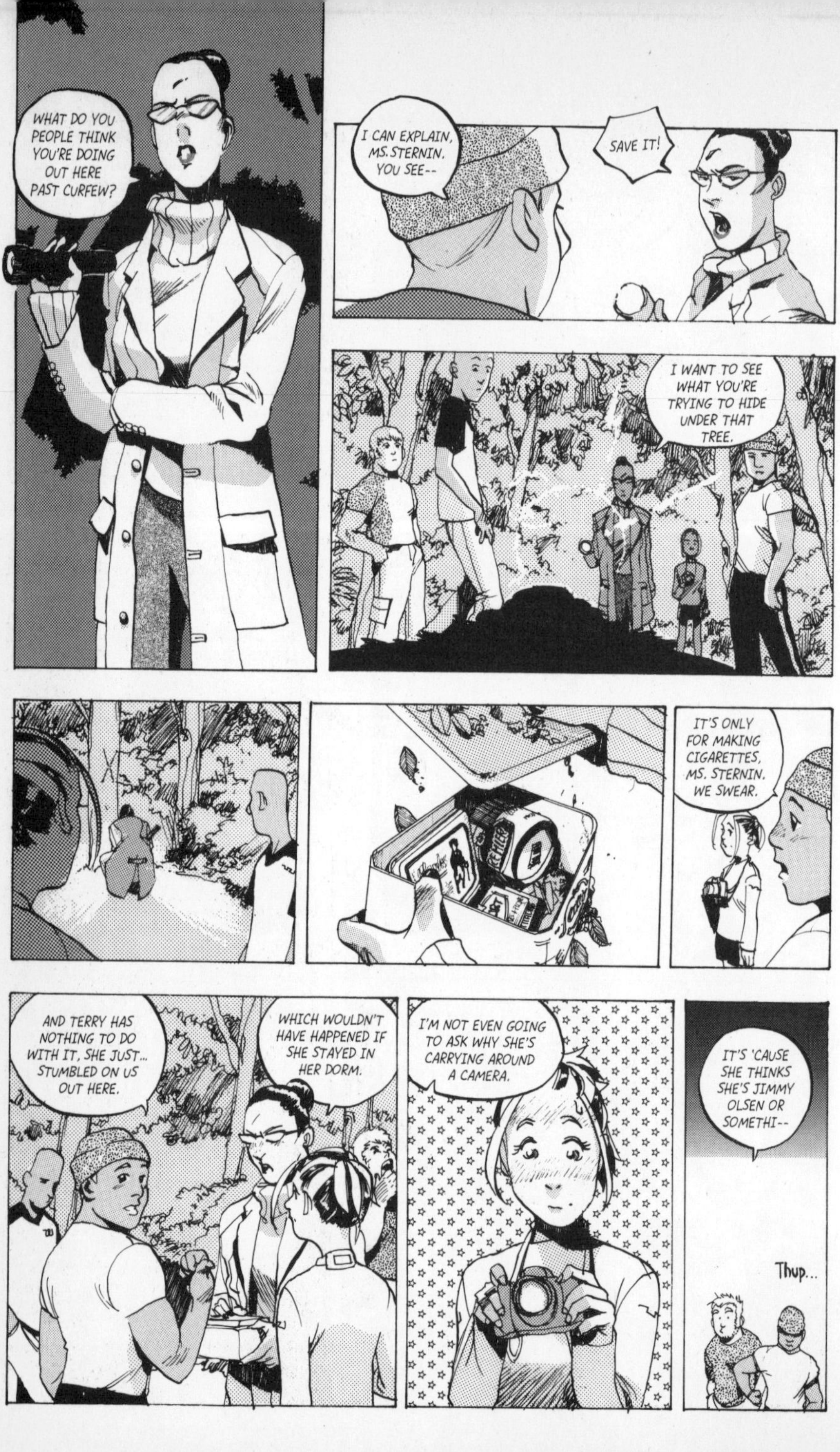
WHAT DO YOU PEOPLE THINK YOU'RE DOING OUT HERE PAST CURFEW?
I CAN EXPLAIN, MS. STERNIN. YOU SEE--
SAVE IT!
I WANT TO SEE WHAT YOU'RE TRYING TO HIDE UNDER THAT TREE.
IT'S ONLY FOR MAKING CIGARETTES, MS. STERNIN. WE SWEAR.
AND TERRY HAS NOTHING TO DO WITH IT, SHE JUST... STUMBLED ON US OUT HERE.
WHICH WOULDN'T HAVE HAPPENED IF SHE STAYED IN HER DORM.
I'M NOT EVEN GOING TO ASK WHY SHE'S CARRYING AROUND A CAMERA.
IT'S 'CAUSE SHE THINKS SHE'S JIMMY OLSEN OR SOMETHI--
Thup...

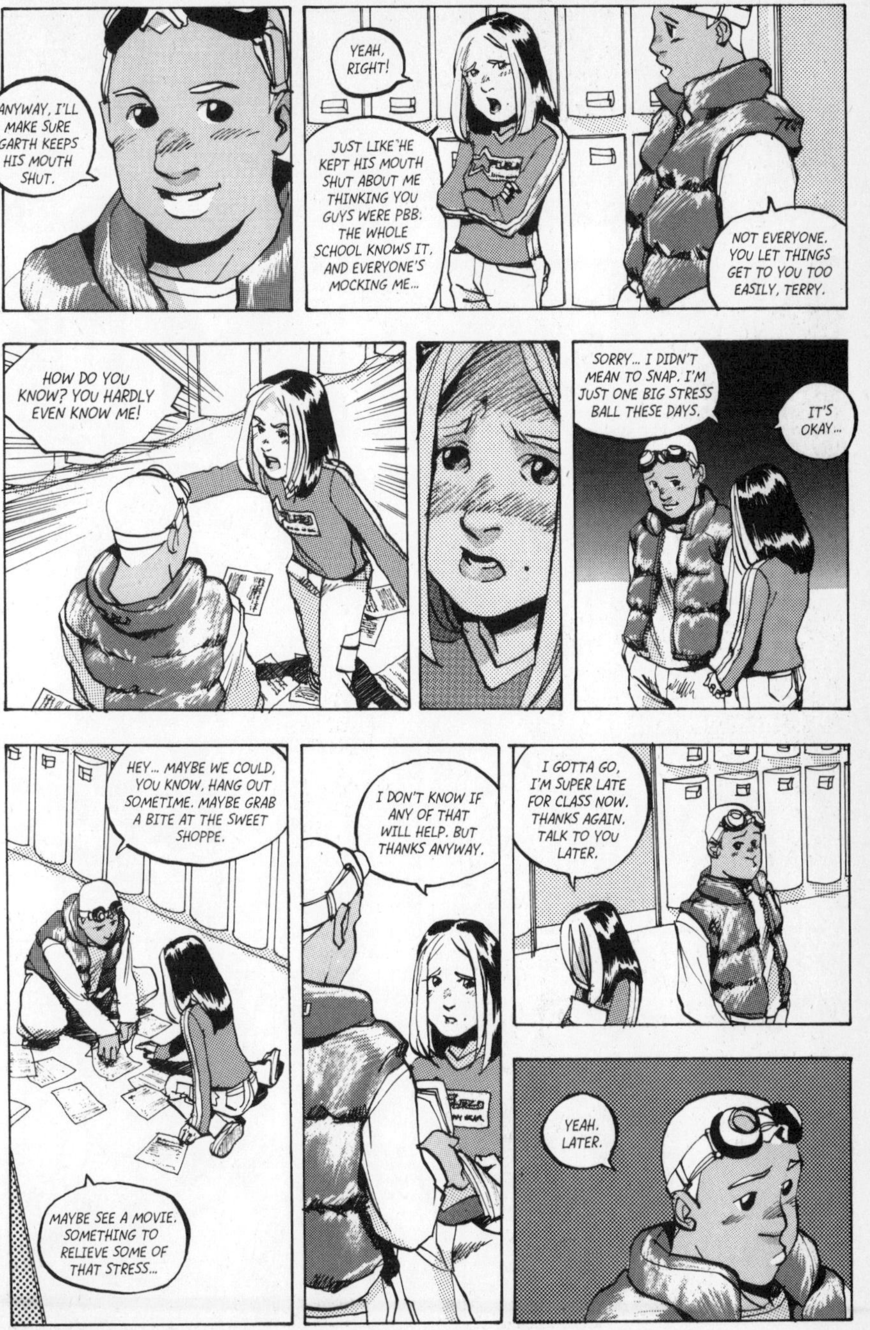
ANYWAY, I'LL MAKE SURE GARTH KEEPS HIS MOUTH SHUT.
YEAH, RIGHT!
JUST LIKE HE KEPT HIS MOUTH SHUT ABOUT ME THINKING YOU GUYS WERE PBB. THE WHOLE SCHOOL KNOWS IT, AND EVERYONE'S MOCKING ME...
NOT EVERYONE. YOU LET THINGS GET TO YOU TOO EASILY, TERRY.
HOW DO YOU KNOW? YOU HARDLY EVEN KNOW ME!
SORRY... I DIDN'T MEAN TO SNAP. I'M JUST ONE BIG STRESS BALL THESE DAYS.
IT'S OKAY...
HEY... MAYBE WE COULD, YOU KNOW, HANG OUT SOMETIME. MAYBE GRAB A BITE AT THE SWEET SHOPPE.
MAYBE SEE A MOVIE. SOMETHING TO RELIEVE SOME OF THAT STRESS...
I DON'T KNOW IF ANY OF THAT WILL HELP. BUT THANKS ANYWAY.
I GOTTA GO, I'M SUPER LATE FOR CLASS NOW. THANKS AGAIN. TALK TO YOU LATER.
YEAH. LATER.

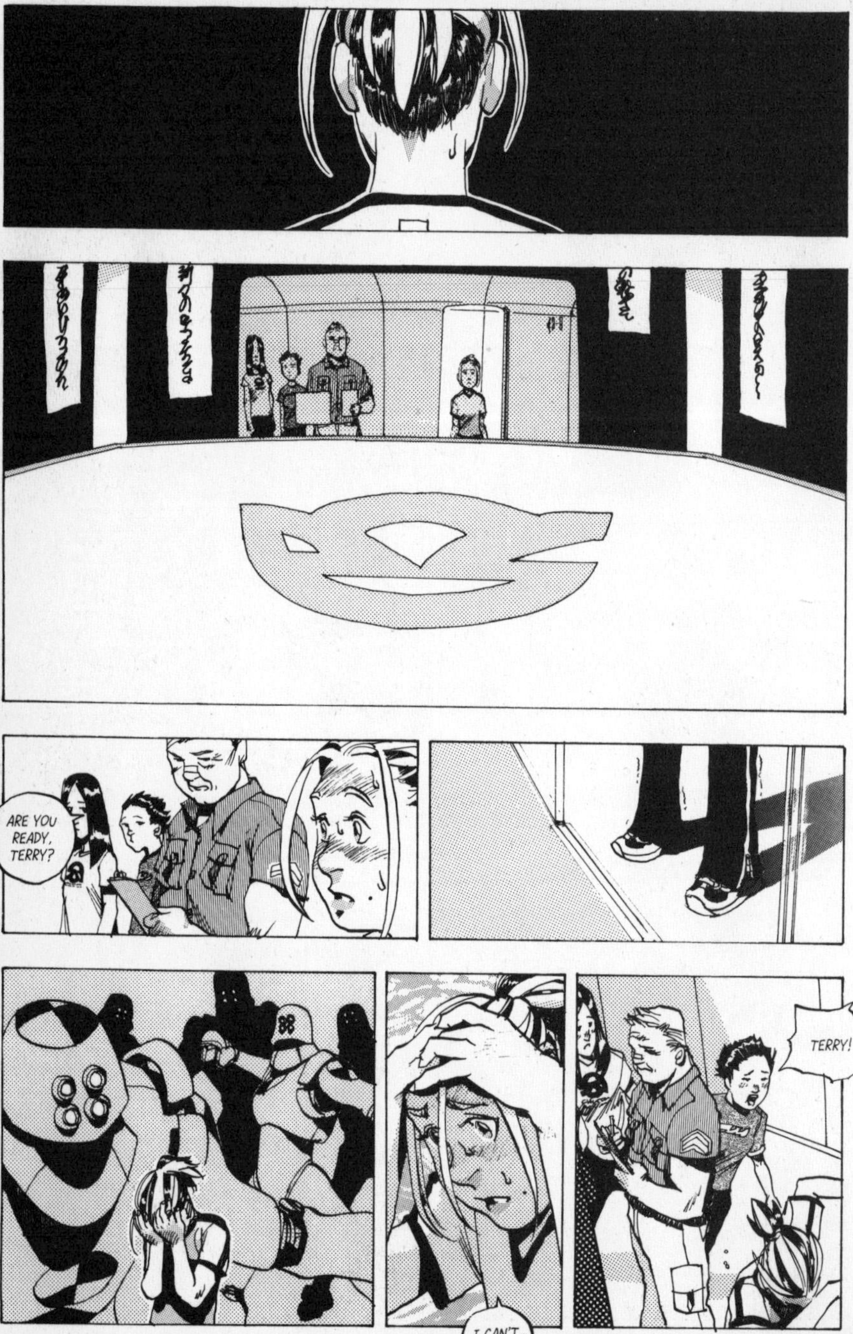
ARE YOU READY, TERRY?
TERRY!
I CAN'T...

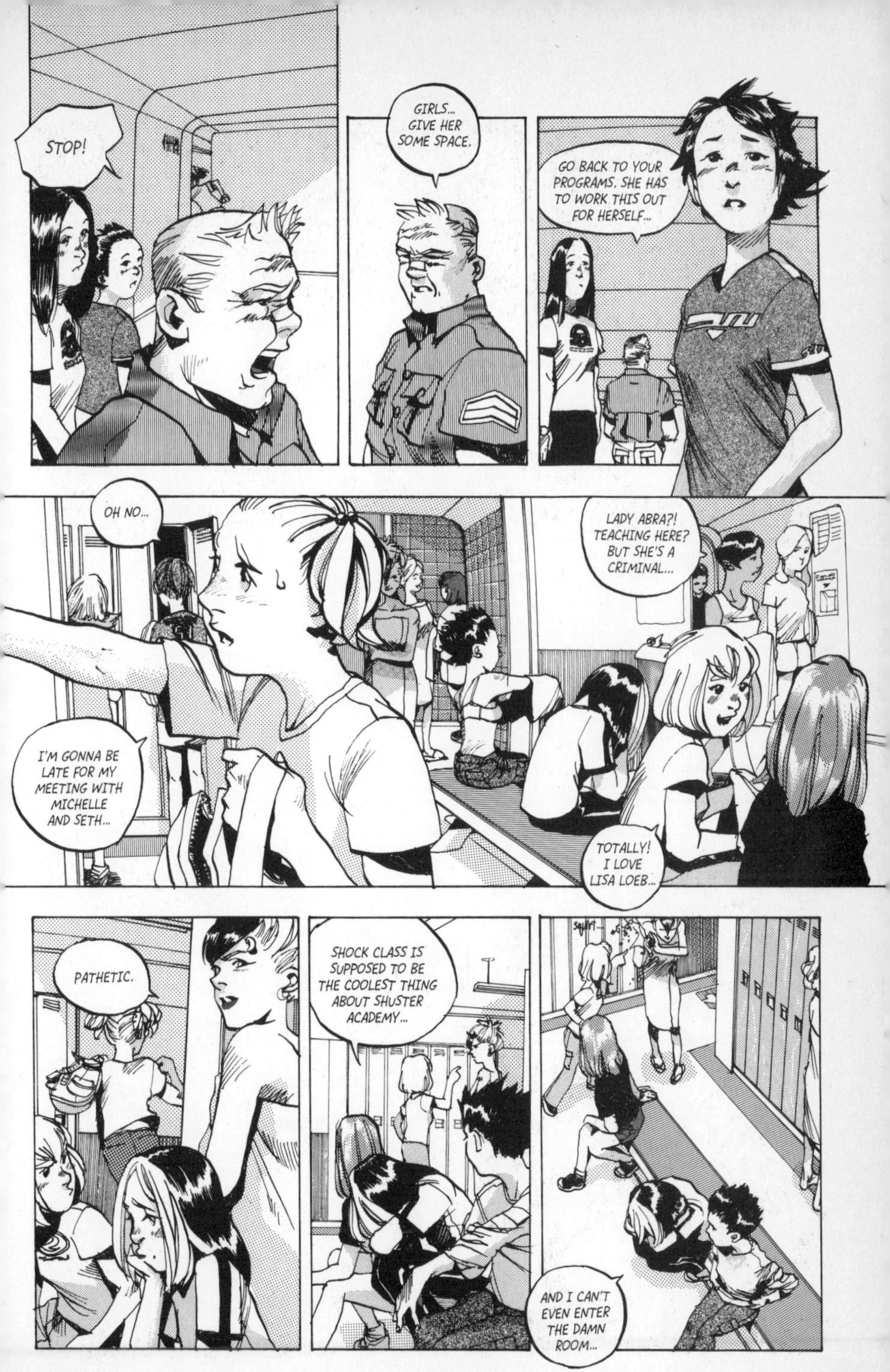
STOP!
GIRLS... GIVE HER SOME SPACE.
GO BACK TO YOUR PROGRAMS. SHE HAS TO WORK THIS OUT FOR HERSELF...
OH NO...
I'M GONNA BE LATE FOR MY MEETING WITH MICHELLE AND SETH...
LADY ABRA?! TEACHING HERE? BUT SHE'S A CRIMINAL...
TOTALLY! I LOVE LISA LOEB...
PATHETIC.
SHOCK CLASS IS SUPPOSED TO BE THE COOLEST THING ABOUT SHUSTER ACADEMY...
AND I CAN'T EVEN ENTER THE DAMN ROOM...

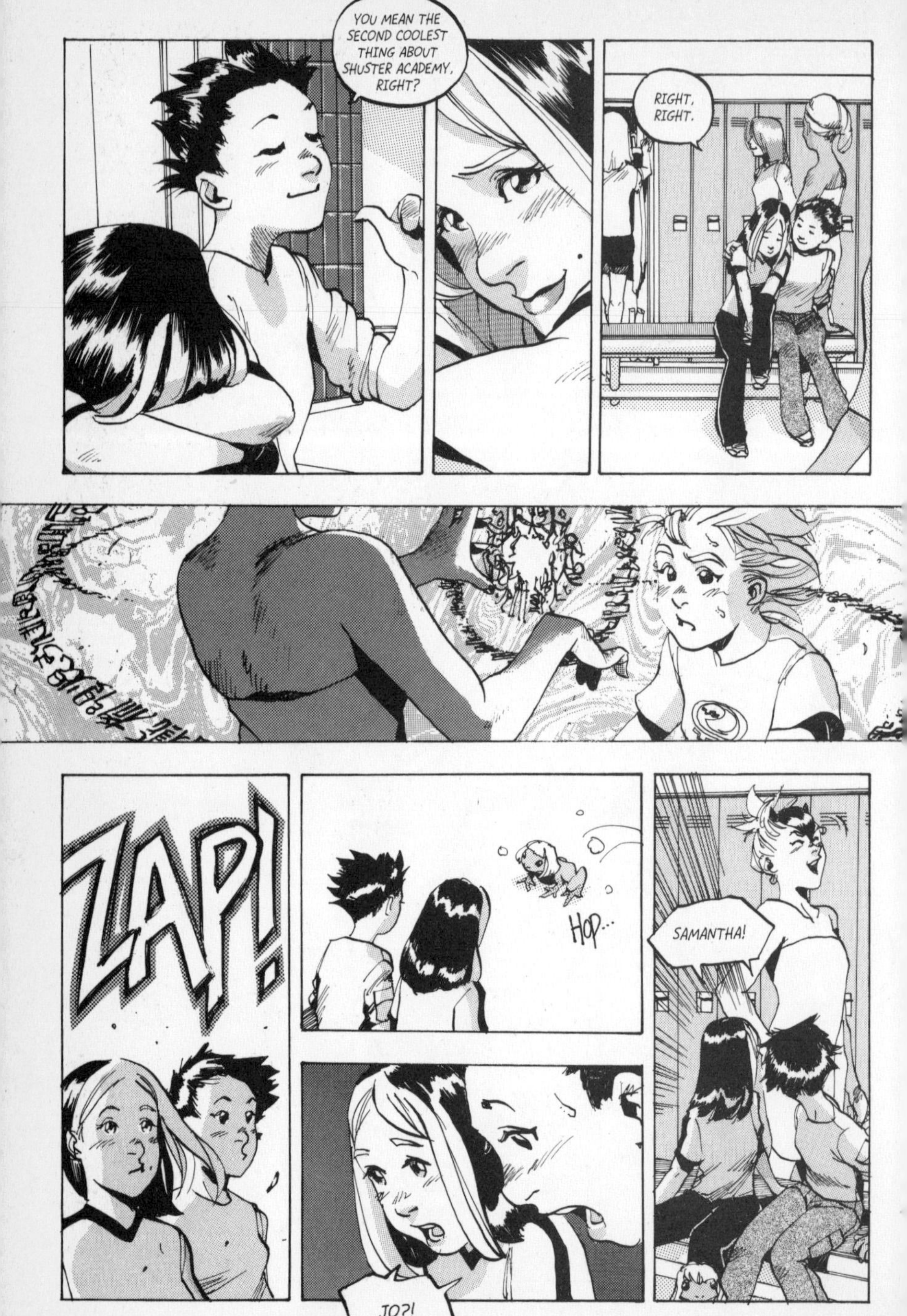
YOU MEAN THE SECOND COOLEST THING ABOUT SHUSTER ACADEMY, RIGHT?
RIGHT, RIGHT.
ZAP!
HOP...
SAMANTHA!
JO?!

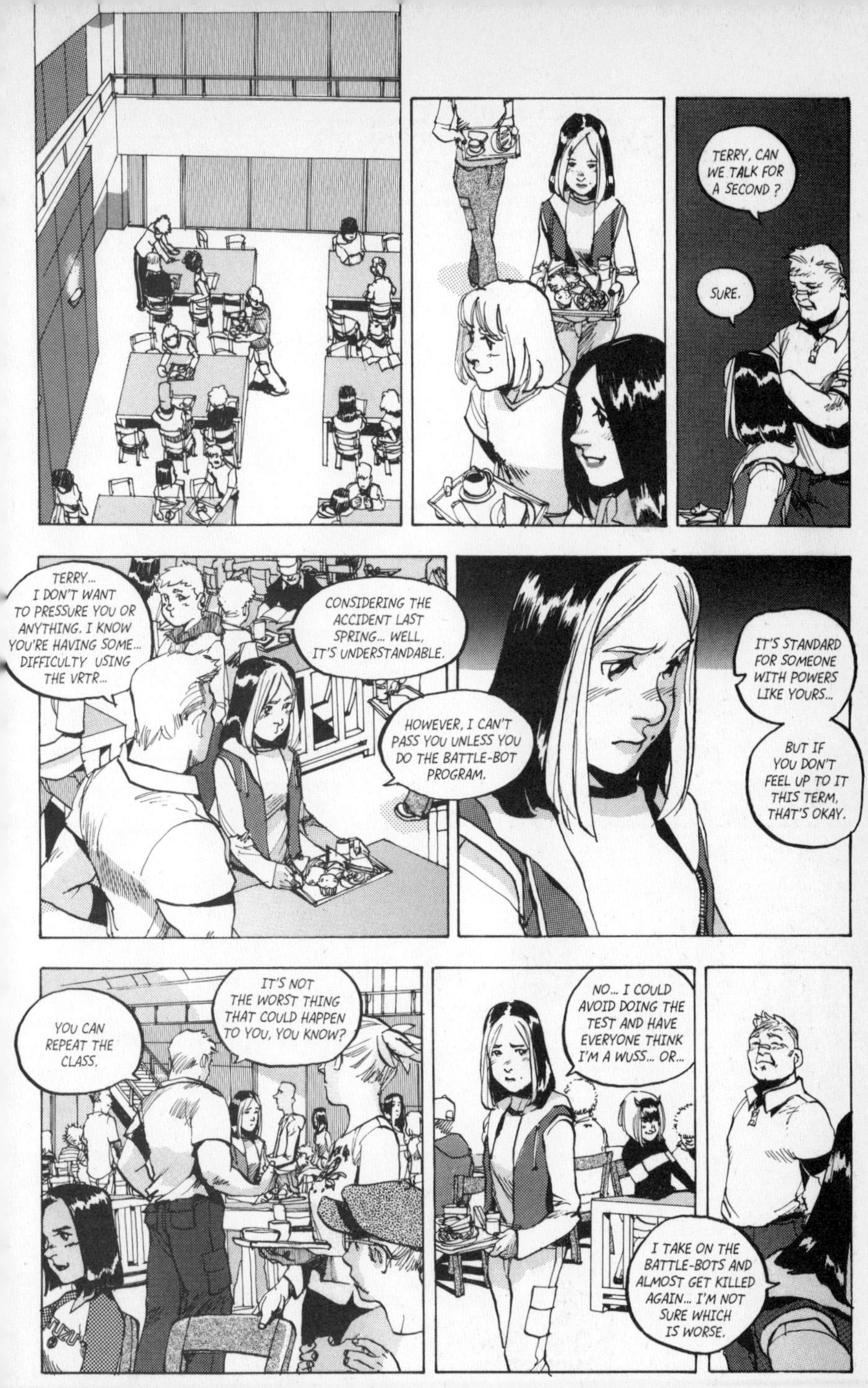
TERRY, CAN WE TALK FOR A SECOND?
SURE.
TERRY... I DON'T WANT TO PRESSURE YOU OR ANYTHING. I KNOW YOU'RE HAVING SOME... DIFFICULTY USING THE VRTR...
CONSIDERING THE ACCIDENT LAST SPRING... WELL, IT'S UNDERSTANDABLE.
HOWEVER, I CAN'T PASS YOU UNLESS YOU DO THE BATTLE-BOT PROGRAM.
IT'S STANDARD FOR SOMEONE WITH POWERS LIKE YOURS...
BUT IF YOU DON'T FEEL UP TO IT THIS TERM, THAT'S OKAY.
YOU CAN REPEAT THE CLASS.
IT'S NOT THE WORST THING THAT COULD HAPPEN TO YOU, YOU KNOW?
NO... I COULD AVOID DOING THE TEST AND HAVE EVERYONE THINK I'M A WUSS... OR...
I TAKE ON THE BATTLE-BOTS AND ALMOST GET KILLED AGAIN... I'M NOT SURE WHICH IS WORSE.

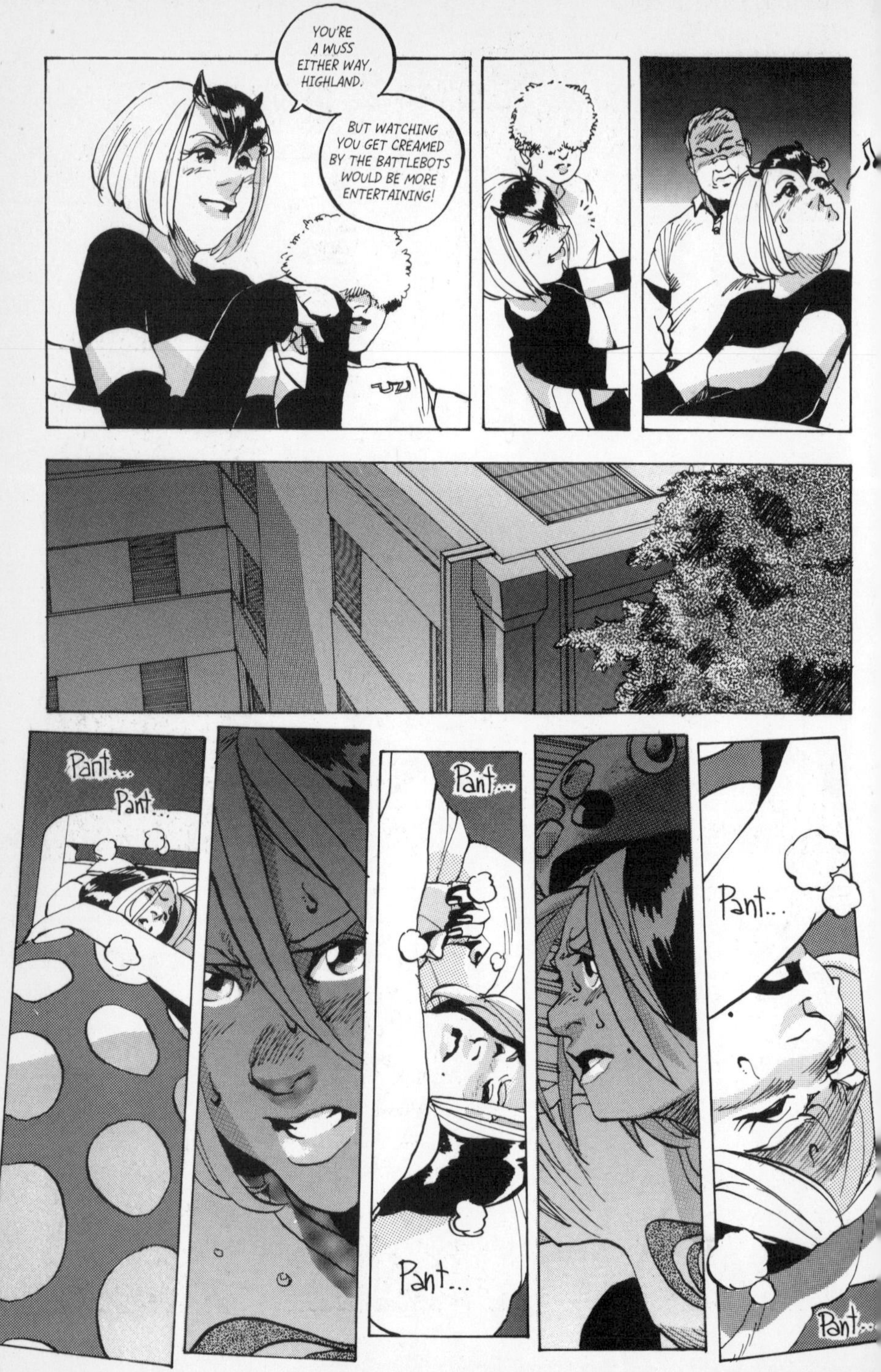
YOU'RE A WUSS EITHER WAY, HIGHLAND.
BUT WATCHING YOU GET CREAMED BY THE BATTLEBOTS WOULD BE MORE ENTERTAINING!
Pant...
Pant...
Pant...
Pant...
Pant...
Pant...

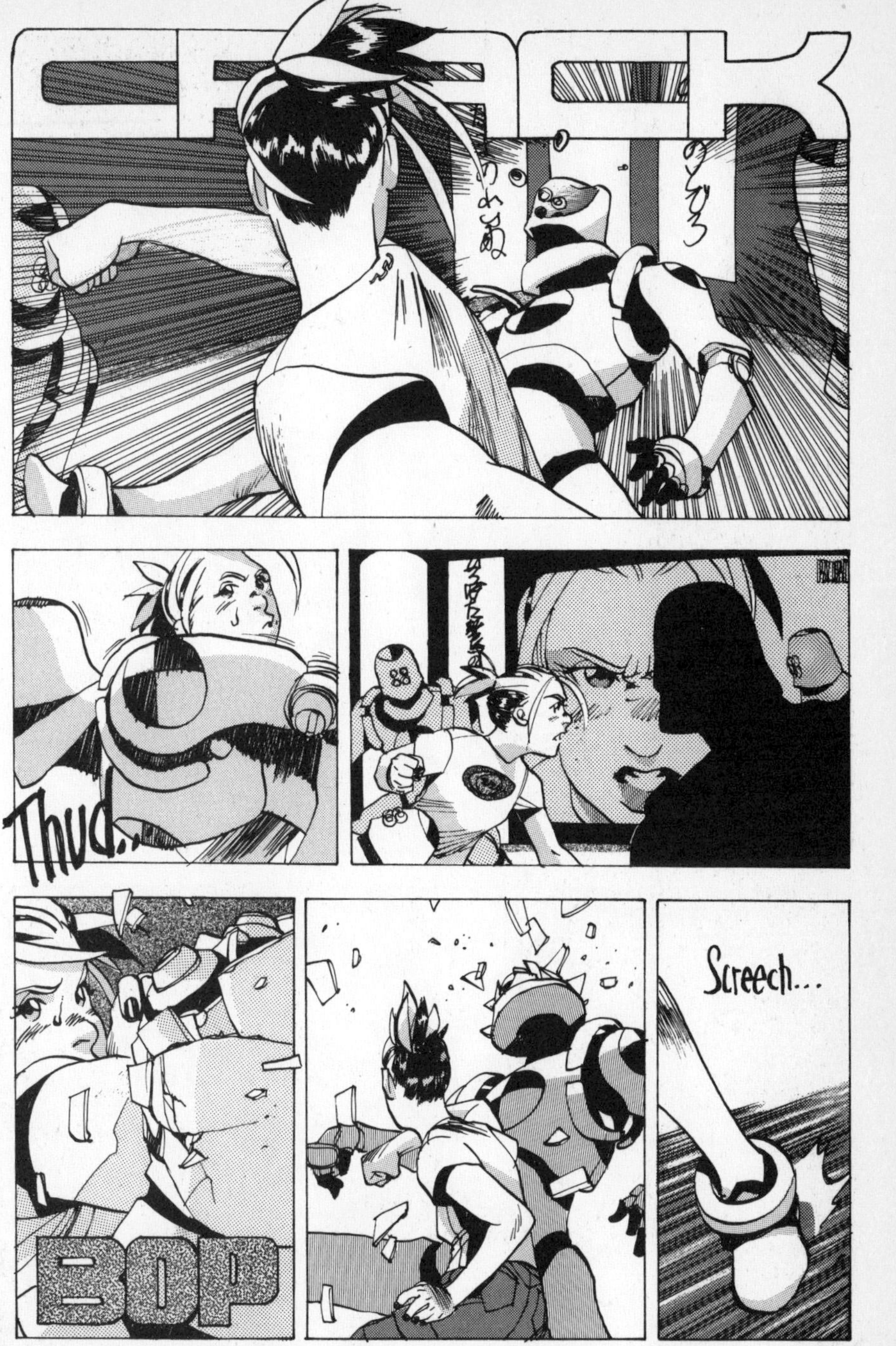
CRACK
Thud...
BOP
Screech...

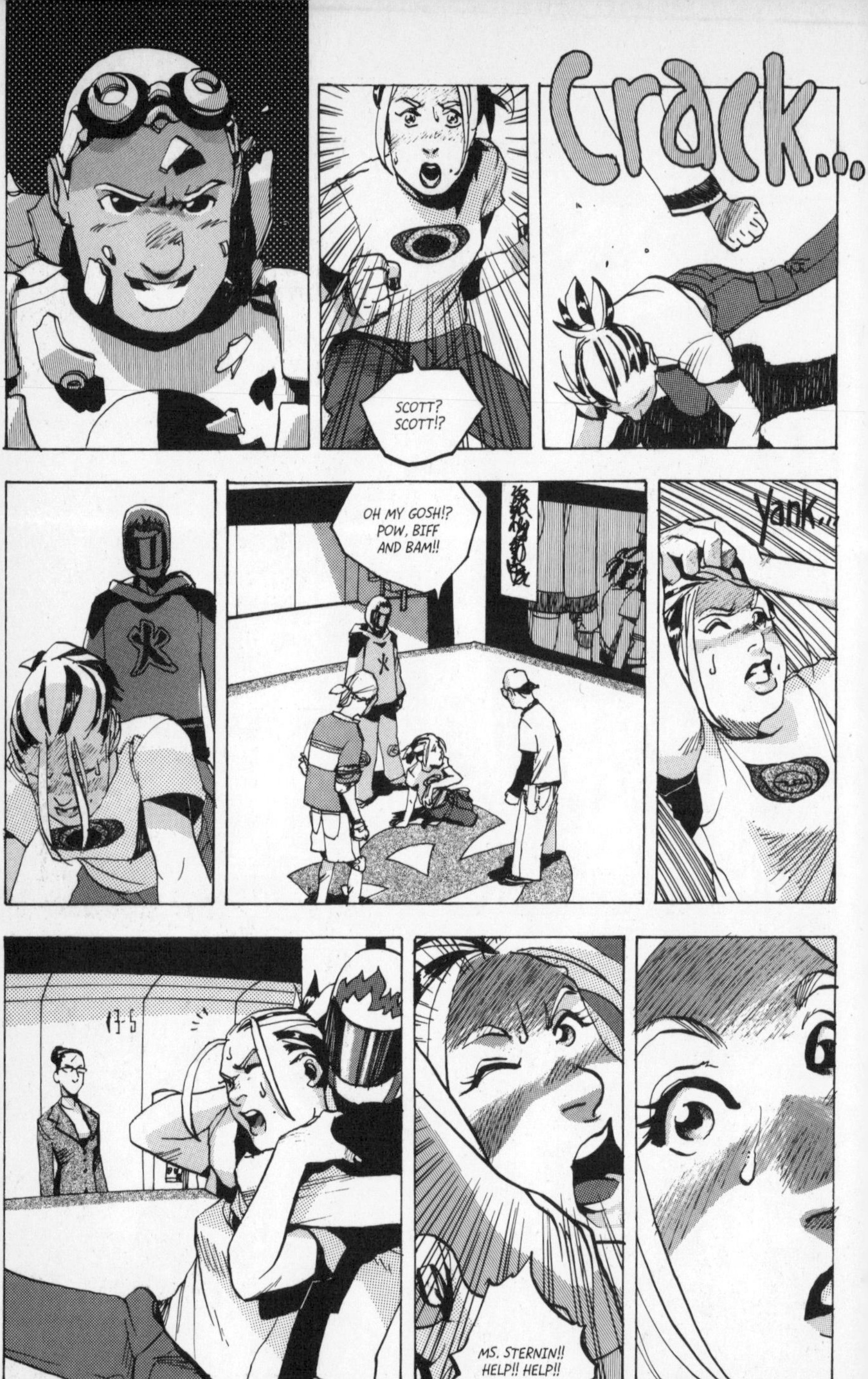

Crack...
SCOTT? SCOTT!?
OH MY GOSH!? POW, BIFF AND BAM!!
yank...
MS. STERNIN!! HELP!! HELP!!

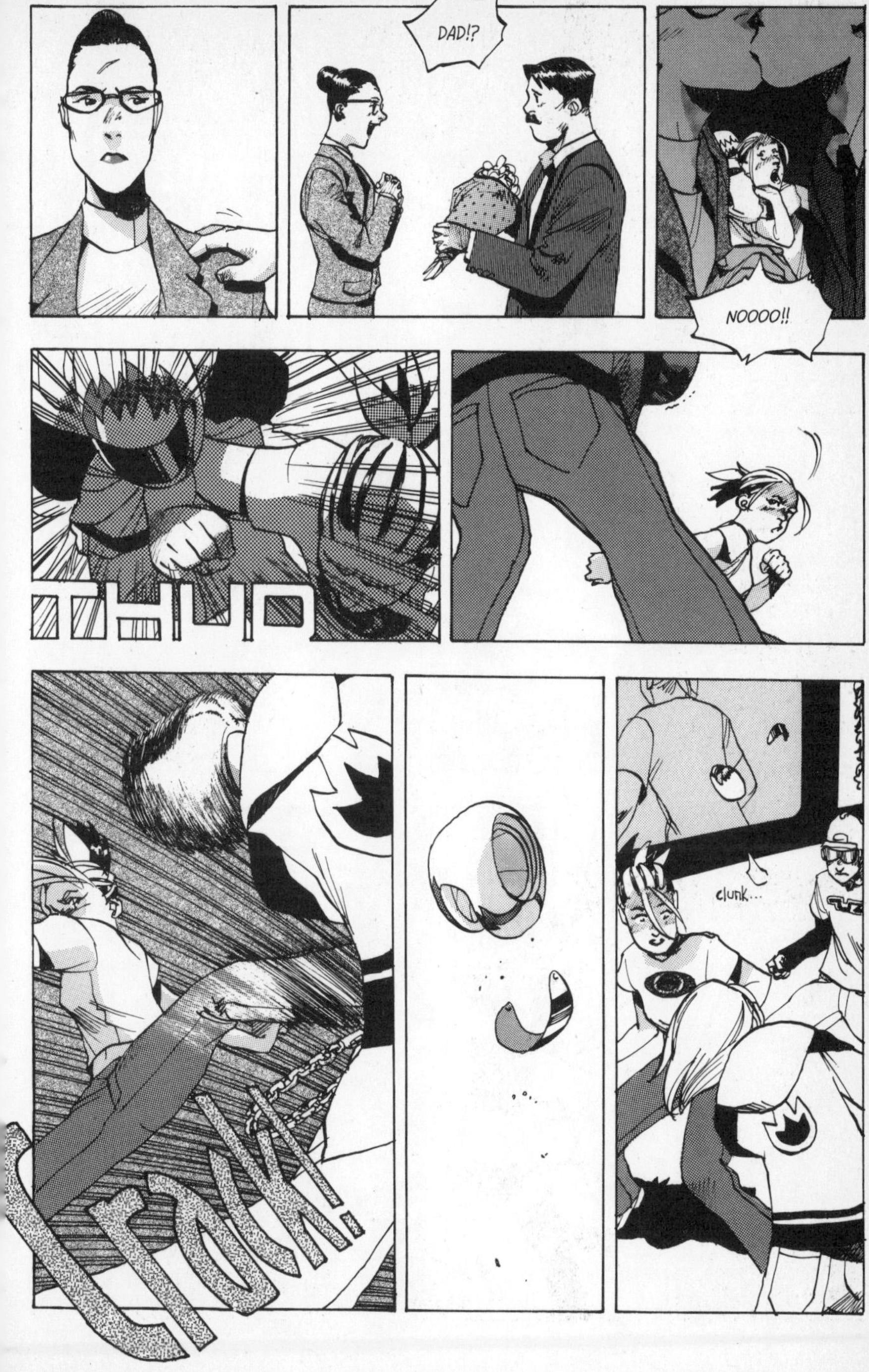

DAD!?
NOOOO!!
THUD
clunk...

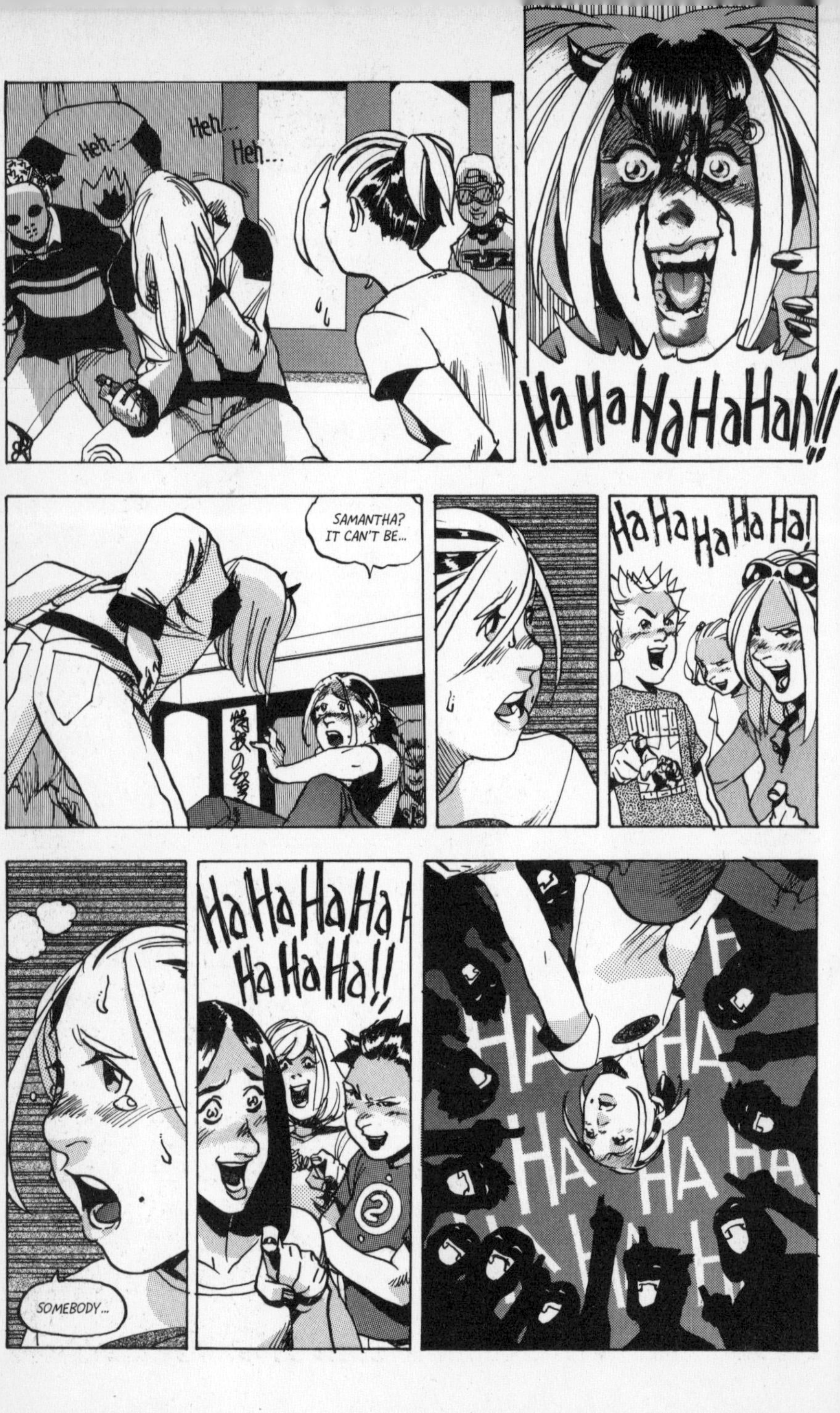
Heh...
Heh...
Heh...
HaHaHaHaHah!!
SAMANTHA? IT CAN'T BE...
HaHaHaHaHa!
SOMEBODY...
HaHaHaHaHa
HaHaHa!!
HA HA HA HA HA HA HA

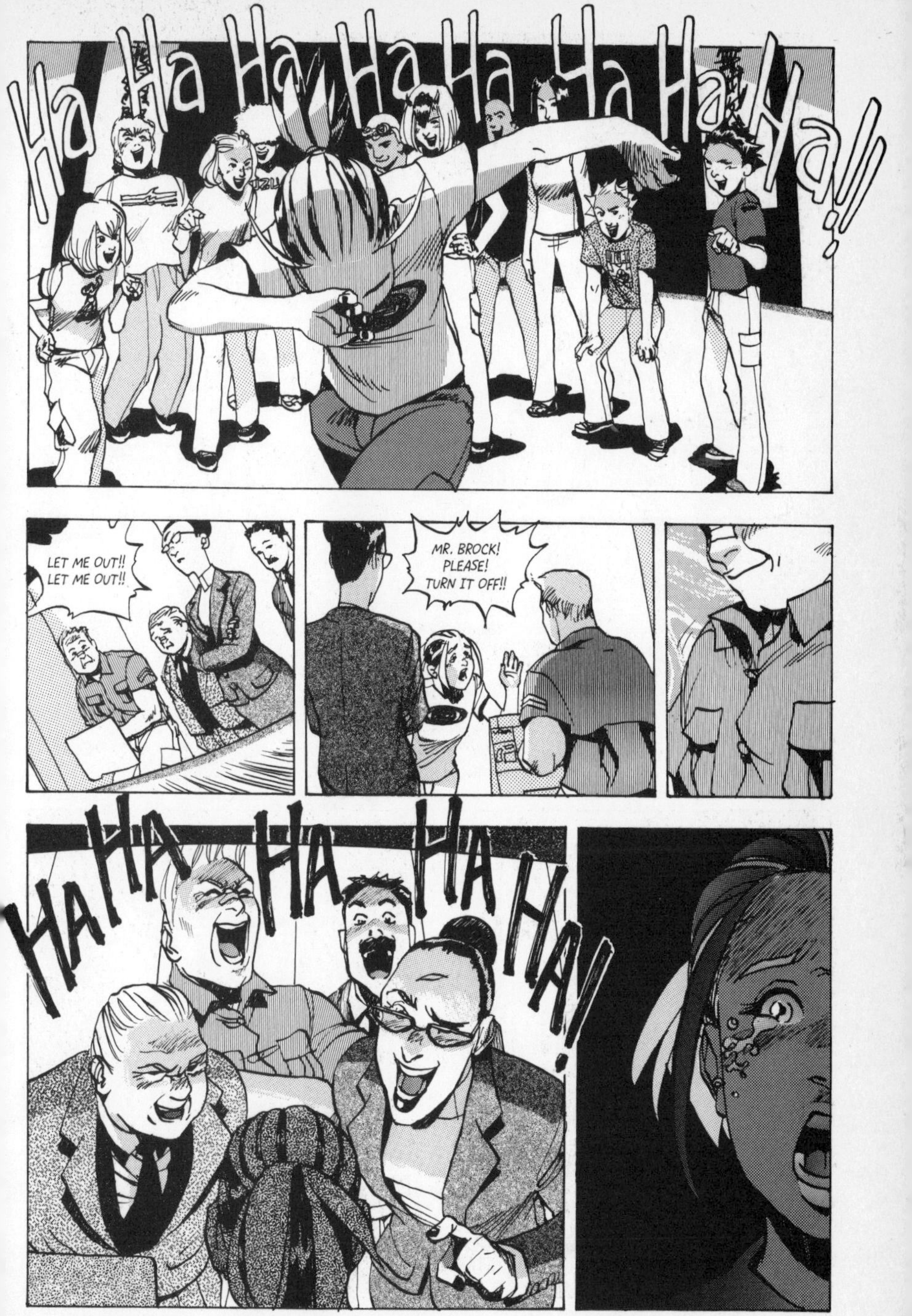
Ha Ha Ha Ha Ha Ha Ha Ha Ha!!
LET ME OUT!! LET ME OUT!!
MR. BROCK! PLEASE! TURN IT OFF!!
HA HA HA HA HA HA!

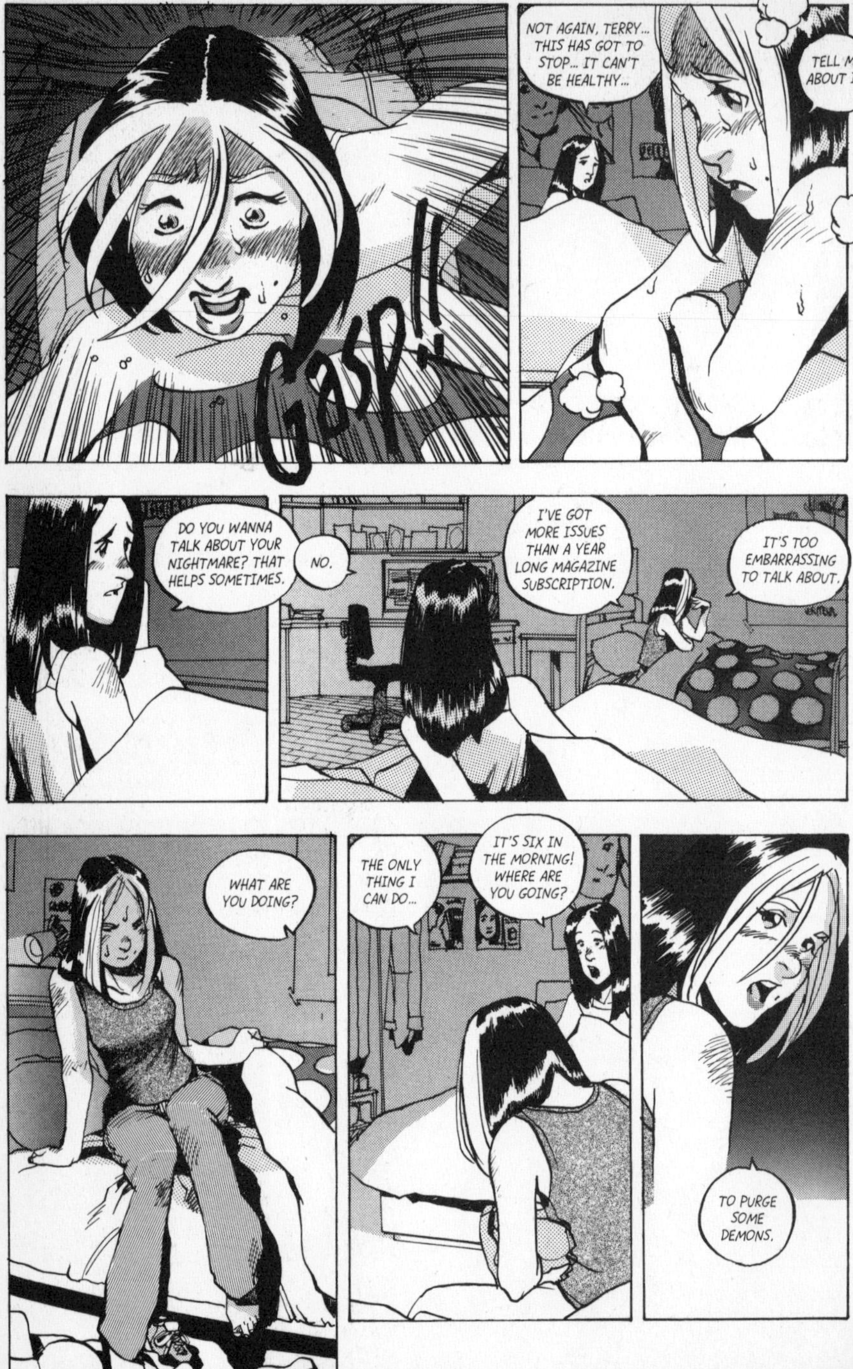
GASP!!
NOT AGAIN, TERRY... THIS HAS GOT TO STOP... IT CAN'T BE HEALTHY...
TELL ME ABOUT IT.
DO YOU WANNA TALK ABOUT YOUR NIGHTMARE? THAT HELPS SOMETIMES.
NO.
I'VE GOT MORE ISSUES THAN A YEAR LONG MAGAZINE SUBSCRIPTION.
IT'S TOO EMBARRASSING TO TALK ABOUT.
WHAT ARE YOU DOING?
THE ONLY THING I CAN DO...
IT'S SIX IN THE MORNING! WHERE ARE YOU GOING?
TO PURGE SOME DEMONS.

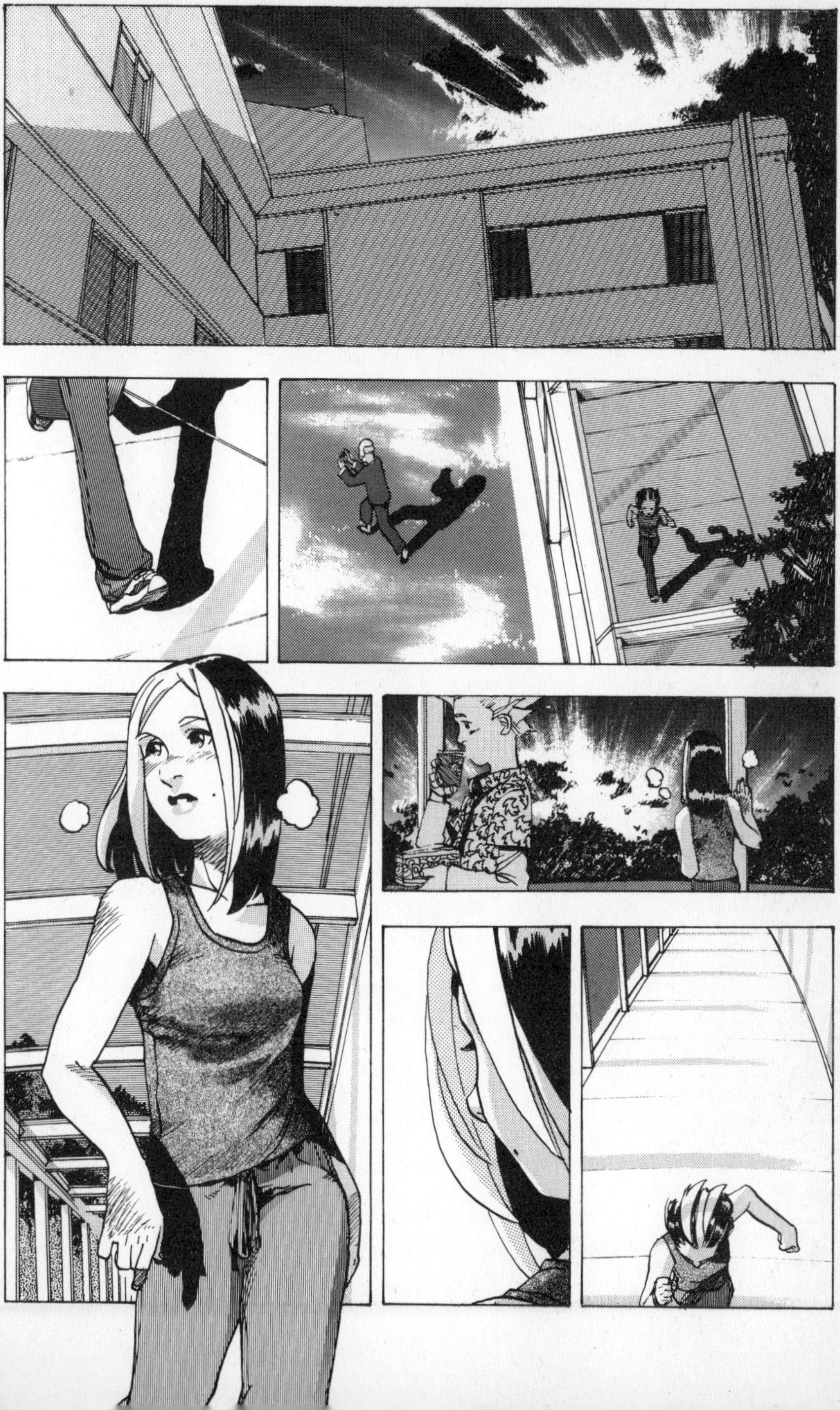

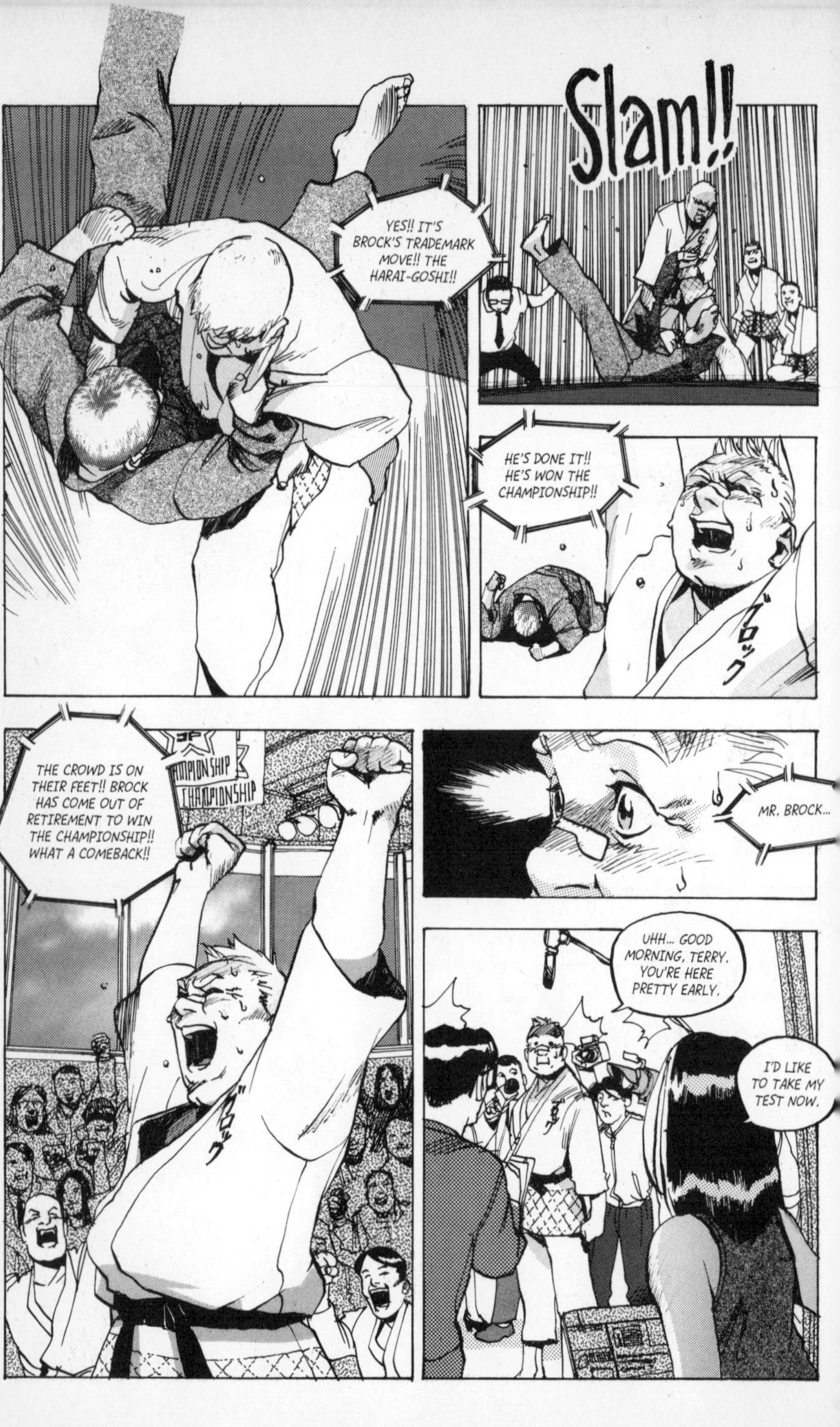
YES!! IT'S BROCK'S TRADEMARK MOVE!! THE HARAI-GOSHI!!
Slam!!
HE'S DONE IT!! HE'S WON THE CHAMPIONSHIP!!
THE CROWD IS ON THEIR FEET!! BROCK HAS COME OUT OF RETIREMENT TO WIN THE CHAMPIONSHIP!! WHAT A COMEBACK!!
CHAMPIONSHIP
MR. BROCK...
UHH... GOOD MORNING, TERRY. YOU'RE HERE PRETTY EARLY.
I'D LIKE TO TAKE MY TEST NOW.

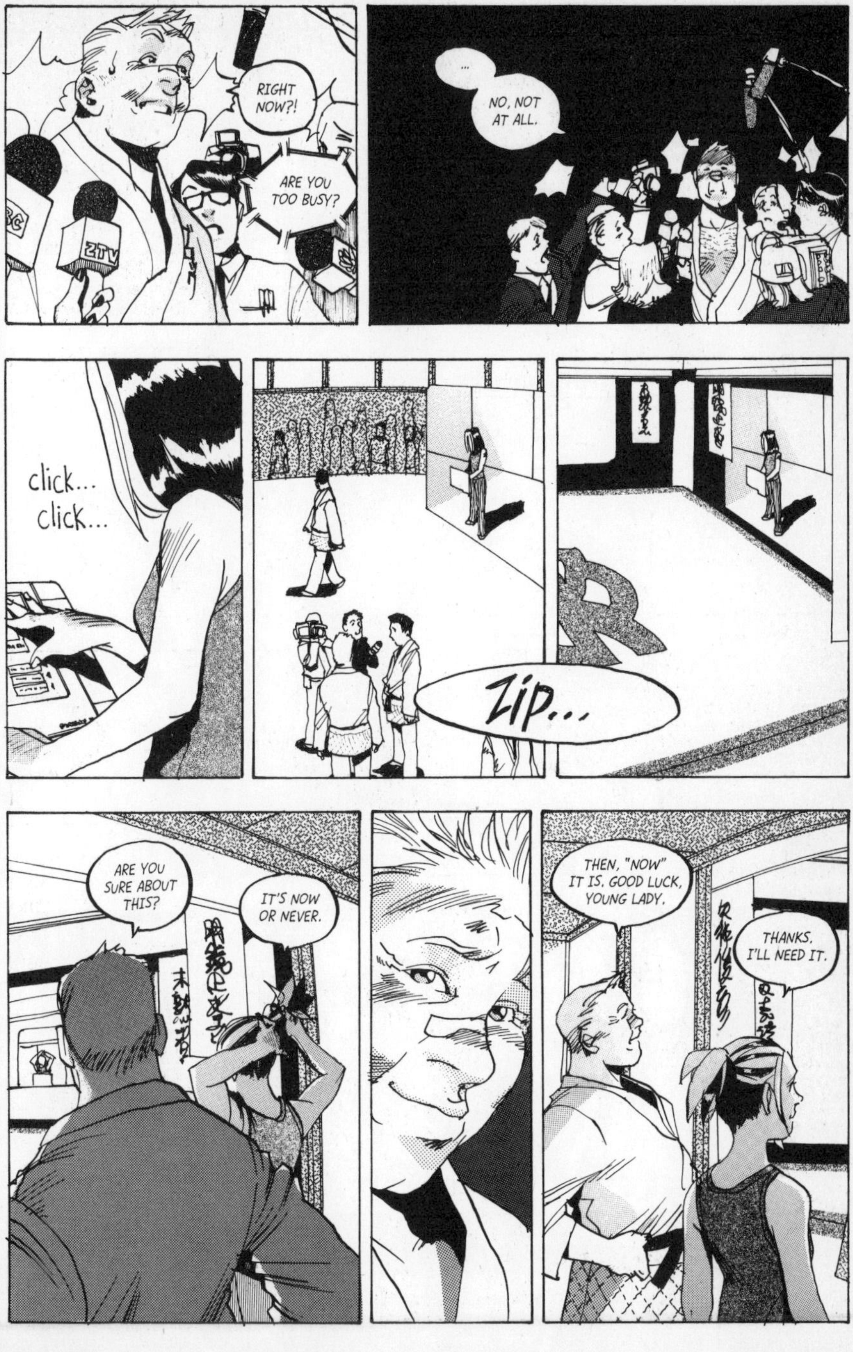
RIGHT NOW?!
ARE YOU TOO BUSY?
...
NO, NOT AT ALL.
click... click...
Zip...
ARE YOU SURE ABOUT THIS?
IT'S NOW OR NEVER.
THEN, "NOW" IT IS. GOOD LUCK, YOUNG LADY.
THANKS, I'LL NEED IT.

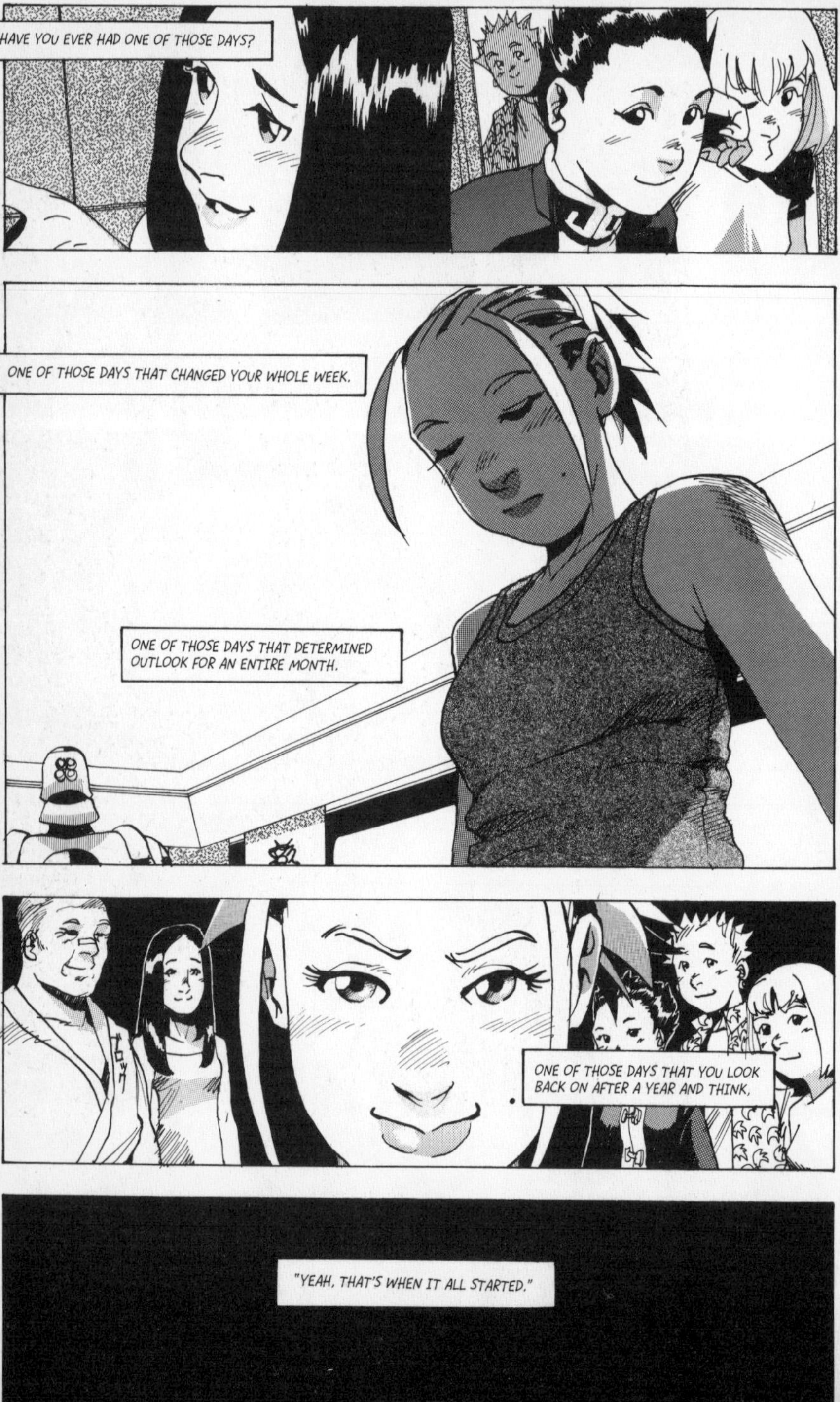
HAVE YOU EVER HAD ONE OF THOSE DAYS?
ONE OF THOSE DAYS THAT CHANGED YOUR WHOLE WEEK.
ONE OF THOSE DAYS THAT DETERMINED OUTLOOK FOR AN ENTIRE MONTH.
ONE OF THOSE DAYS THAT YOU LOOK BACK ON AFTER A YEAR AND THINK,
"YEAH, THAT'S WHEN IT ALL STARTED."

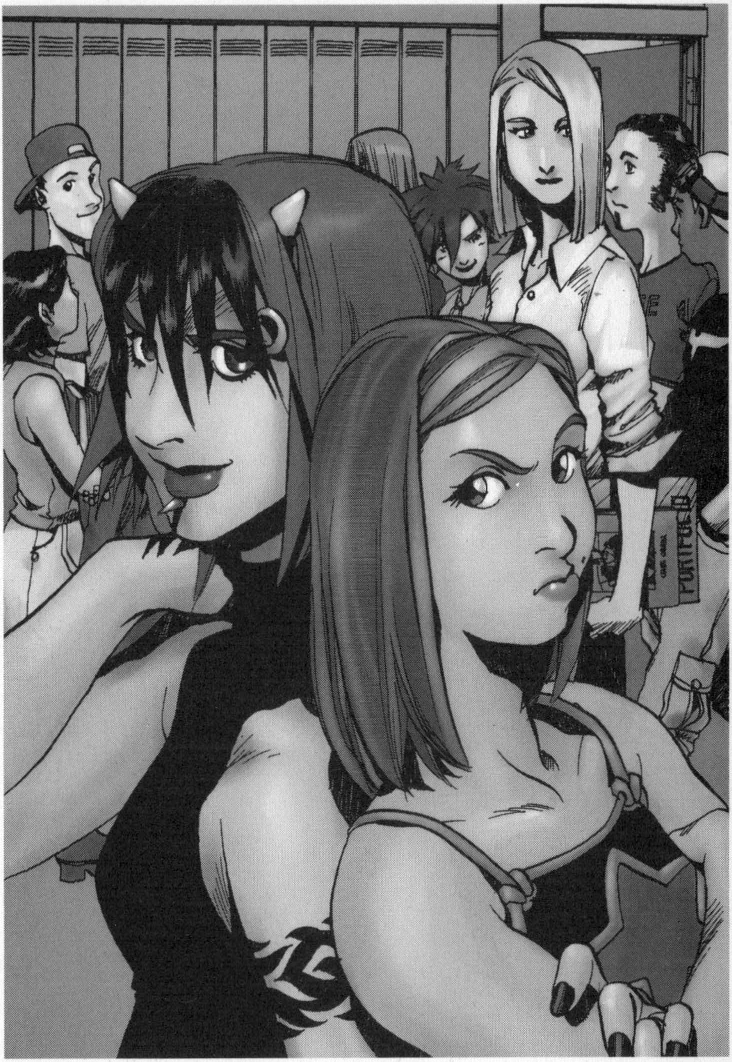
PORTFOLIO

The Substitute

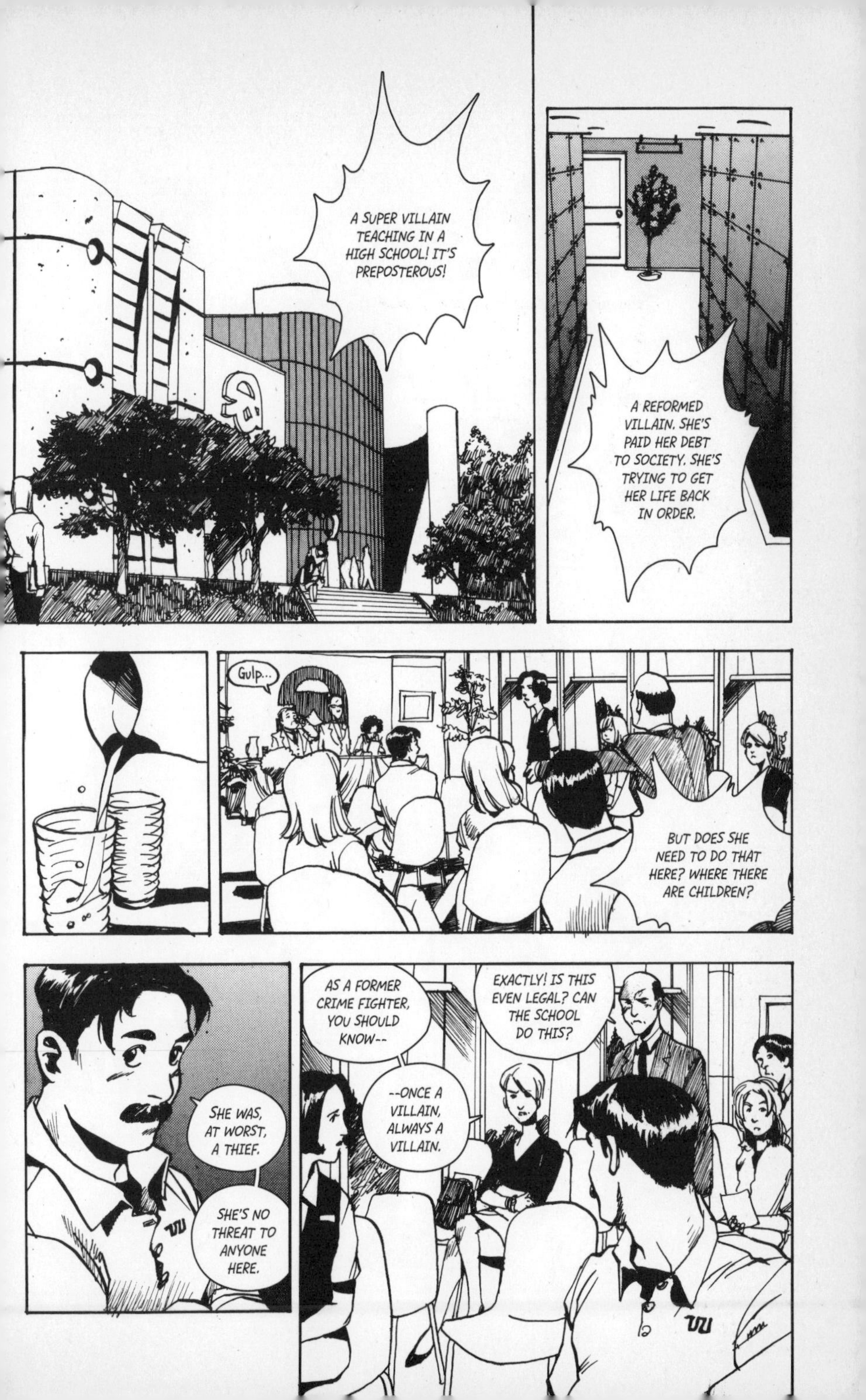
A SUPER VILLAIN TEACHING IN A HIGH SCHOOL! IT'S PREPOSTEROUS!
A REFORMED VILLAIN. SHE'S PAID HER DEBT TO SOCIETY. SHE'S TRYING TO GET HER LIFE BACK IN ORDER.
Gulp...
BUT DOES SHE NEED TO DO THAT HERE? WHERE THERE ARE CHILDREN?
SHE WAS, AT WORST, A THIEF.
SHE'S NO THREAT TO ANYONE HERE.
AS A FORMER CRIME FIGHTER, YOU SHOULD KNOW--
--ONCE A VILLAIN, ALWAYS A VILLAIN.
EXACTLY! IS THIS EVEN LEGAL? CAN THE SCHOOL DO THIS?

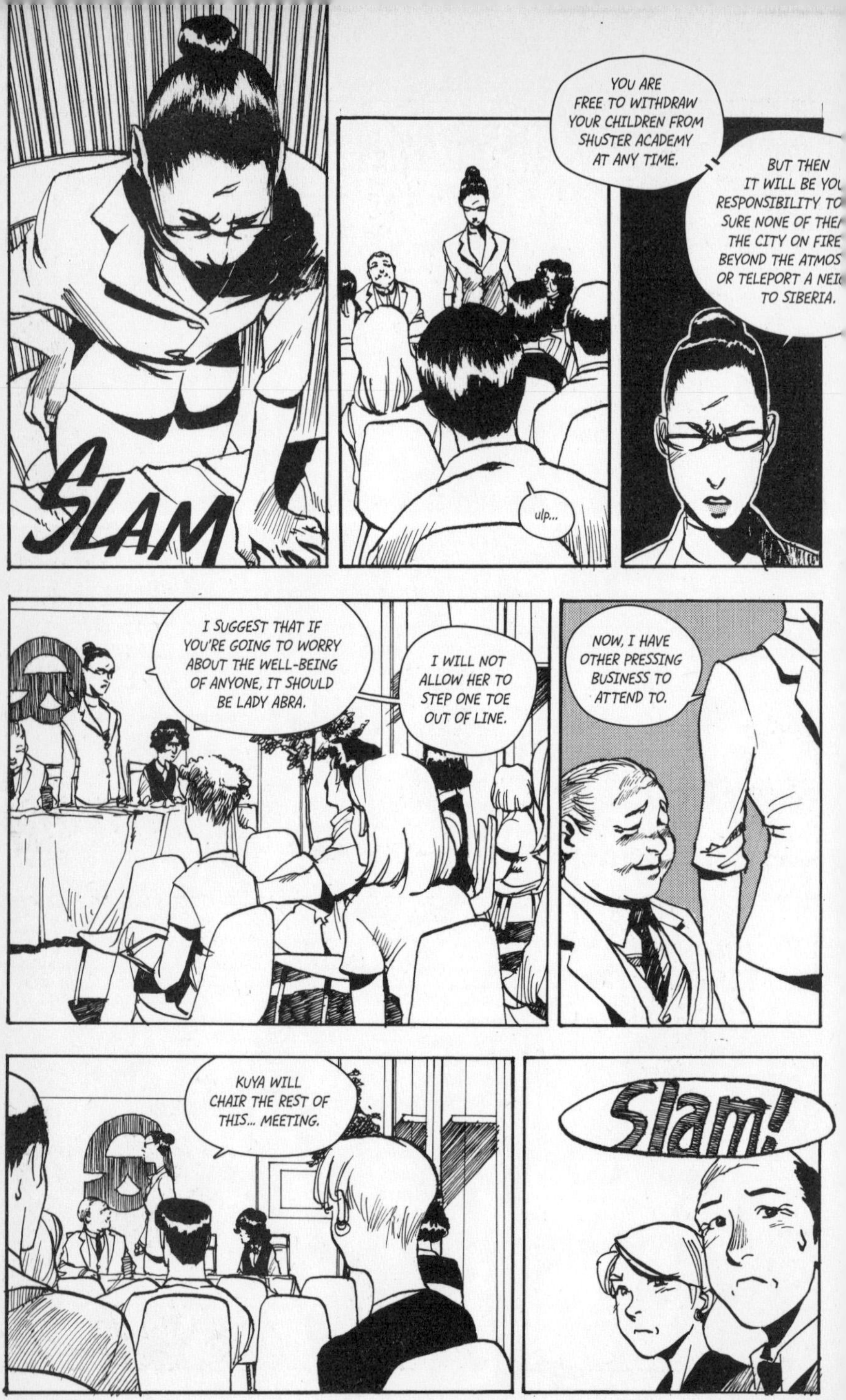
SLAM
YOU ARE FREE TO WITHDRAW YOUR CHILDREN FROM SHUSTER ACADEMY AT ANY TIME.
BUT THEN IT WILL BE YO RESPONSIBILITY TO SURE NONE OF THE THE CITY ON FIRE BEYOND THE ATMOS OR TELEPORT A NEI TO SIBERIA.
ulp...
I SUGGEST THAT IF YOU'RE GOING TO WORRY ABOUT THE WELL-BEING OF ANYONE, IT SHOULD BE LADY ABRA.
I WILL NOT ALLOW HER TO STEP ONE TOE OUT OF LINE.
NOW, I HAVE OTHER PRESSING BUSINESS TO ATTEND TO.
KUYA WILL CHAIR THE REST OF THIS... MEETING.
Slam!

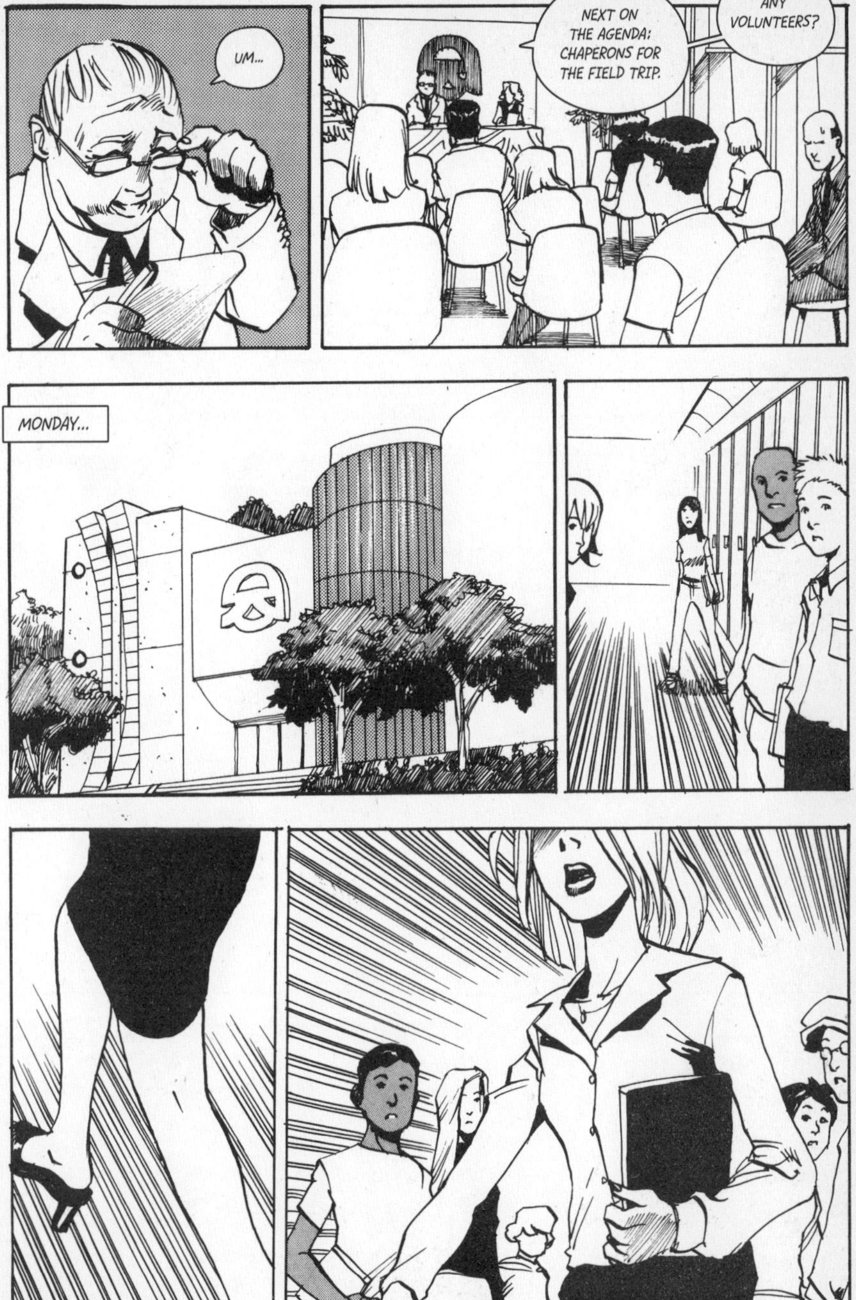
UM...
NEXT ON THE AGENDA: CHAPERONS FOR THE FIELD TRIP.
ANY VOLUNTEERS?
MONDAY...

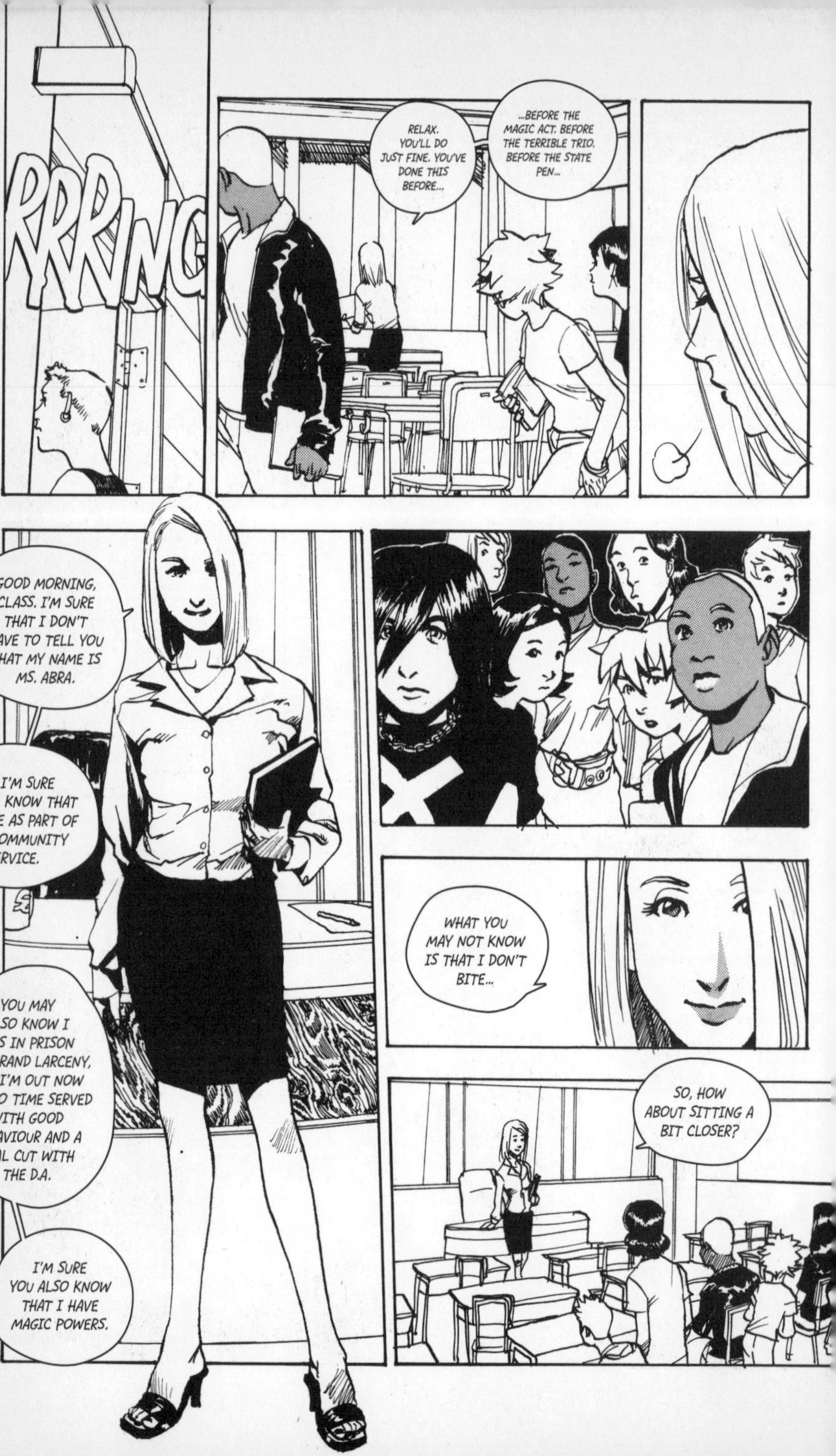
RRRING
RELAX. YOU'LL DO JUST FINE. YOU'VE DONE THIS BEFORE...
...BEFORE THE MAGIC ACT. BEFORE THE TERRIBLE TRIO. BEFORE THE STATE PEN...
GOOD MORNING, CLASS. I'M SURE THAT I DON'T HAVE TO TELL YOU THAT MY NAME IS MS. ABRA.
AND I'M SURE YOU ALL KNOW THAT I'M HERE AS PART OF MY... COMMUNITY SERVICE.
YOU MAY ALSO KNOW I WAS IN PRISON FOR GRAND LARCENY, BUT I'M OUT NOW DUE TO TIME SERVED WITH GOOD BEHAVIOUR AND A DEAL CUT WITH THE D.A.
I'M SURE YOU ALSO KNOW THAT I HAVE MAGIC POWERS.
WHAT YOU MAY NOT KNOW IS THAT I DON'T BITE...
SO, HOW ABOUT SITTING A BIT CLOSER?

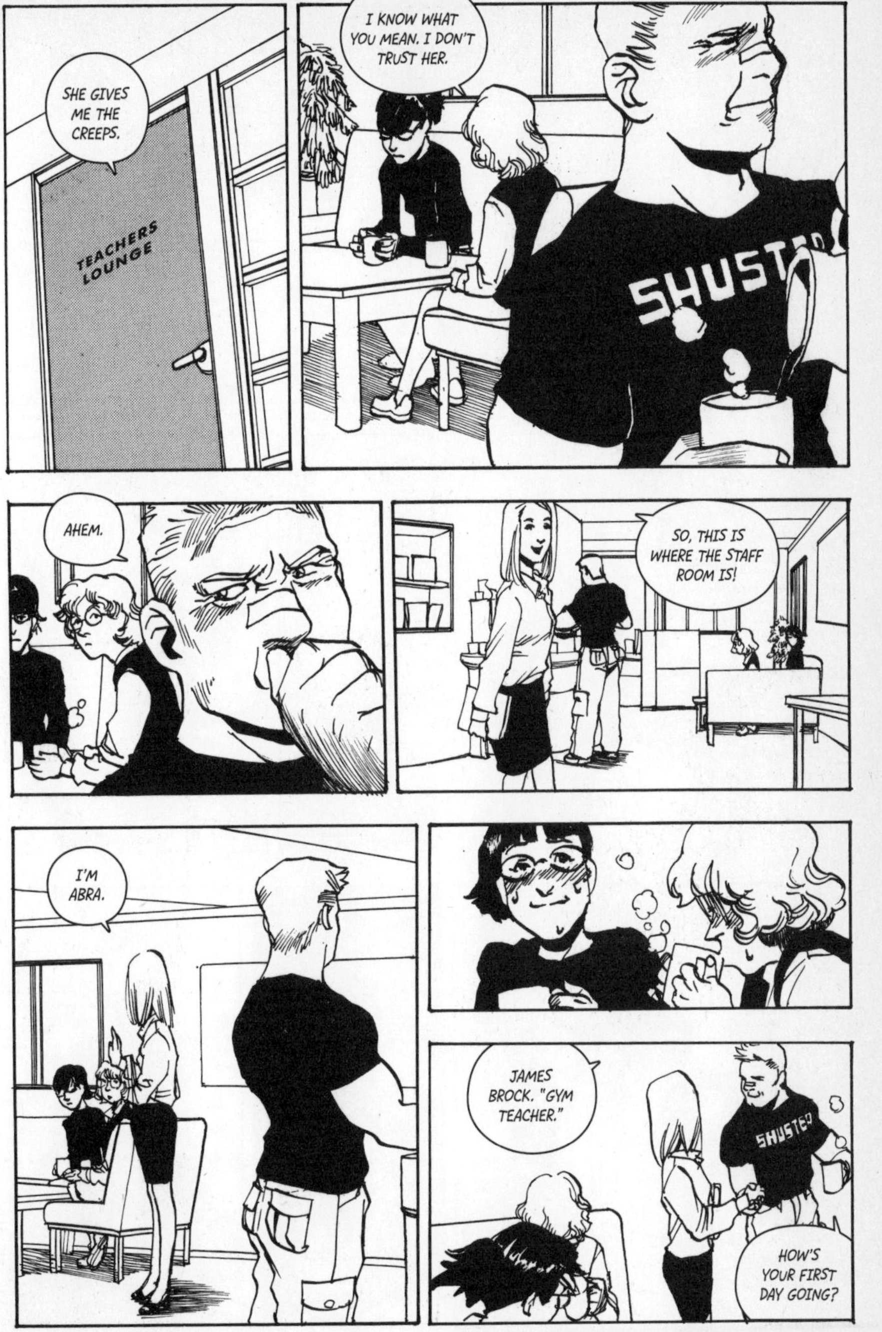
SHE GIVES ME THE CREEPS.
TEACHERS LOUNGE
I KNOW WHAT YOU MEAN. I DON'T TRUST HER.
SHUSTED
AHEM.
SO, THIS IS WHERE THE STAFF ROOM IS!
I'M ABRA.
JAMES BROCK. "GYM TEACHER."
SHUSTED
HOW'S YOUR FIRST DAY GOING?

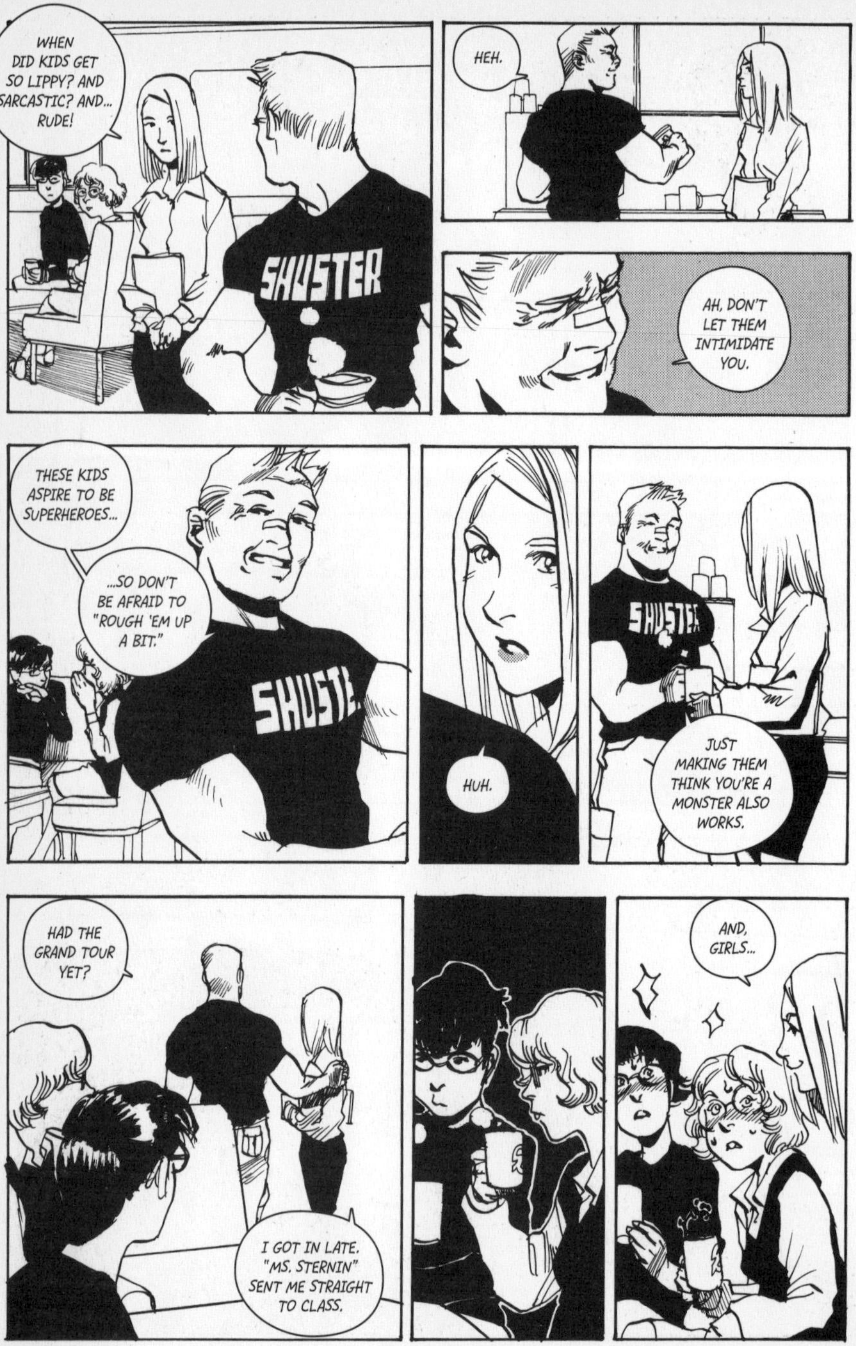
WHEN DID KIDS GET SO LIPPY? AND SARCASTIC? AND... RUDE!
SHUSTER
HEH.
AH, DON'T LET THEM INTIMIDATE YOU.
THESE KIDS ASPIRE TO BE SUPERHEROES...
...SO DON'T BE AFRAID TO "ROUGH 'EM UP A BIT."
HUH.
JUST MAKING THEM THINK YOU'RE A MONSTER ALSO WORKS.
HAD THE GRAND TOUR YET?
I GOT IN LATE. "MS. STERNIN" SENT ME STRAIGHT TO CLASS.
AND, GIRLS...

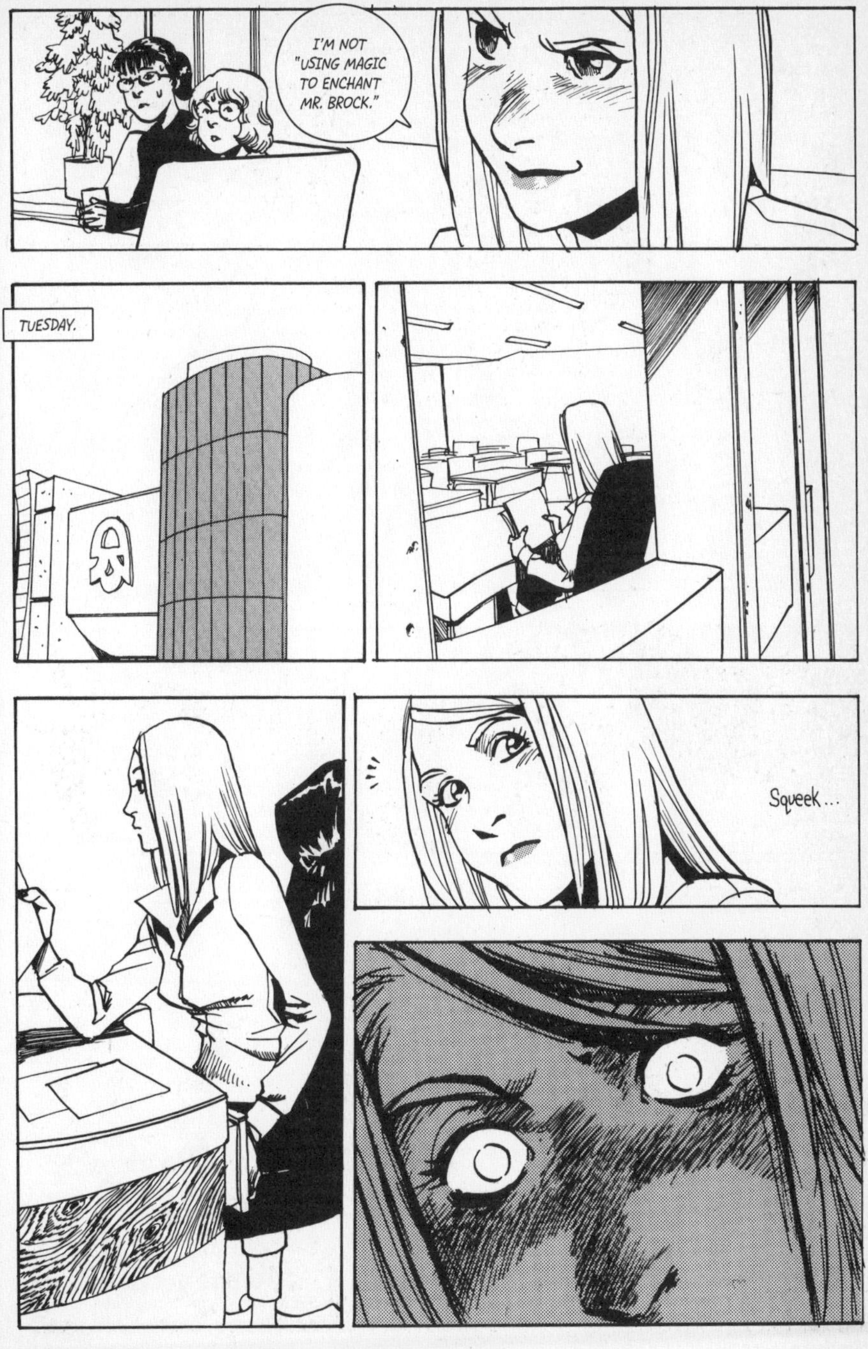
I'M NOT "USING MAGIC TO ENCHANT MR. BROCK."
TUESDAY.
Squeek...

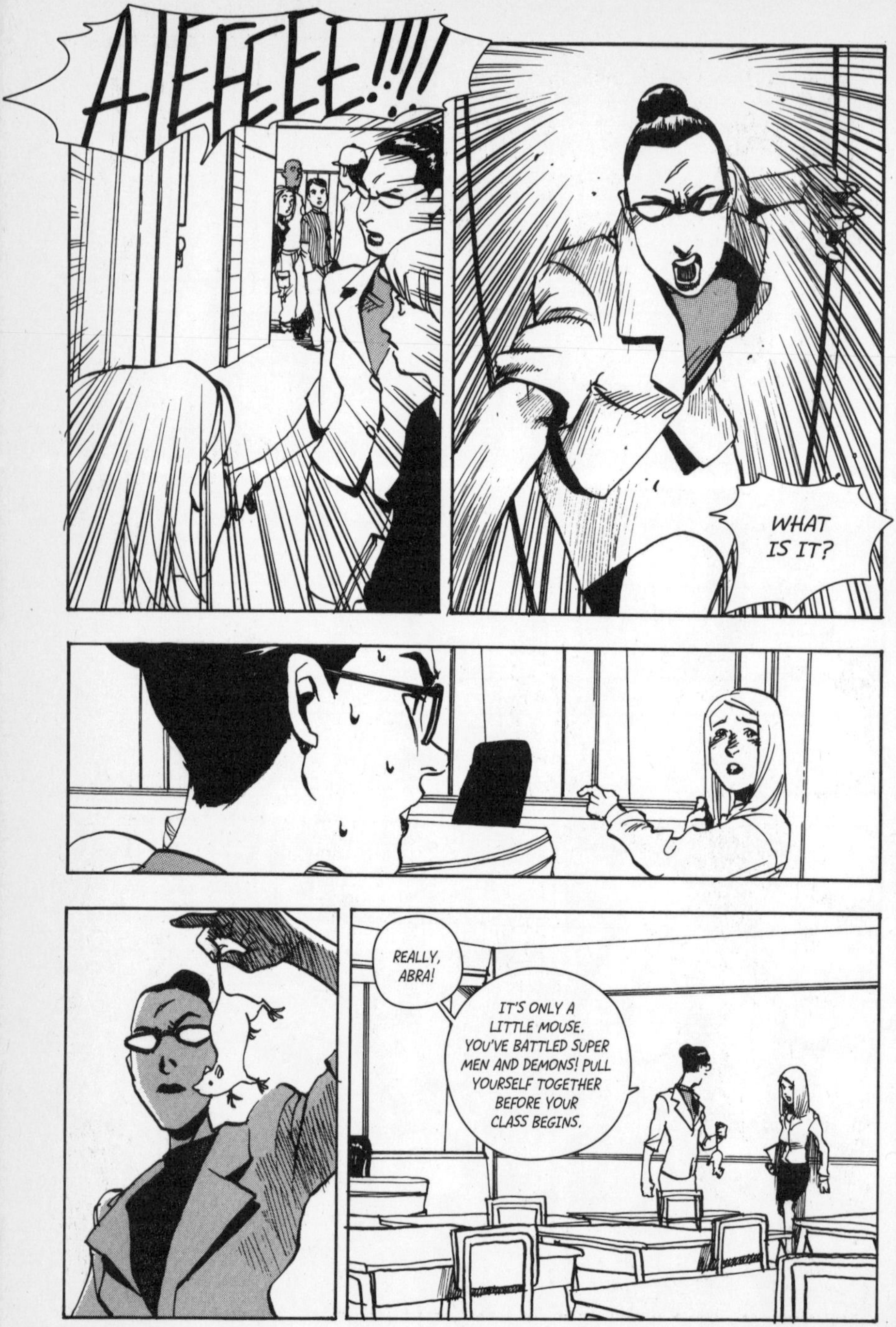
AIEEEEE!!!!
WHAT IS IT?
REALLY, ABRA!
IT'S ONLY A LITTLE MOUSE. YOU'VE BATTLED SUPER MEN AND DEMONS! PULL YOURSELF TOGETHER BEFORE YOUR CLASS BEGINS.

I'LL TAKE CARE OF THE PESTS!

YOU OKAY, MISS?

YES... YES, I'M FINE.

JUST EMBARRASSED EVERYONE NOW KNOWS THAT MY WEAKNESS ISN'T CRYSTANITE.

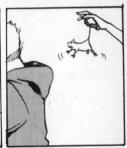

THIS MOUSE SEEMS TO KNOW YOU, GARTH DUPONT.

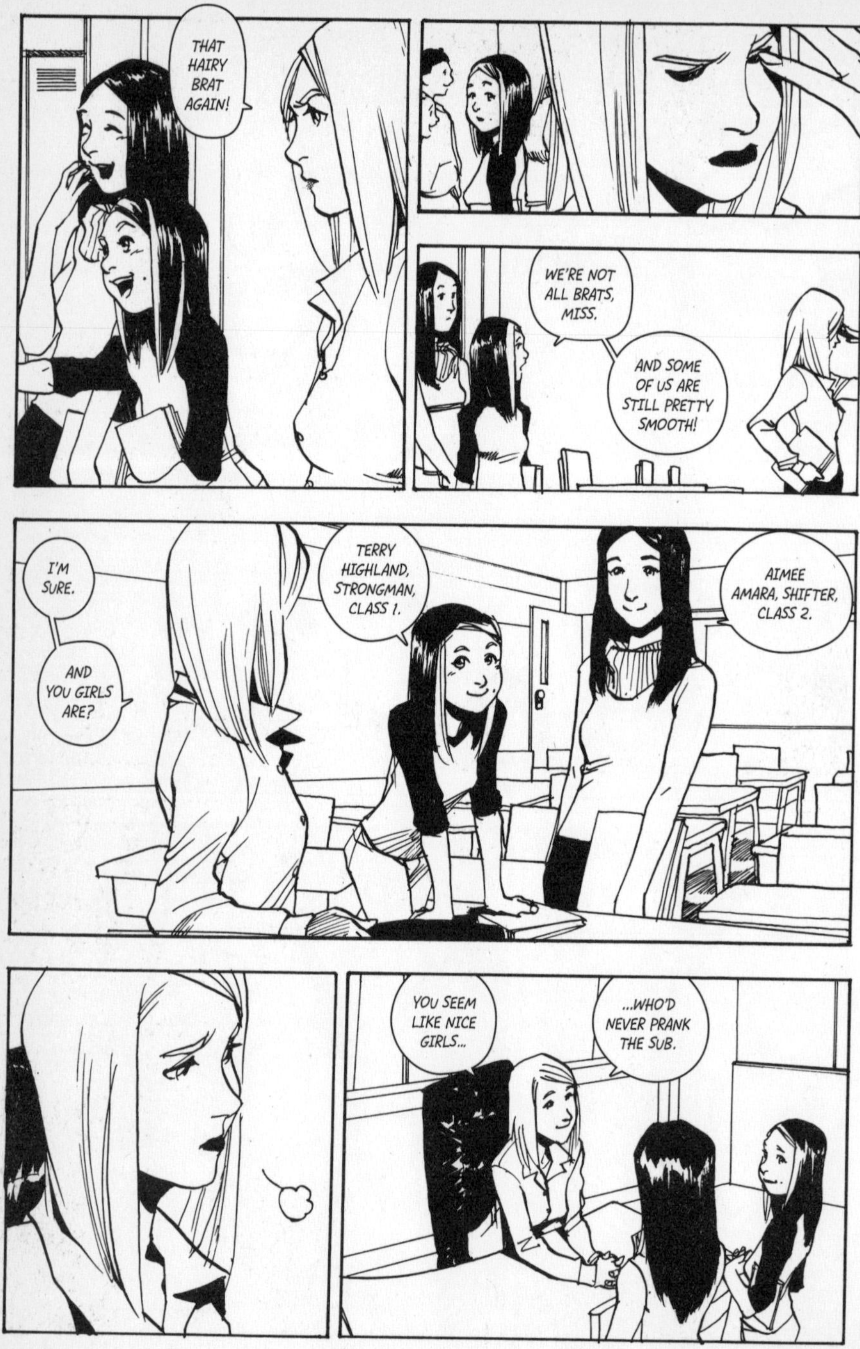
THAT HAIRY BRAT AGAIN!
WE'RE NOT ALL BRATS, MISS.
AND SOME OF US ARE STILL PRETTY SMOOTH!
I'M SURE.
AND YOU GIRLS ARE?
TERRY HIGHLAND, STRONGMAN, CLASS 1.
AIMEE AMARA, SHIFTER, CLASS 2.
YOU SEEM LIKE NICE GIRLS...
...WHO'D NEVER PRANK THE SUB.

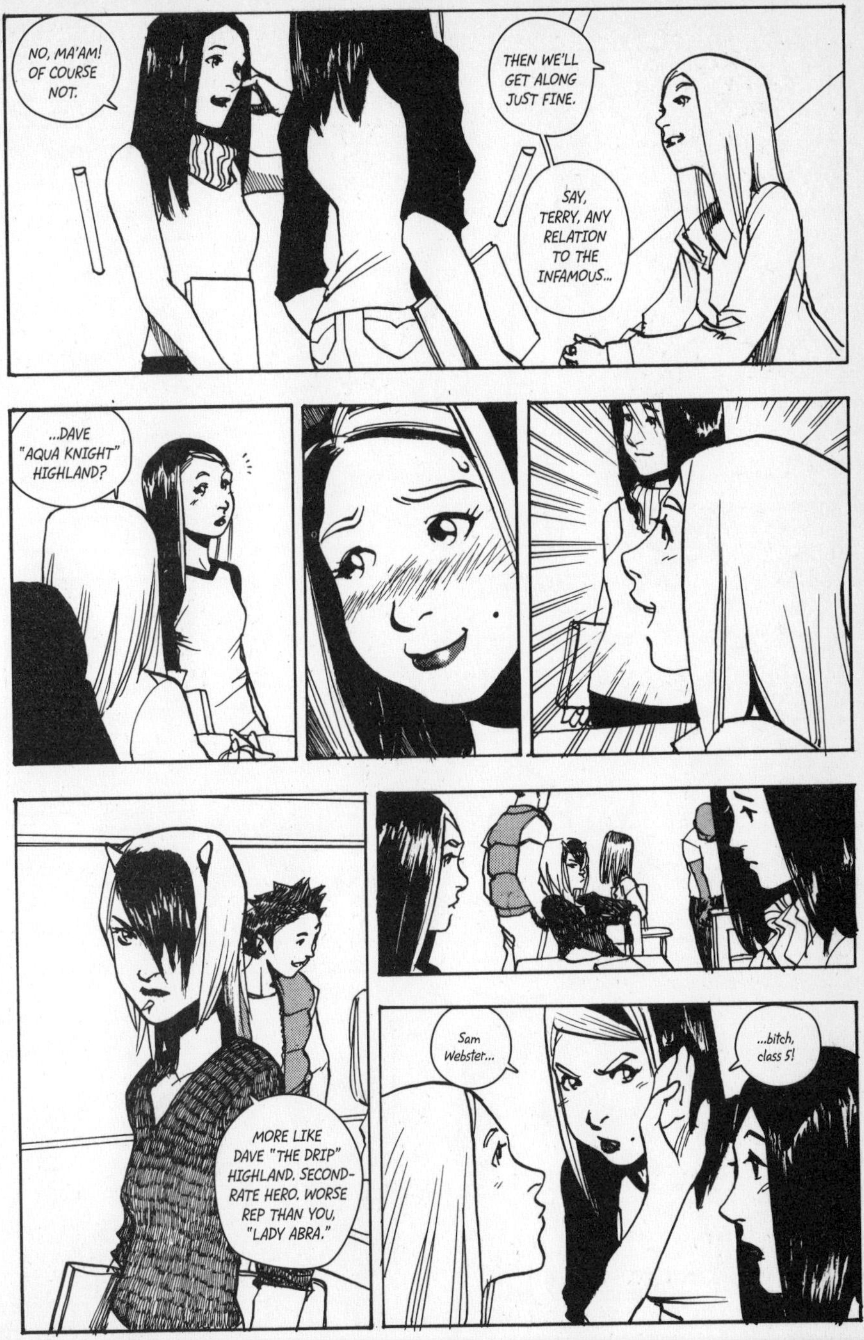
NO, MA'AM! OF COURSE NOT.
THEN WE'LL GET ALONG JUST FINE.
SAY, TERRY, ANY RELATION TO THE INFAMOUS...
...DAVE "AQUA KNIGHT" HIGHLAND?
MORE LIKE DAVE "THE DRIP" HIGHLAND. SECOND-RATE HERO. WORSE REP THAN YOU, "LADY ABRA."
Sam Webster...
...bitch, class 5!

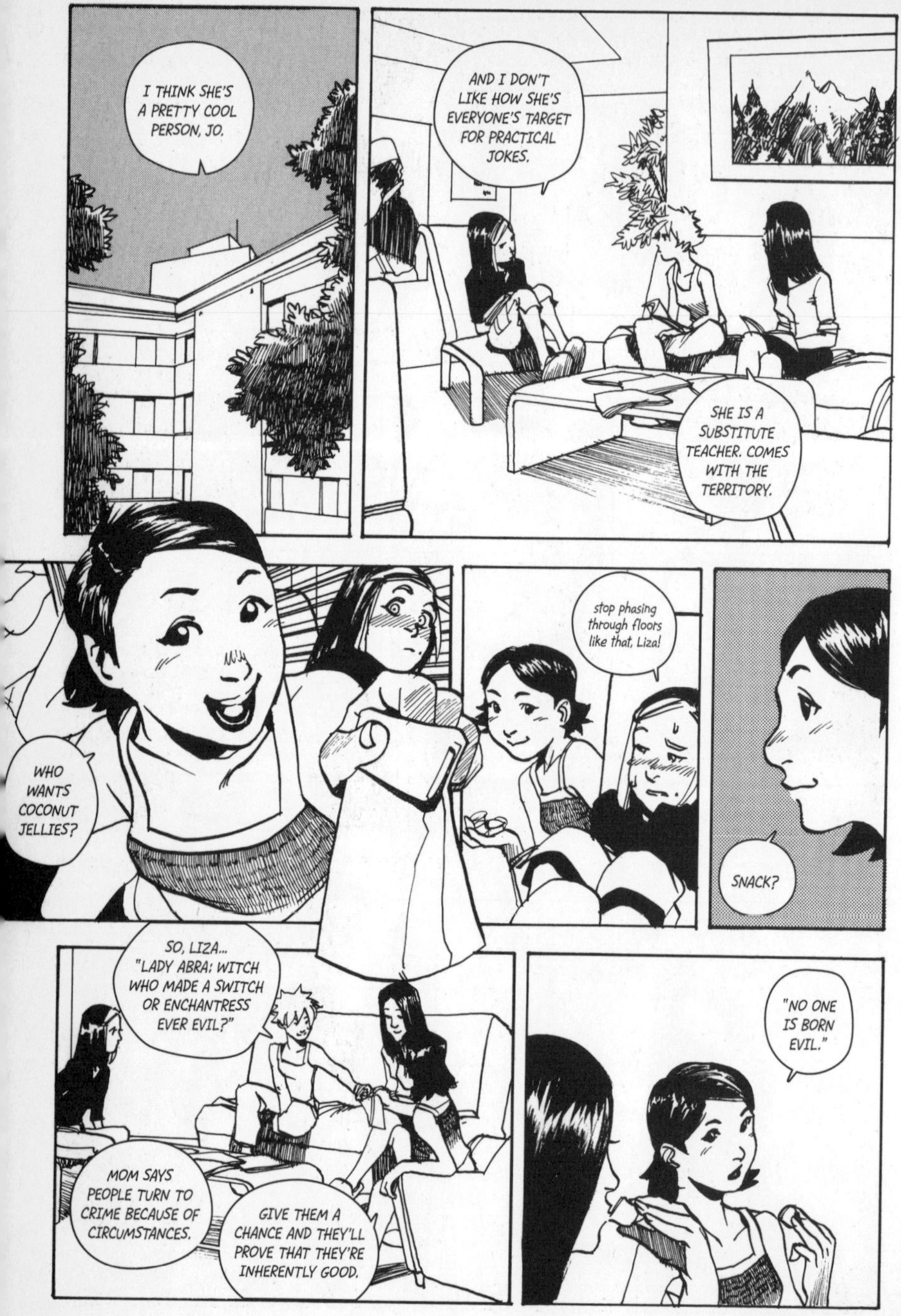
I THINK SHE'S A PRETTY COOL PERSON, JO.
AND I DON'T LIKE HOW SHE'S EVERYONE'S TARGET FOR PRACTICAL JOKES.
SHE IS A SUBSTITUTE TEACHER. COMES WITH THE TERRITORY.
WHO WANTS COCONUT JELLIES?
stop phasing through floors like that, Liza!
SNACK?
SO, LIZA... "LADY ABRA: WITCH WHO MADE A SWITCH OR ENCHANTRESS EVER EVIL?"
MOM SAYS PEOPLE TURN TO CRIME BECAUSE OF CIRCUMSTANCES.
GIVE THEM A CHANCE AND THEY'LL PROVE THAT THEY'RE INHERENTLY GOOD.
"NO ONE IS BORN EVIL."

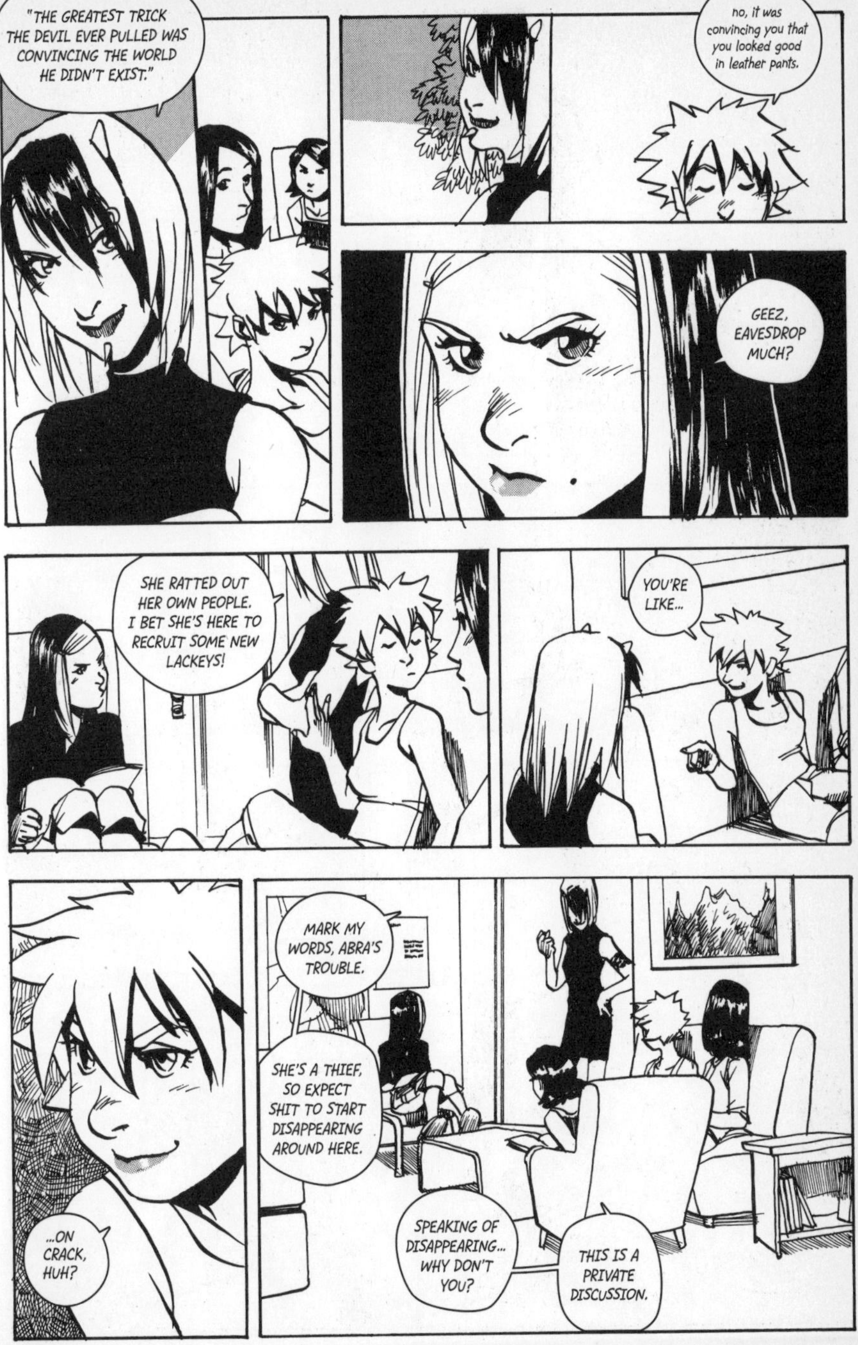
"THE GREATEST TRICK THE DEVIL EVER PULLED WAS CONVINCING THE WORLD HE DIDN'T EXIST."
no, it was convincing you that you looked good in leather pants.
GEEZ, EAVESDROP MUCH?
SHE RATTED OUT HER OWN PEOPLE. I BET SHE'S HERE TO RECRUIT SOME NEW LACKEYS!
YOU'RE LIKE...
...ON CRACK, HUH?
MARK MY WORDS, ABRA'S TROUBLE.
SHE'S A THIEF, SO EXPECT SHIT TO START DISAPPEARING AROUND HERE.
SPEAKING OF DISAPPEARING... WHY DON'T YOU?
THIS IS A PRIVATE DISCUSSION.

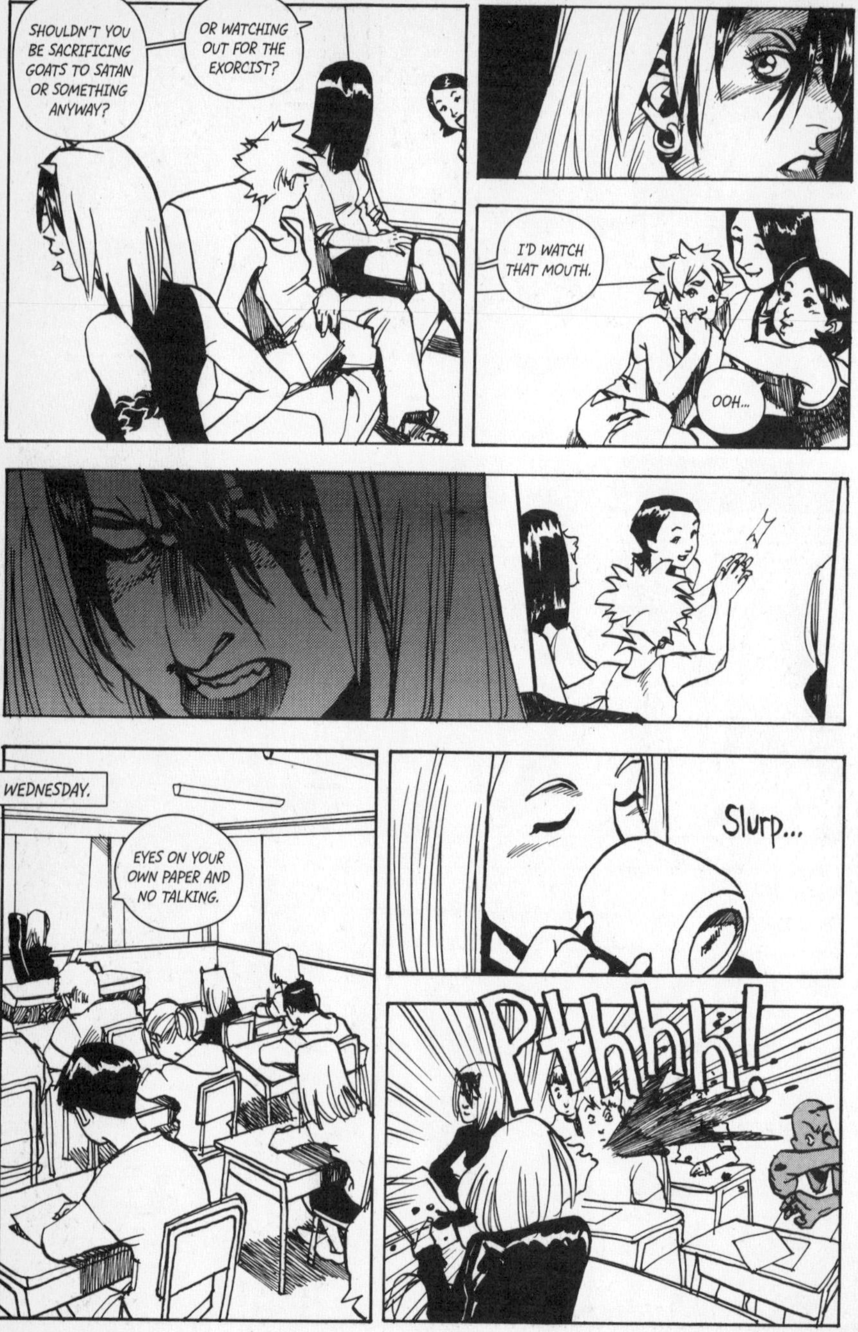
SHOULDN'T YOU BE SACRIFICING GOATS TO SATAN OR SOMETHING ANYWAY?
OR WATCHING OUT FOR THE EXORCIST?
I'D WATCH THAT MOUTH.
OOH...
WEDNESDAY.
EYES ON YOUR OWN PAPER AND NO TALKING.
Slurp...
Pthhh!

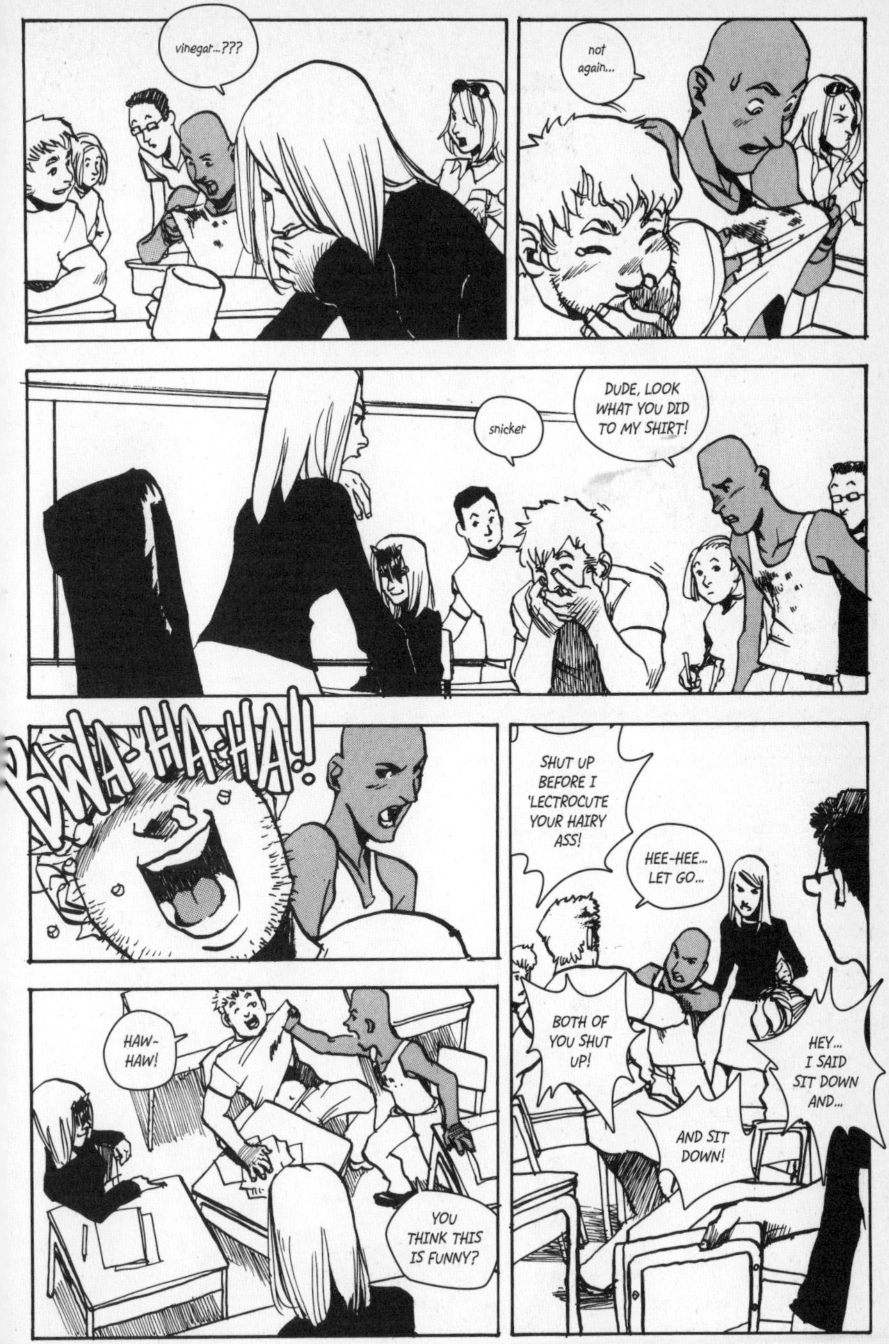
vinegar...???
not again...
snicker
DUDE, LOOK WHAT YOU DID TO MY SHIRT!
BWA-HA-HA!!
SHUT UP BEFORE I 'LECTROCUTE YOUR HAIRY ASS!
HEE-HEE... LET GO...
HAW-HAW!
YOU THINK THIS IS FUNNY?
BOTH OF YOU SHUT UP!
HEY... I SAID SIT DOWN AND...
AND SIT DOWN!

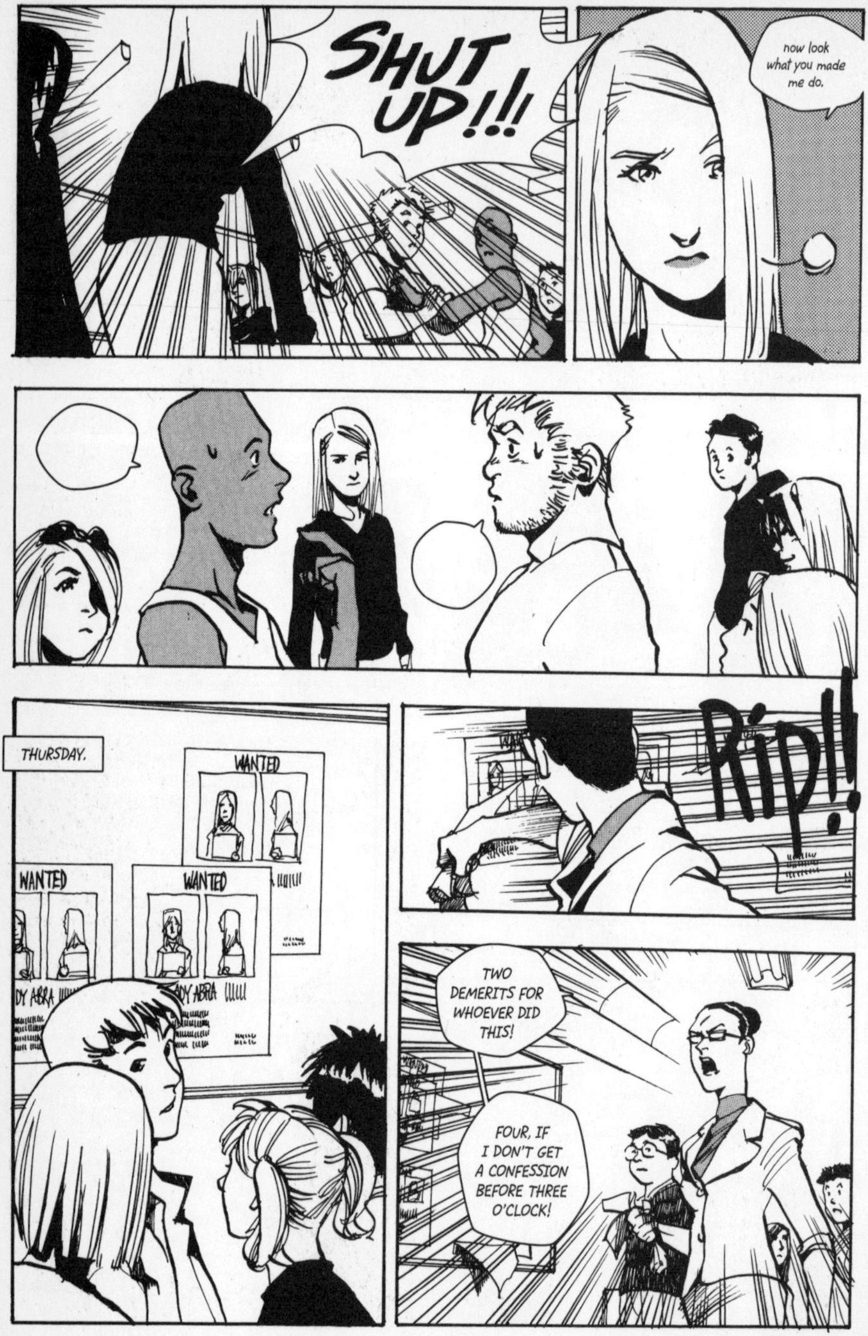
SHUT UP!!!
now look what you made me do.
THURSDAY.
WANTED
WANTED
WANTED
RIP!!
TWO DEMERITS FOR WHOEVER DID THIS!
FOUR, IF I DON'T GET A CONFESSION BEFORE THREE O'CLOCK!

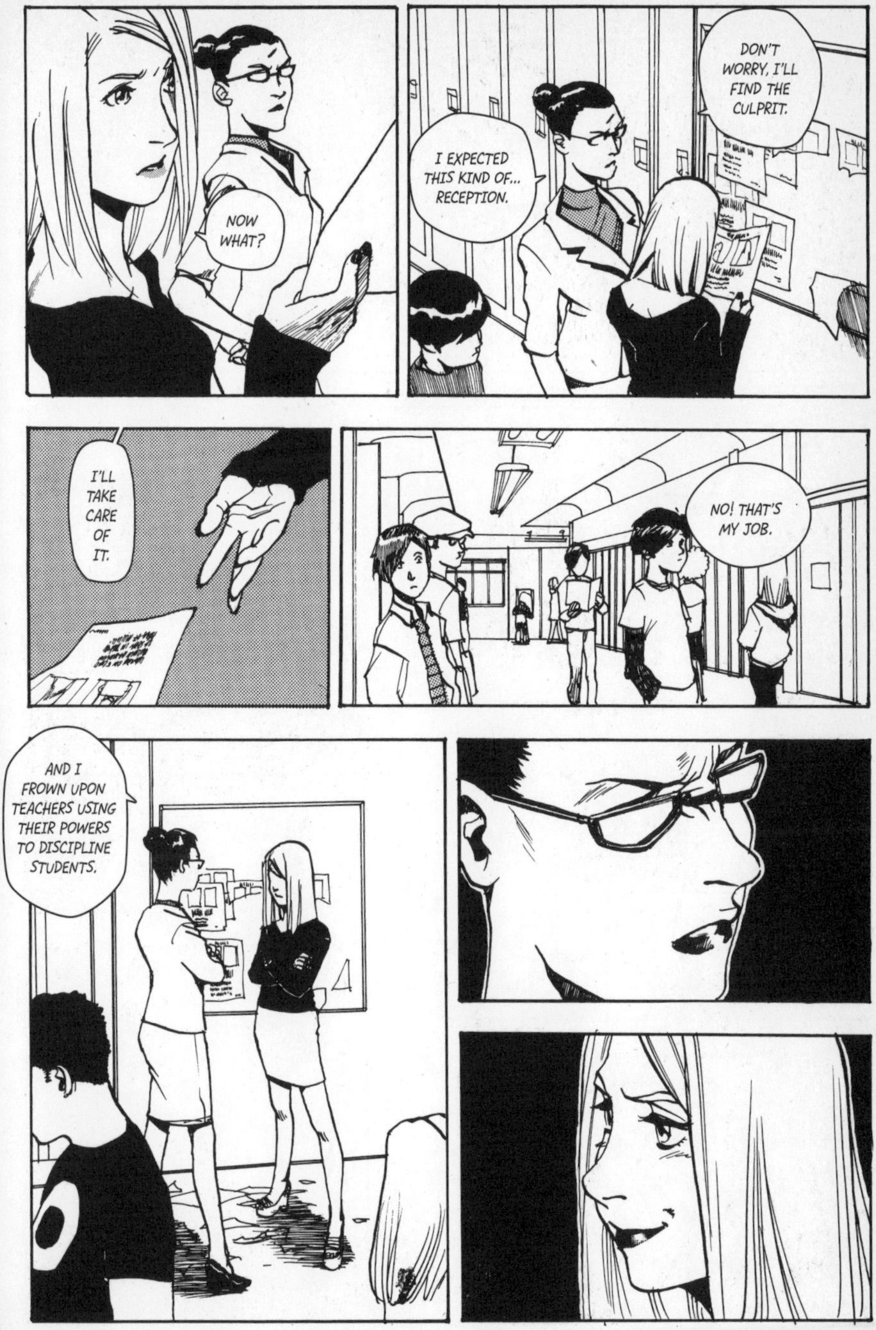
NOW WHAT?
I EXPECTED THIS KIND OF... RECEPTION.
DON'T WORRY, I'LL FIND THE CULPRIT.
I'LL TAKE CARE OF IT.
NO! THAT'S MY JOB.
AND I FROWN UPON TEACHERS USING THEIR POWERS TO DISCIPLINE STUDENTS.

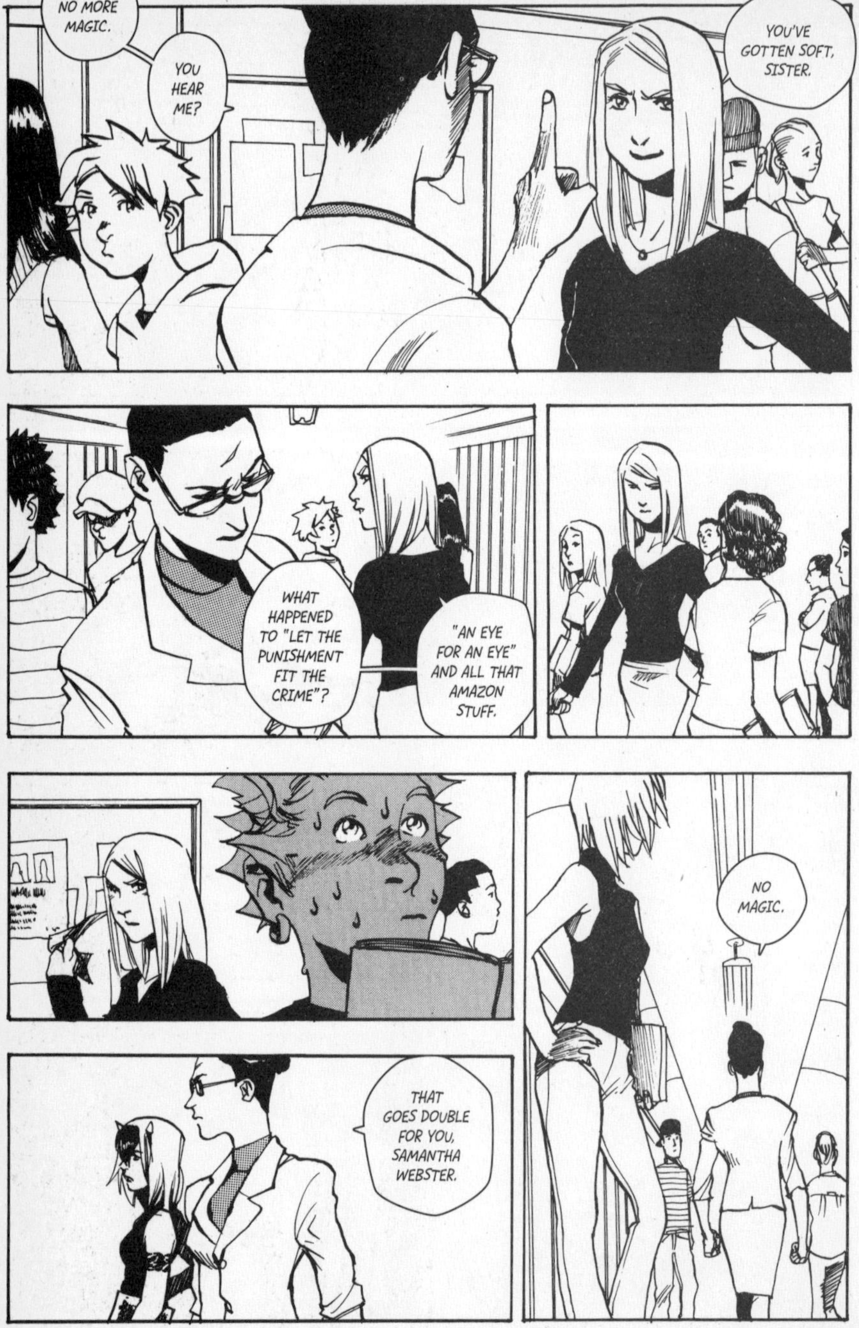
NO MORE MAGIC.
YOU HEAR ME?
YOU'VE GOTTEN SOFT, SISTER.
WHAT HAPPENED TO "LET THE PUNISHMENT FIT THE CRIME"?
"AN EYE FOR AN EYE" AND ALL THAT AMAZON STUFF.
NO MAGIC.
THAT GOES DOUBLE FOR YOU, SAMANTHA WEBSTER.

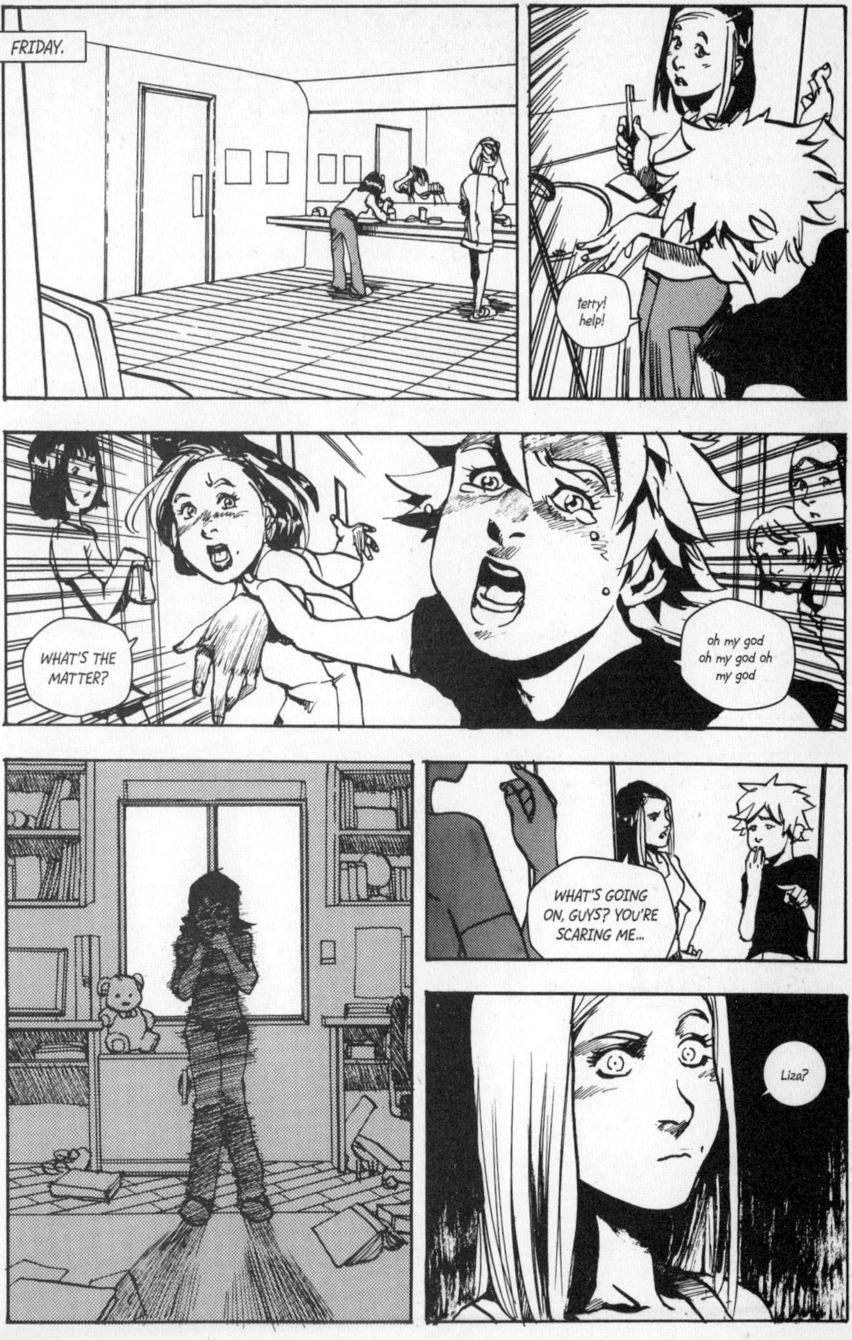
FRIDAY.
terry! help!
WHAT'S THE MATTER?
oh my god oh my god oh my god
WHAT'S GOING ON, GUYS? YOU'RE SCARING ME...
Liza?

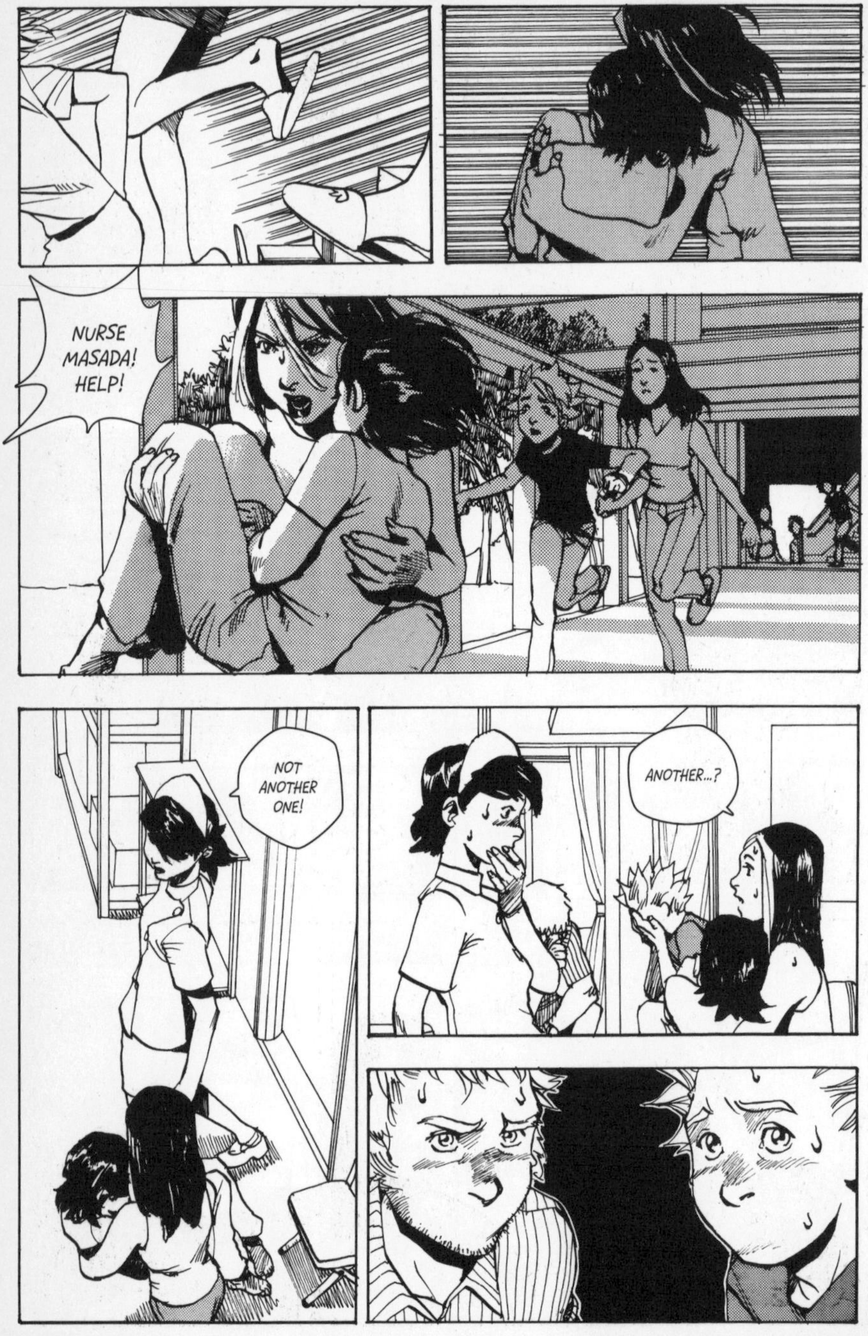
NURSE MASADA! HELP!
NOT ANOTHER ONE!
ANOTHER...?

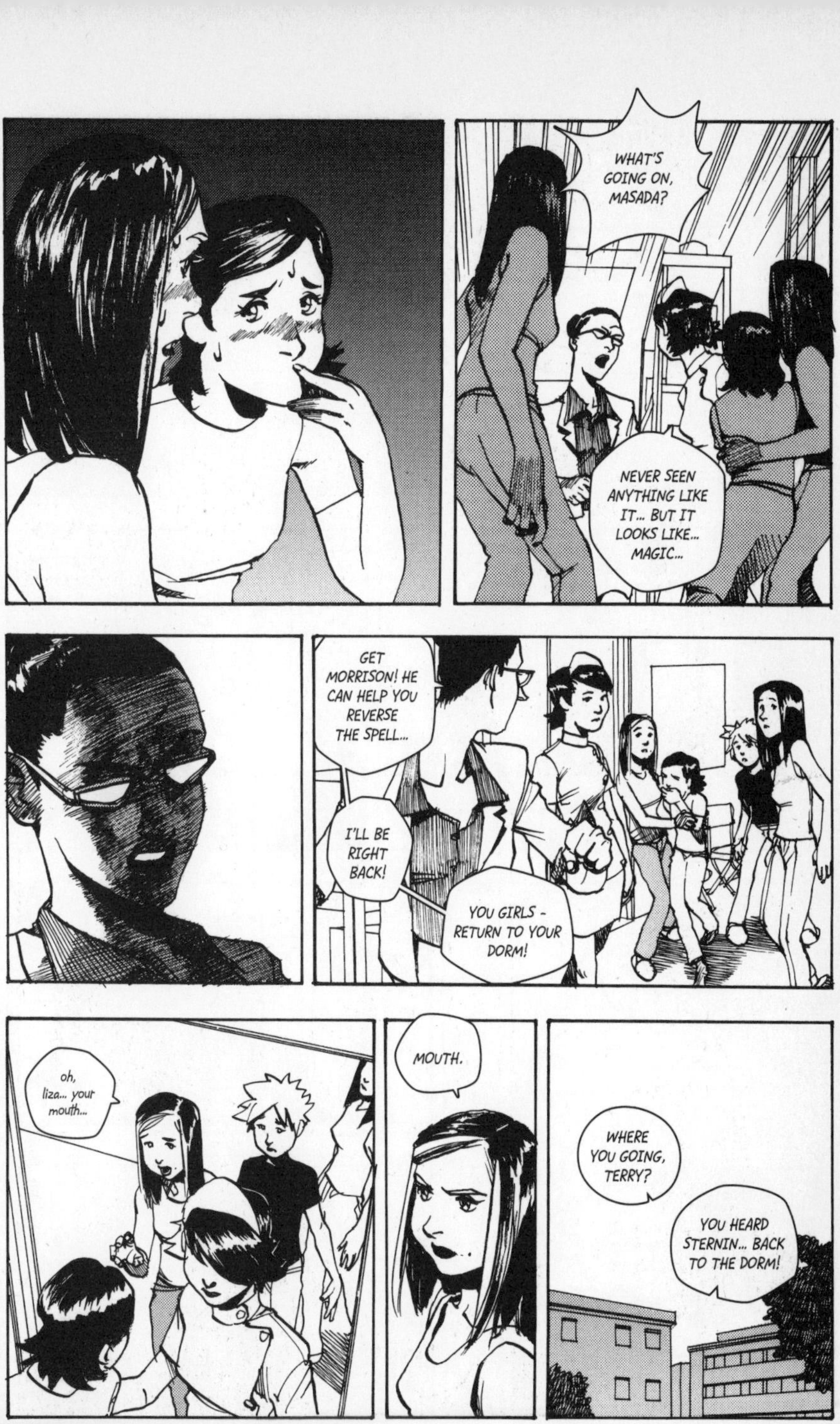
WHAT'S GOING ON, MASADA?
NEVER SEEN ANYTHING LIKE IT... BUT IT LOOKS LIKE... MAGIC...
GET MORRISON! HE CAN HELP YOU REVERSE THE SPELL...
I'LL BE RIGHT BACK!
YOU GIRLS - RETURN TO YOUR DORM!
oh, liza... your mouth...
MOUTH.
WHERE YOU GOING, TERRY?
YOU HEARD STERNIN... BACK TO THE DORM!

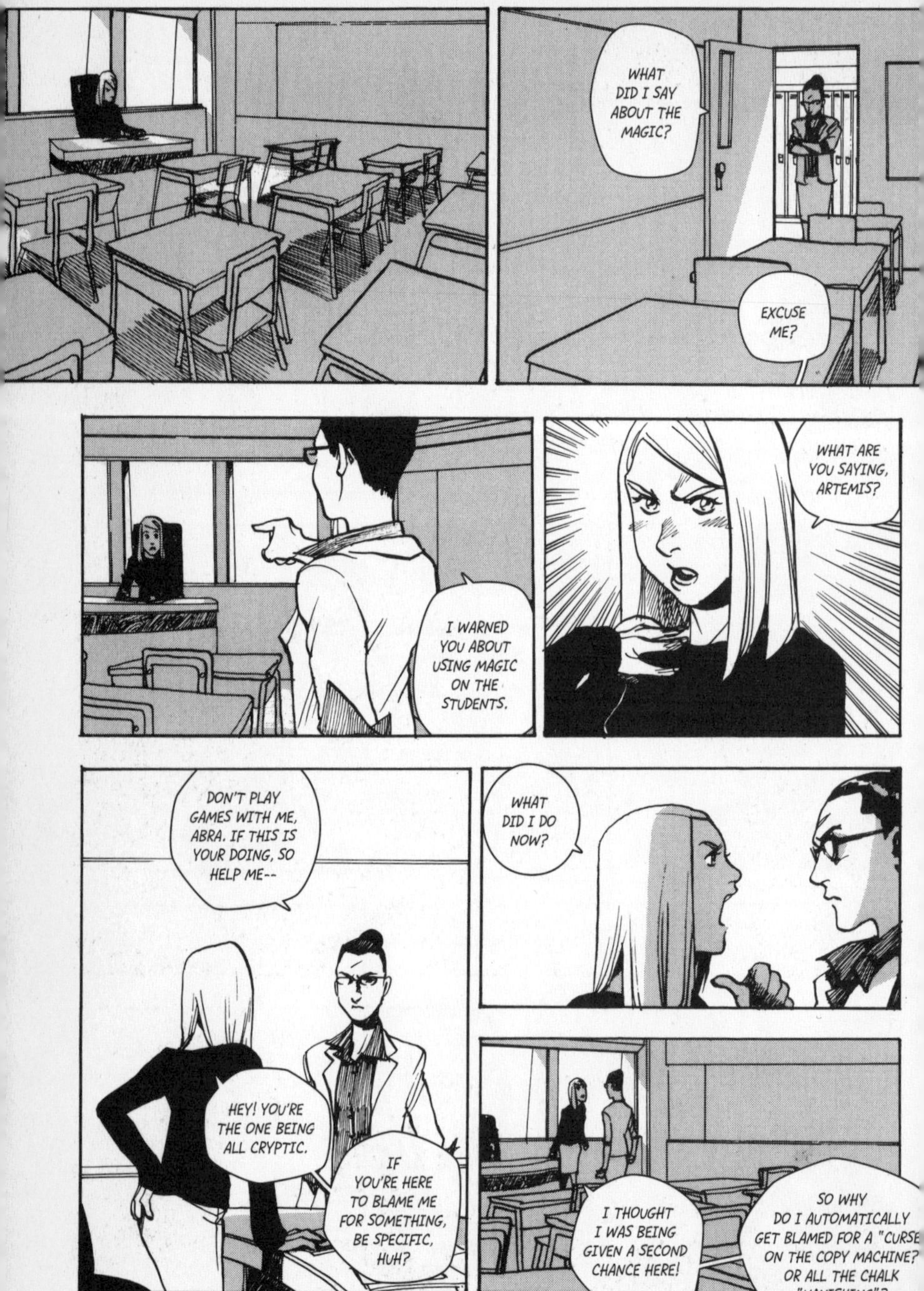
WHAT DID I SAY ABOUT THE MAGIC?
EXCUSE ME?
I WARNED YOU ABOUT USING MAGIC ON THE STUDENTS.
WHAT ARE YOU SAYING, ARTEMIS?
DON'T PLAY GAMES WITH ME, ABRA. IF THIS IS YOUR DOING, SO HELP ME--
HEY! YOU'RE THE ONE BEING ALL CRYPTIC.
IF YOU'RE HERE TO BLAME ME FOR SOMETHING, BE SPECIFIC, HUH?
WHAT DID I DO NOW?
I THOUGHT I WAS BEING GIVEN A SECOND CHANCE HERE!
SO WHY DO I AUTOMATICALLY GET BLAMED FOR A "CURSE" ON THE COPY MACHINE? OR ALL THE CHALK "VANISHING"?

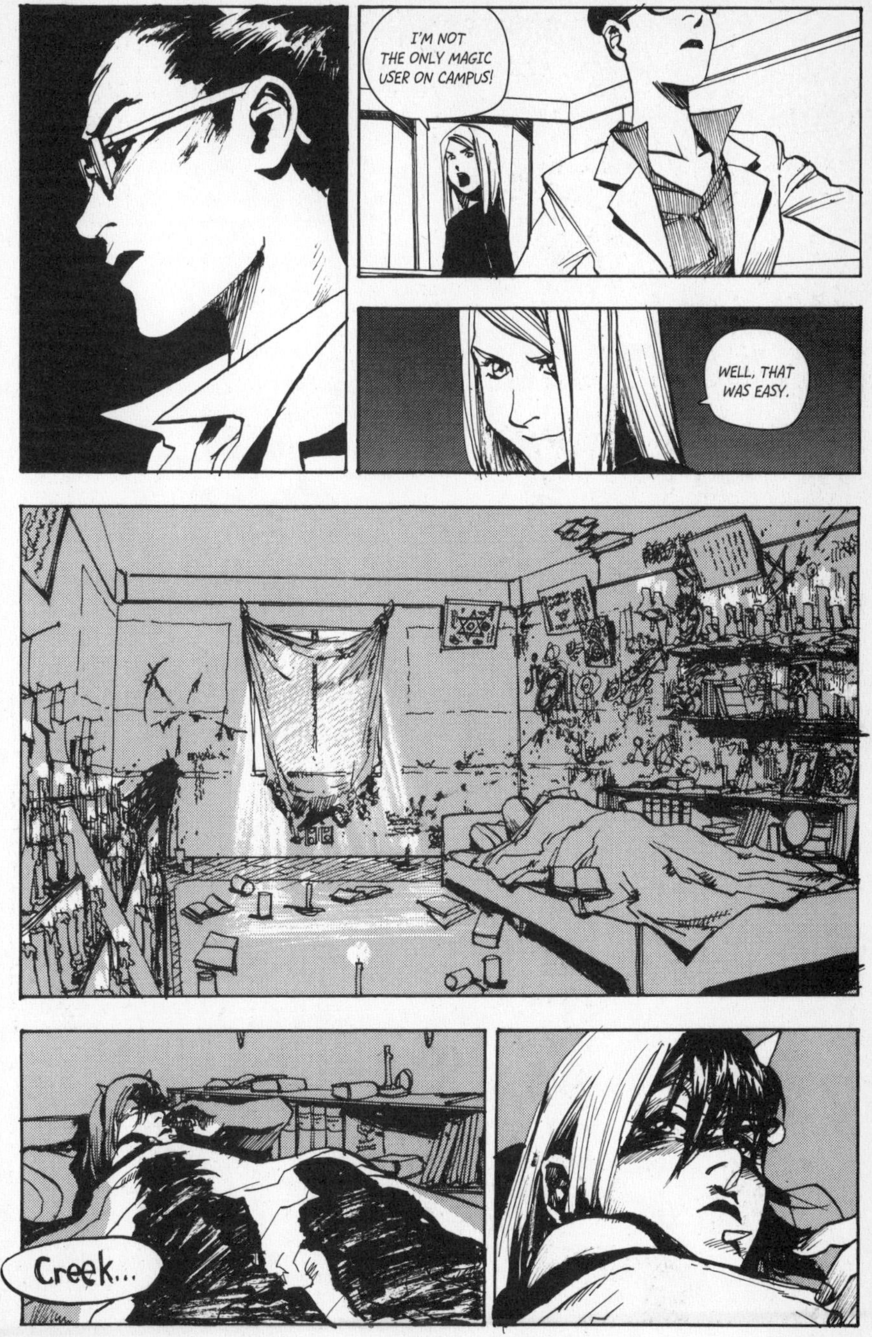
I'M NOT THE ONLY MAGIC USER ON CAMPUS!
WELL, THAT WAS EASY.
Creek...

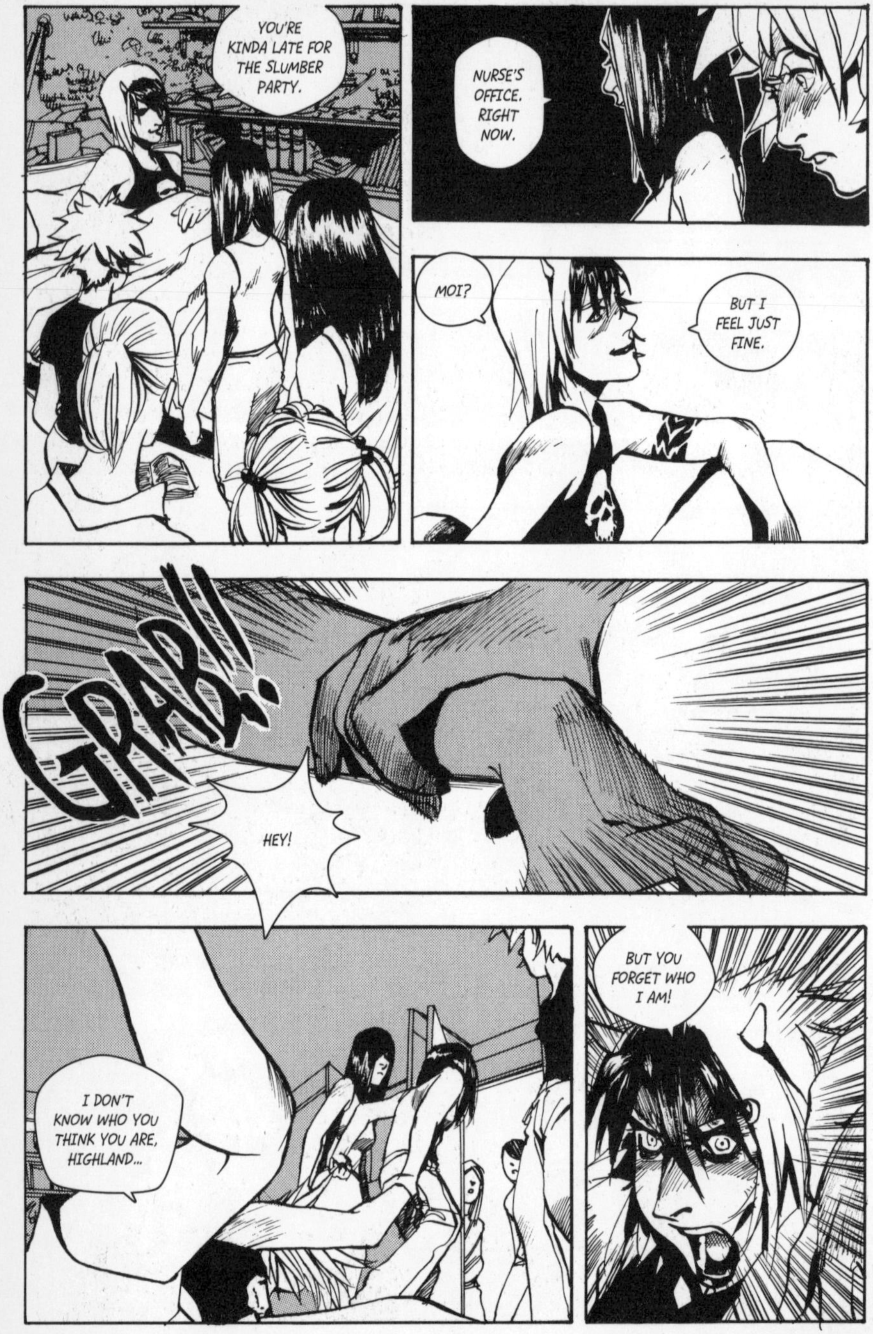
YOU'RE KINDA LATE FOR THE SLUMBER PARTY.
NURSE'S OFFICE. RIGHT NOW.
MOI?
BUT I FEEL JUST FINE.
GRAB!!
HEY!
I DON'T KNOW WHO YOU THINK YOU ARE, HIGHLAND...
BUT YOU FORGET WHO I AM!

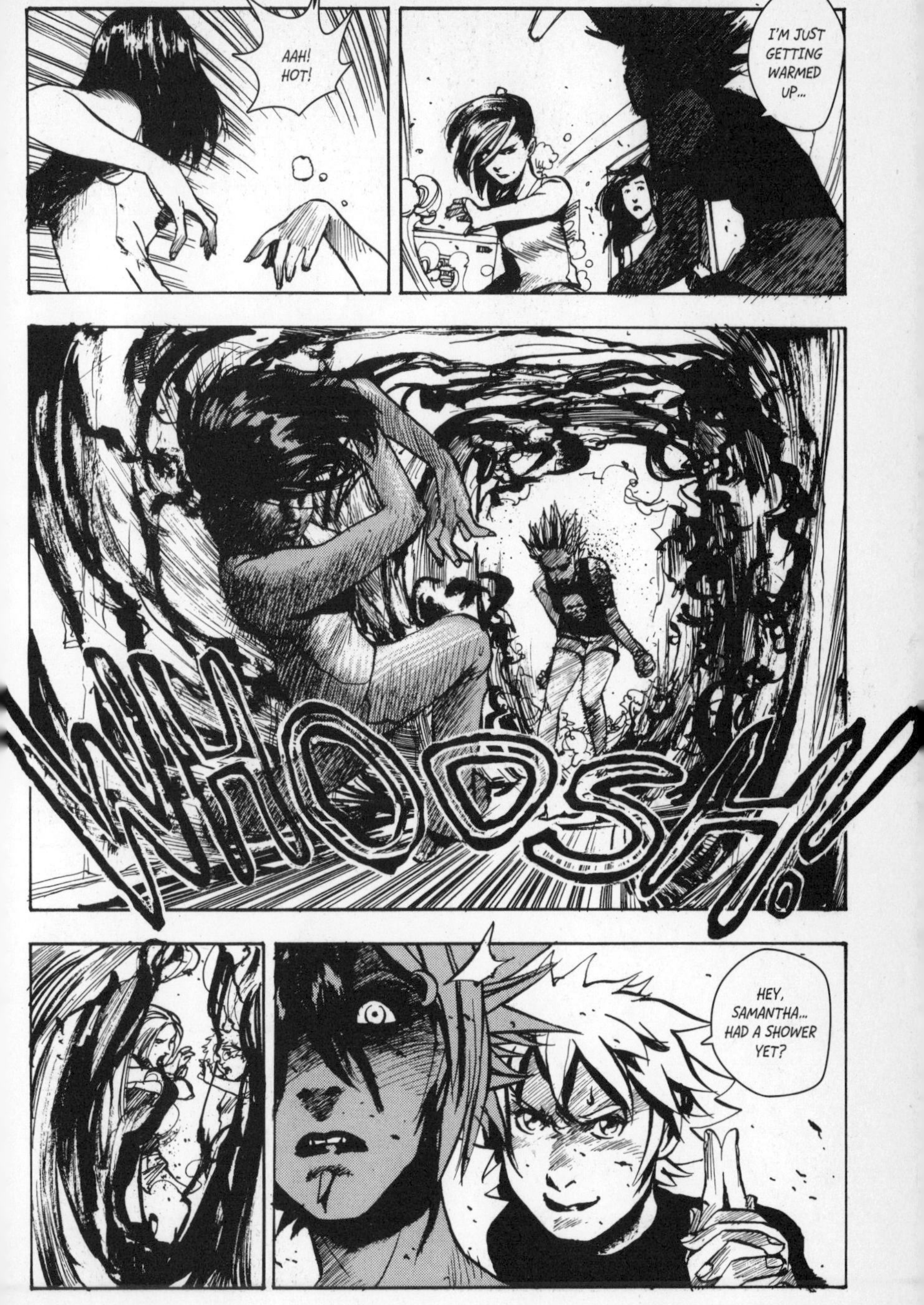
AAH! HOT!
I'M JUST GETTING WARMED UP...
WHOOSH!
HEY, SAMANTHA... HAD A SHOWER YET?

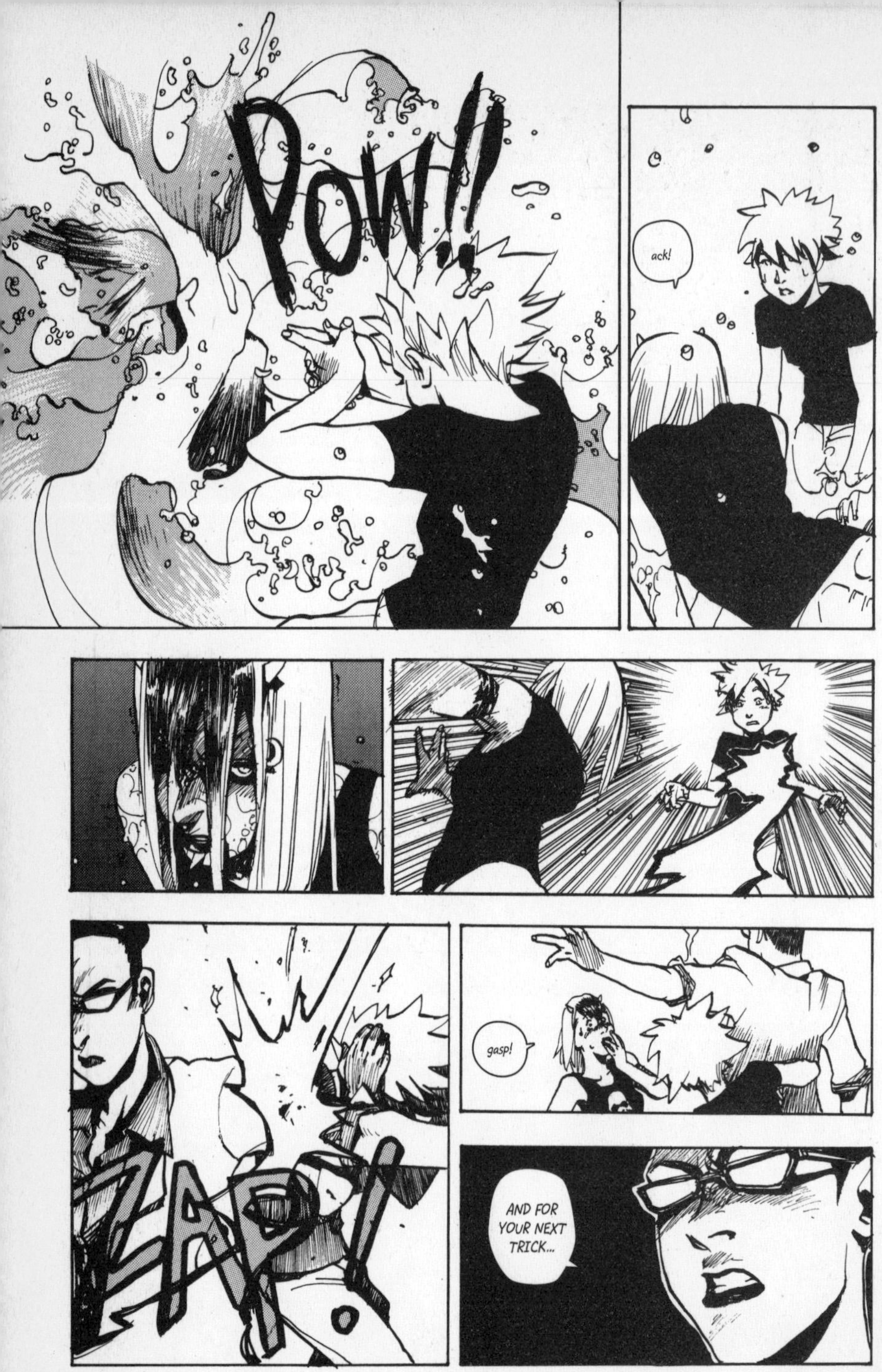
POW!!
ack!
ZAP!
gasp!
AND FOR YOUR NEXT TRICK...

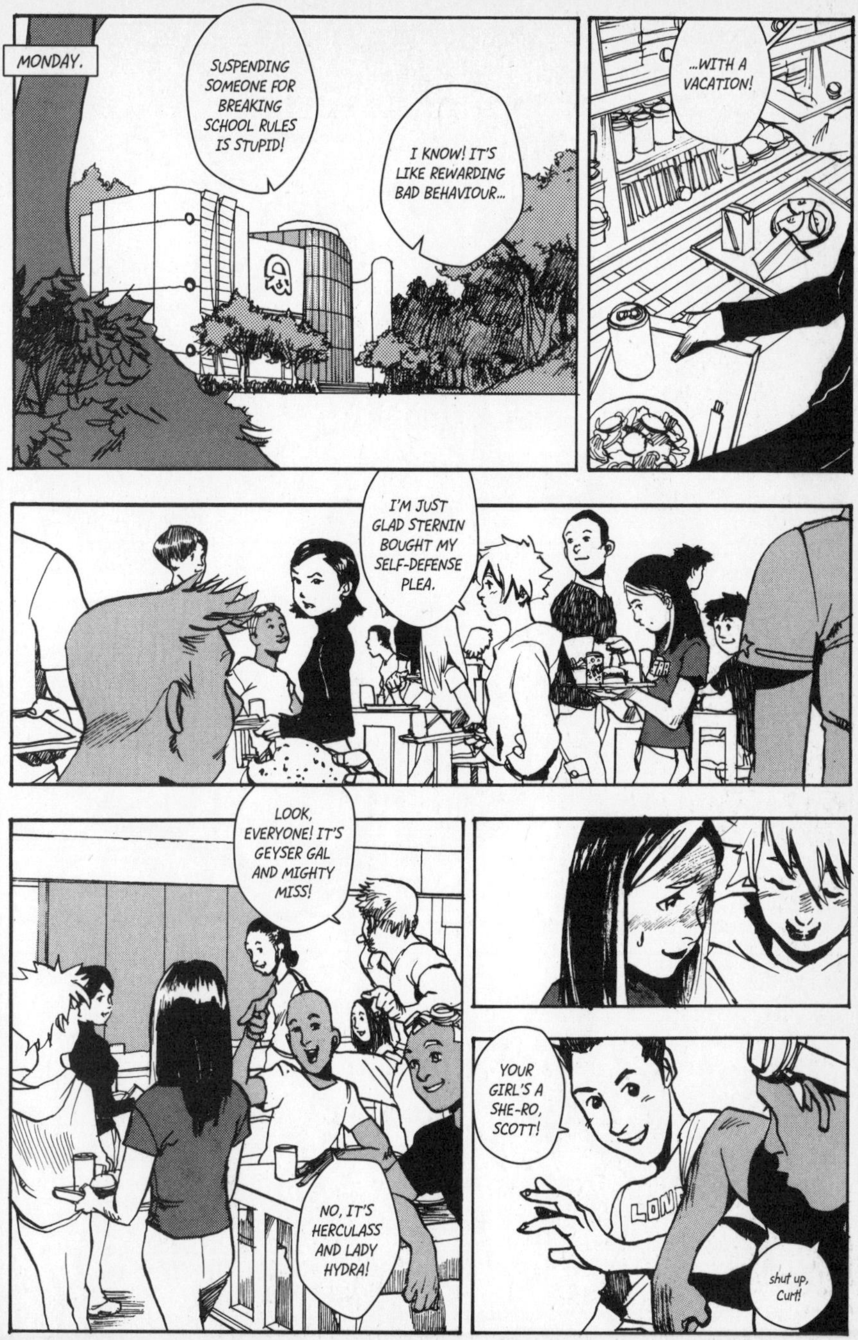
MONDAY.
SUSPENDING SOMEONE FOR BREAKING SCHOOL RULES IS STUPID!
I KNOW! IT'S LIKE REWARDING BAD BEHAVIOUR...
...WITH A VACATION!
I'M JUST GLAD STERNIN BOUGHT MY SELF-DEFENSE PLEA.
LOOK, EVERYONE! IT'S GEYSER GAL AND MIGHTY MISS!
NO, IT'S HERCULASS AND LADY HYDRA!
YOUR GIRL'S A SHE-RO, SCOTT!
shut up, Curt!

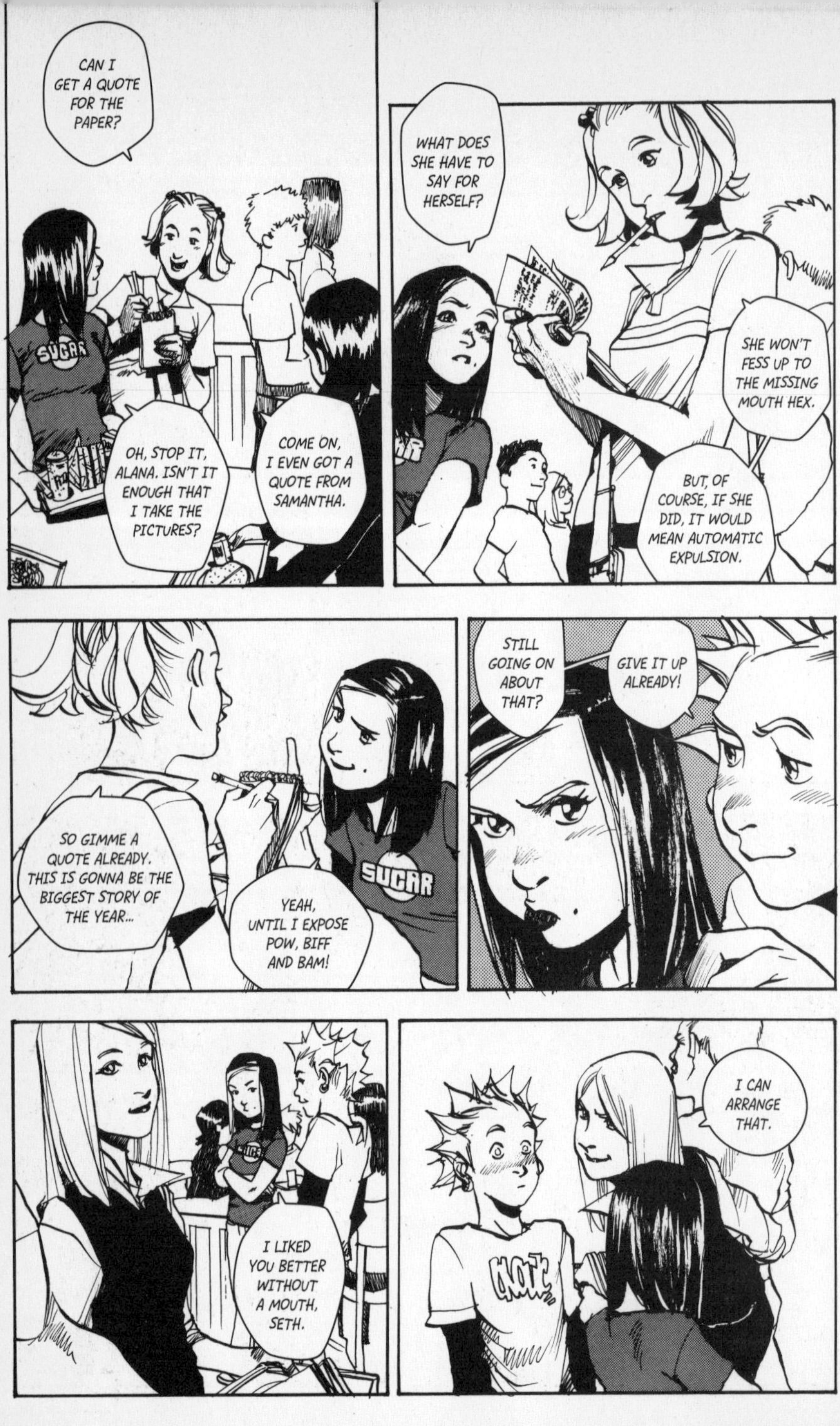
CAN I GET A QUOTE FOR THE PAPER?
OH, STOP IT, ALANA. ISN'T IT ENOUGH THAT I TAKE THE PICTURES?
COME ON, I EVEN GOT A QUOTE FROM SAMANTHA.
WHAT DOES SHE HAVE TO SAY FOR HERSELF?
SHE WON'T FESS UP TO THE MISSING MOUTH HEX.
BUT, OF COURSE, IF SHE DID, IT WOULD MEAN AUTOMATIC EXPULSION.
SO GIMME A QUOTE ALREADY. THIS IS GONNA BE THE BIGGEST STORY OF THE YEAR...
YEAH, UNTIL I EXPOSE POW, BIFF AND BAM!
STILL GOING ON ABOUT THAT?
GIVE IT UP ALREADY!
I LIKED YOU BETTER WITHOUT A MOUTH, SETH.
I CAN ARRANGE THAT.

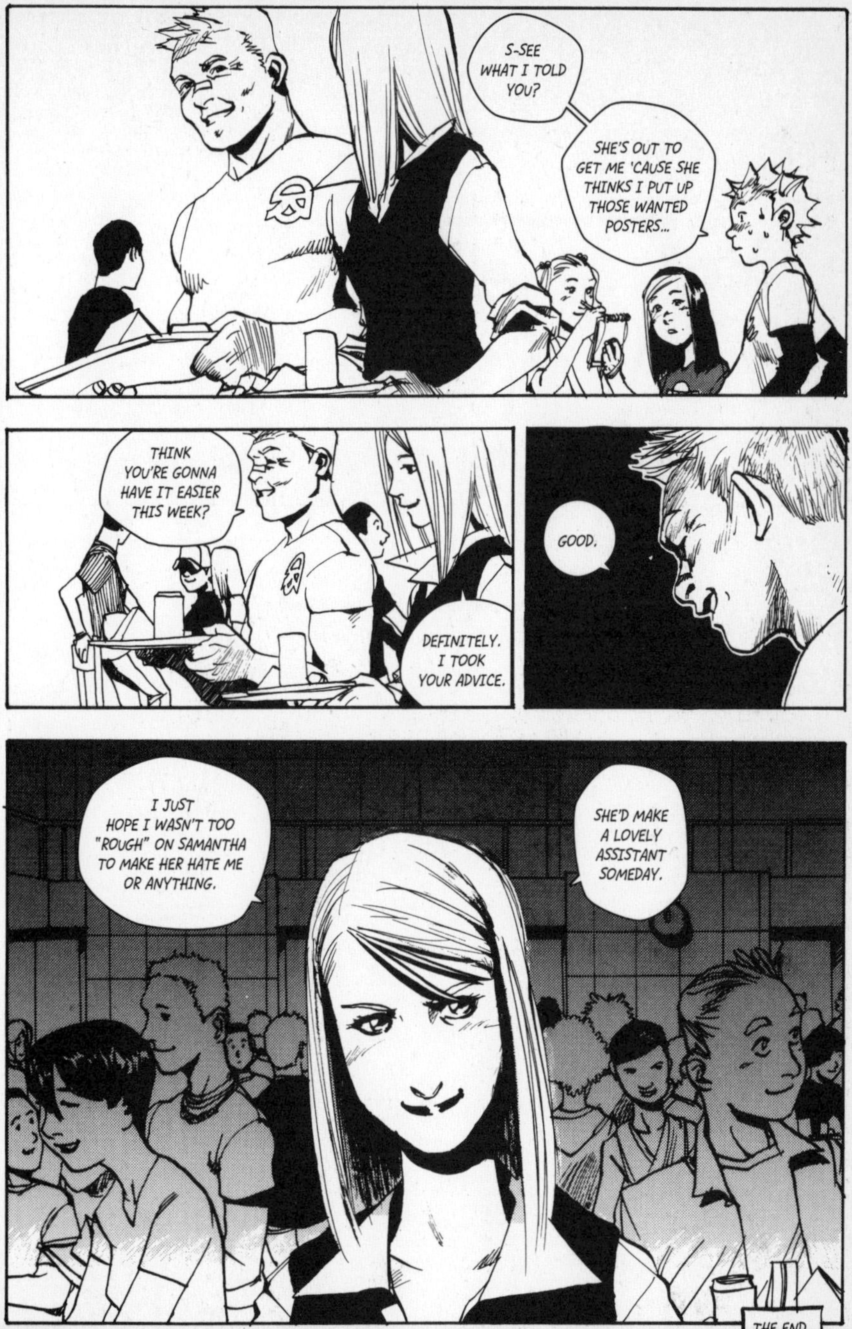
S-SEE WHAT I TOLD YOU?
SHE'S OUT TO GET ME 'CAUSE SHE THINKS I PUT UP THOSE WANTED POSTERS...
THINK YOU'RE GONNA HAVE IT EASIER THIS WEEK?
DEFINITELY. I TOOK YOUR ADVICE.
GOOD.
I JUST HOPE I WASN'T TOO "ROUGH" ON SAMANTHA TO MAKE HER HATE ME OR ANYTHING.
SHE'D MAKE A LOVELY ASSISTANT SOMEDAY.
THE END.

Crash Course

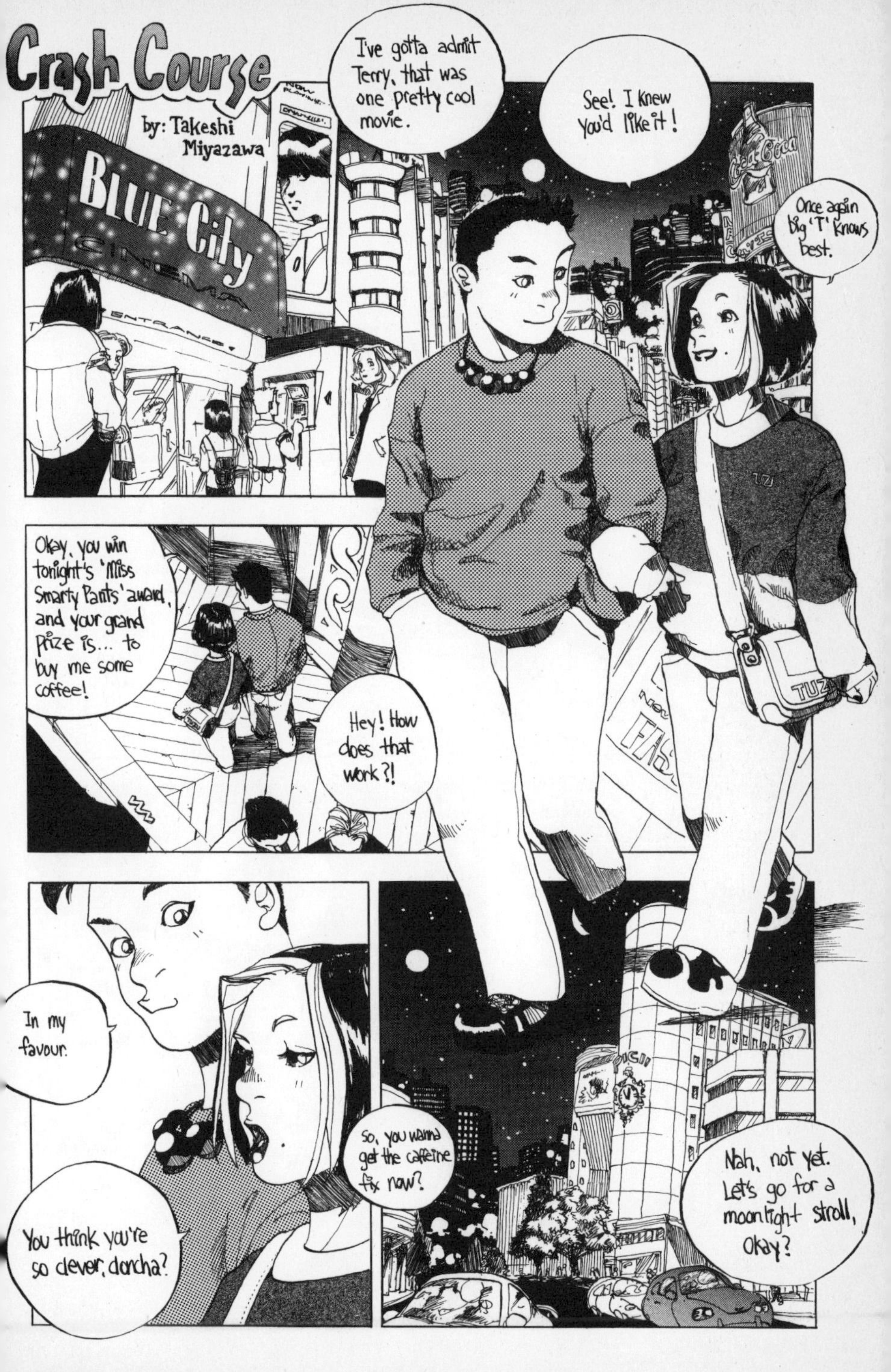

Crash Course
by: Takeshi Miyazawa
BLUE City
CINEMA
ENTRANCE
I've gotta admit Terry, that was one pretty cool movie.
See! I knew you'd like it!
Once again big 'T' knows best.
Okay, you win tonight's 'Miss Smarty Pants' award, and your grand prize is... to buy me some coffee!
Hey! How does that work?!
In my favour.
You think you're so clever, doncha?
So, you wanna get the caffeine fix now?
Nah, not yet. Let's go for a moonlight stroll, Okay?

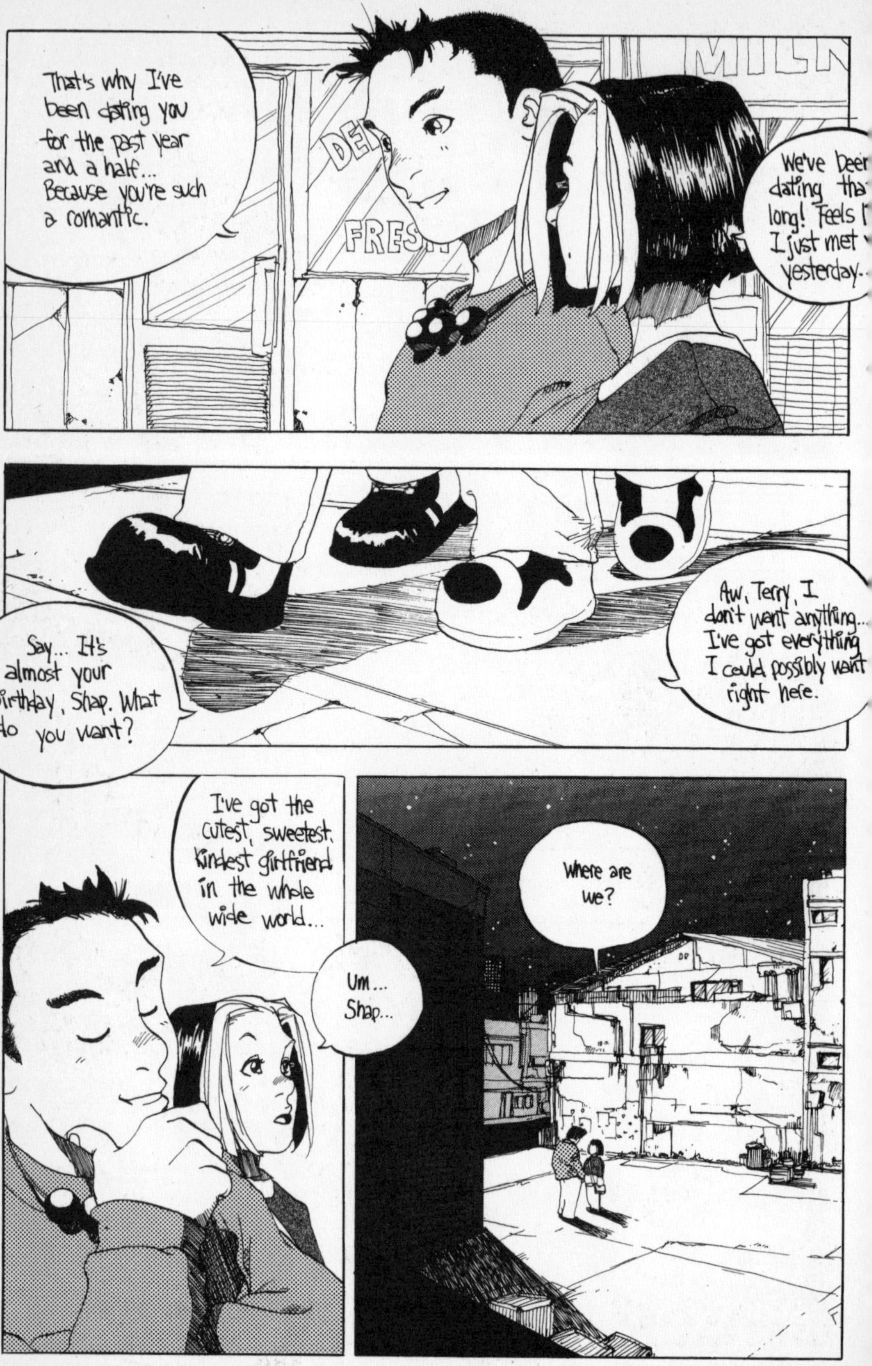
MILK
DELI
FRESH
That's why I've been dating you for the past year and a half... Because you're such a romantic.
We've beer dating tha long! Feels l I just met yesterday..
Say... It's almost your birthday, Shap. What do you want?
Aw, Terry, I don't want anything... I've got everything I could possibly want right here.
I've got the cutest, sweetest, kindest girlfriend in the whole wide world...
Um... Shap...
Where are we?

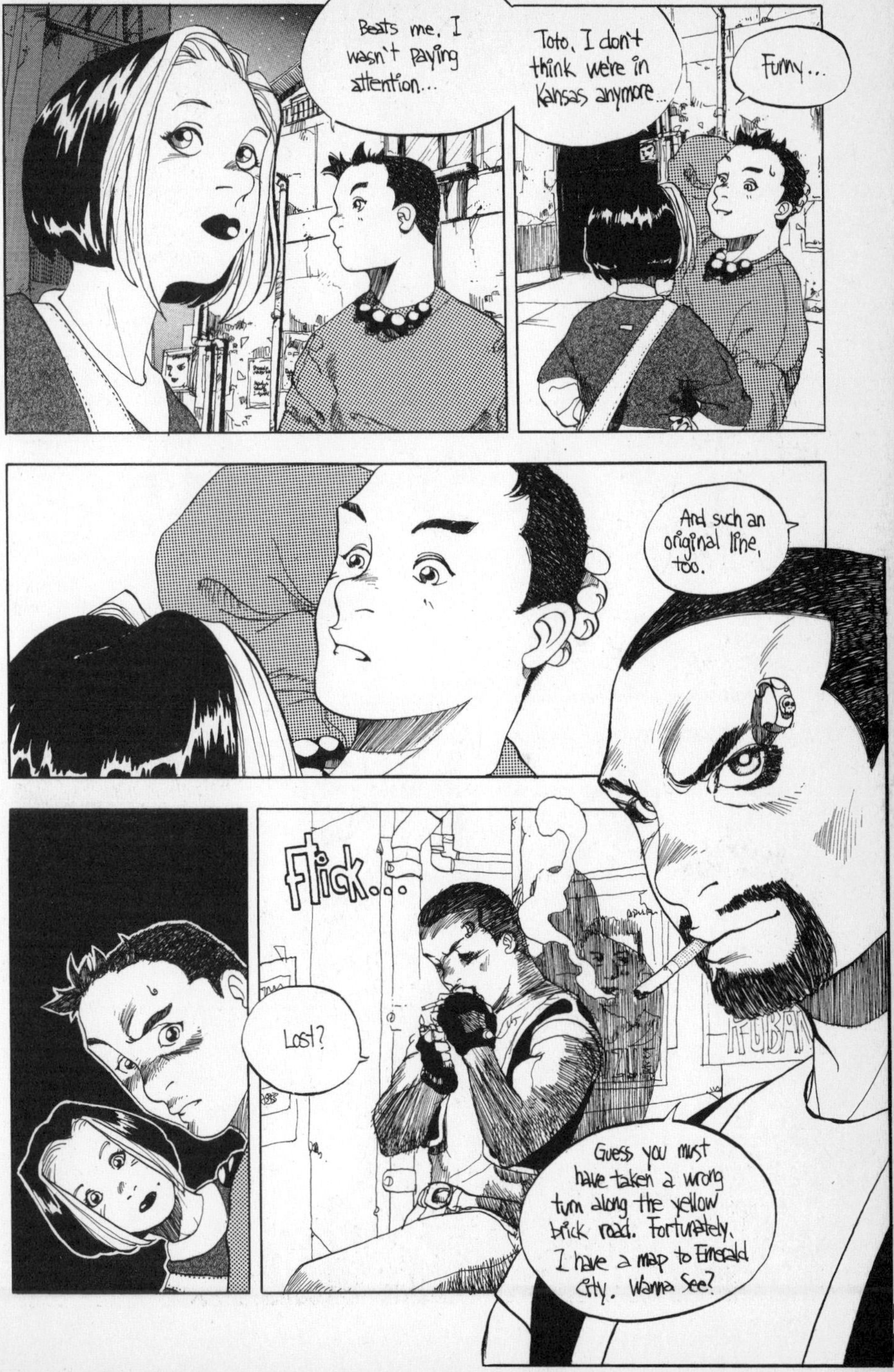
Beats me. I wasn't paying attention...
Toto, I don't think we're in Kansas anymore...
Funny...
And such an original line, too.
Flick...
Lost?
Guess you must have taken a wrong turn along the yellow brick road. Fortunately, I have a map to Emerald City. Wanna see?

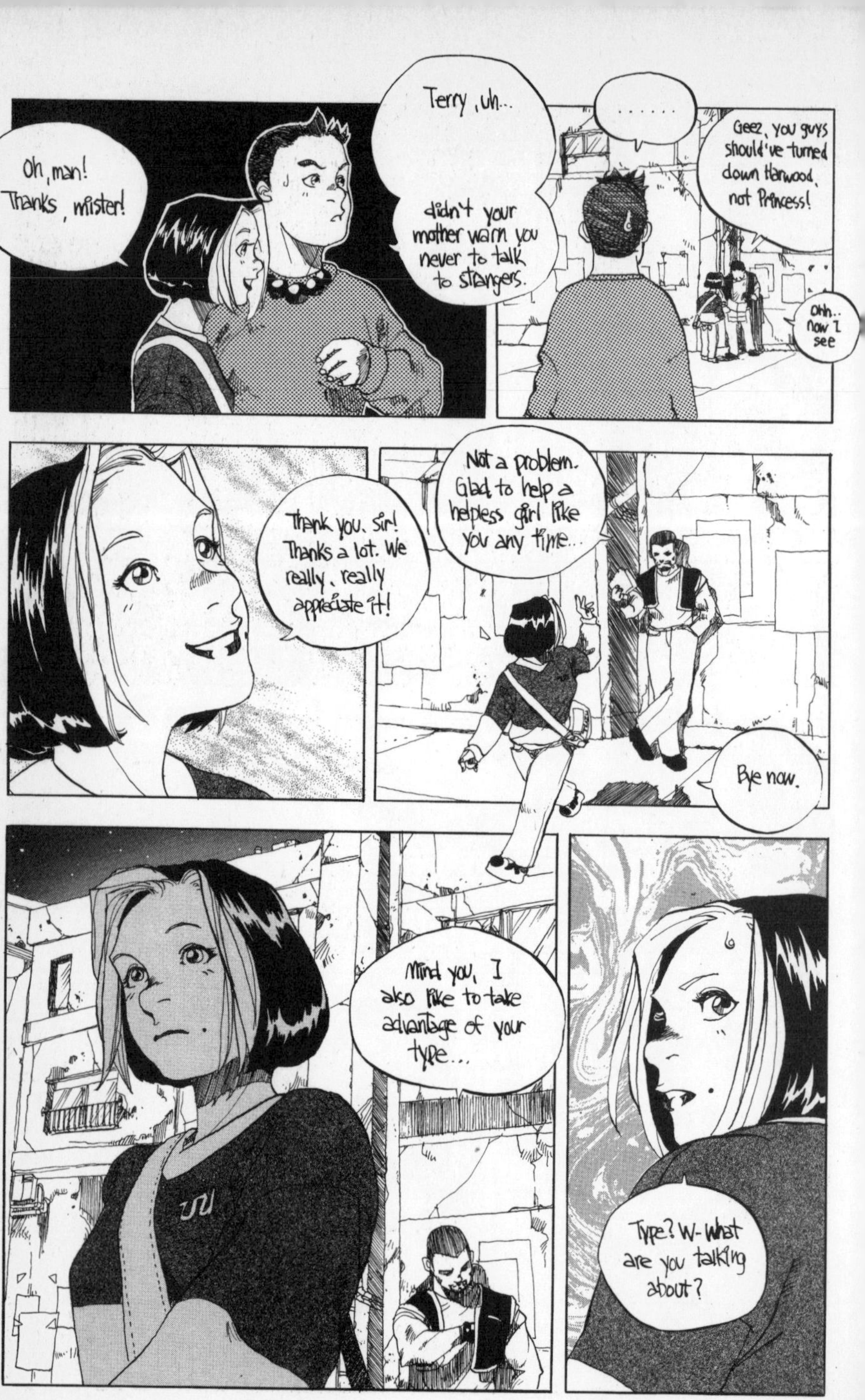
Oh, man! Thanks, mister!
Terry, uh...
didn't your mother warn you never to talk to strangers.
. . . . . .
Geez, you guys should've turned down Harwood, not Princess!
Ohh.. now I see
Thank you, sir! Thanks a lot. We really, really appreciate it!
Not a problem. Glad to help a helpless girl like you any time...
Bye now.
Mind you, I also like to take advantage of your type...
Type? W-what are you talking about?

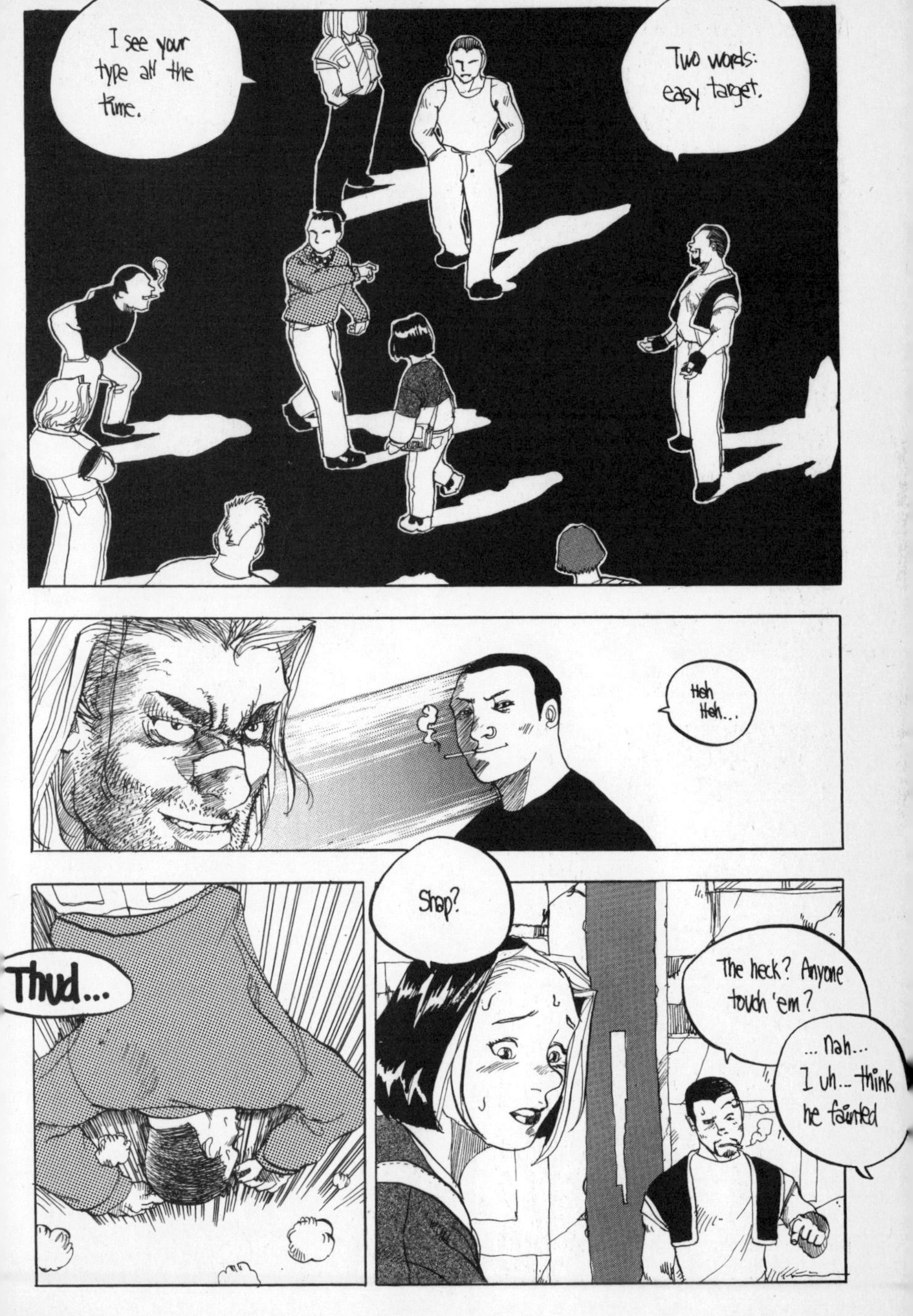
I see your type all the time.
Two words: easy target.
Heh Heh...
Thud...
Snap?
The heck? Anyone touch 'em?
... nah... I uh... think he fainted

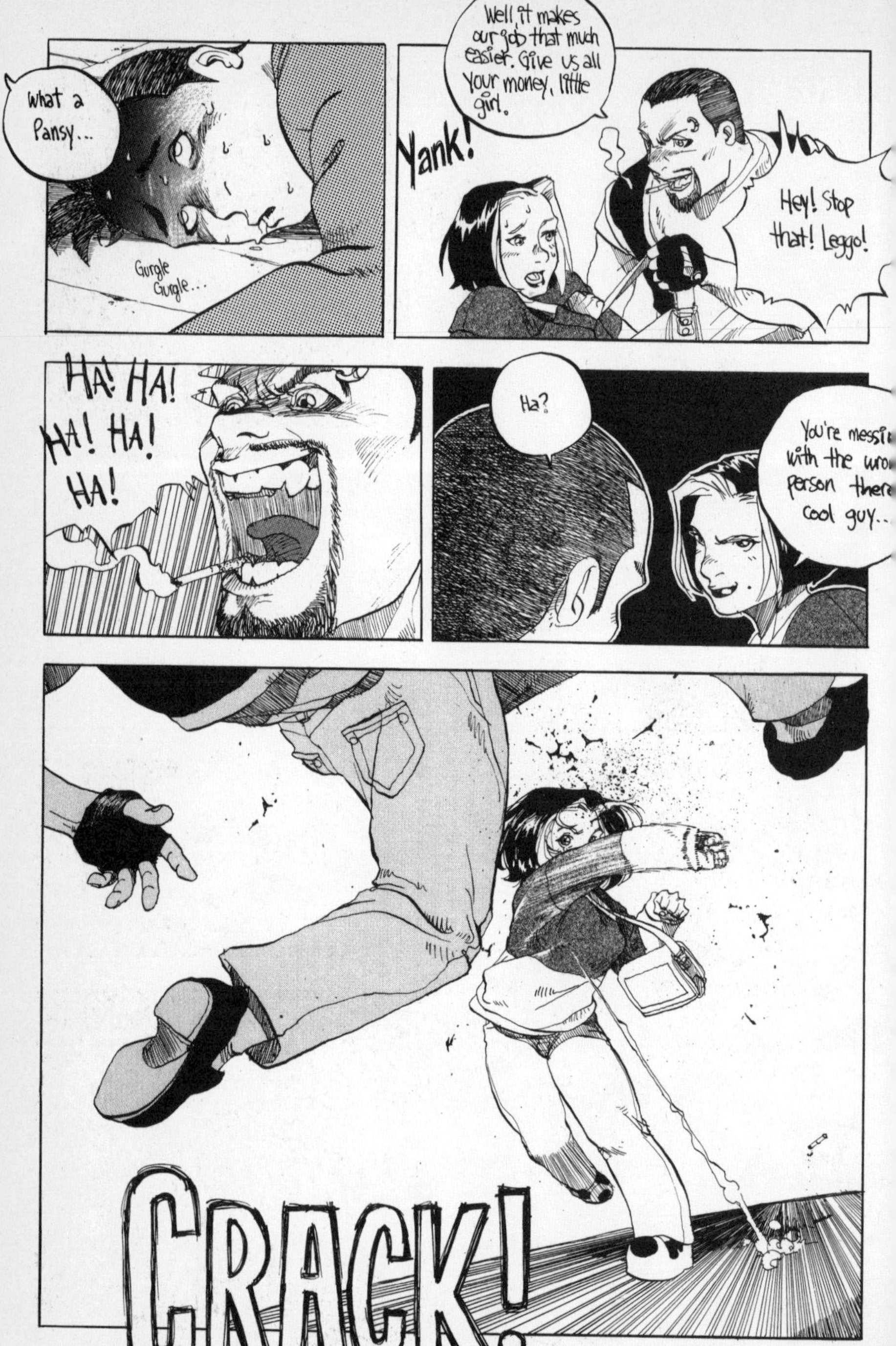
what a Pansy...
Gurgle Gurgle...
Well, it makes our job that much easier. Give us all your money, little girl.
Yank!
Hey! Stop that! Leggo!
HA! HA! HA! HA! HA!
Ha?
CRACK!

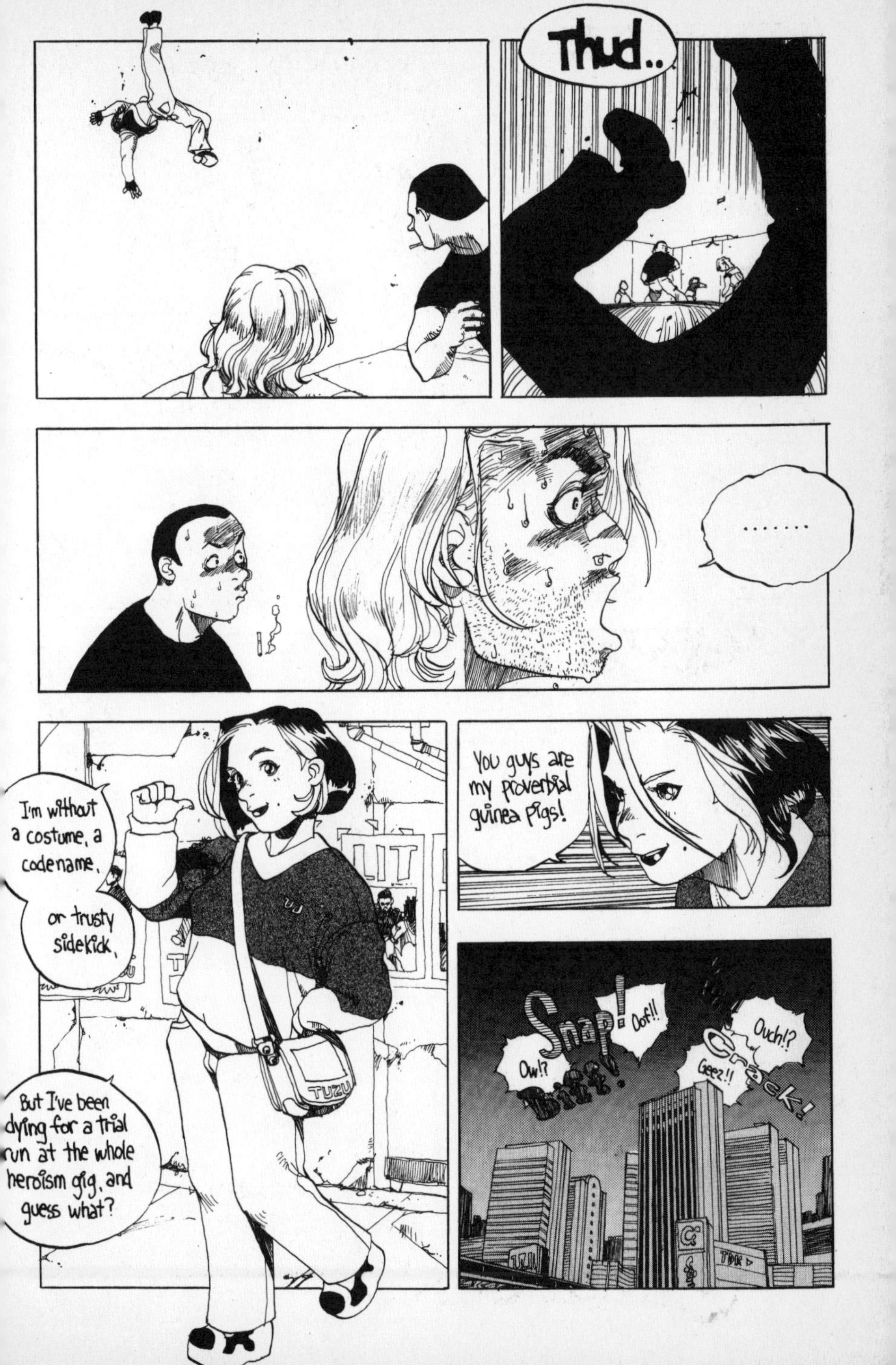
Thud..
....
I'm without a costume, a codename,
or trusty sidekick,
But I've been dying for a trial run at the whole heroism gig, and guess what?
You guys are my proverbial guinea pigs!
Snap!
Oof!!
Ouch!?
Ow!?
Geez!!
Crack!

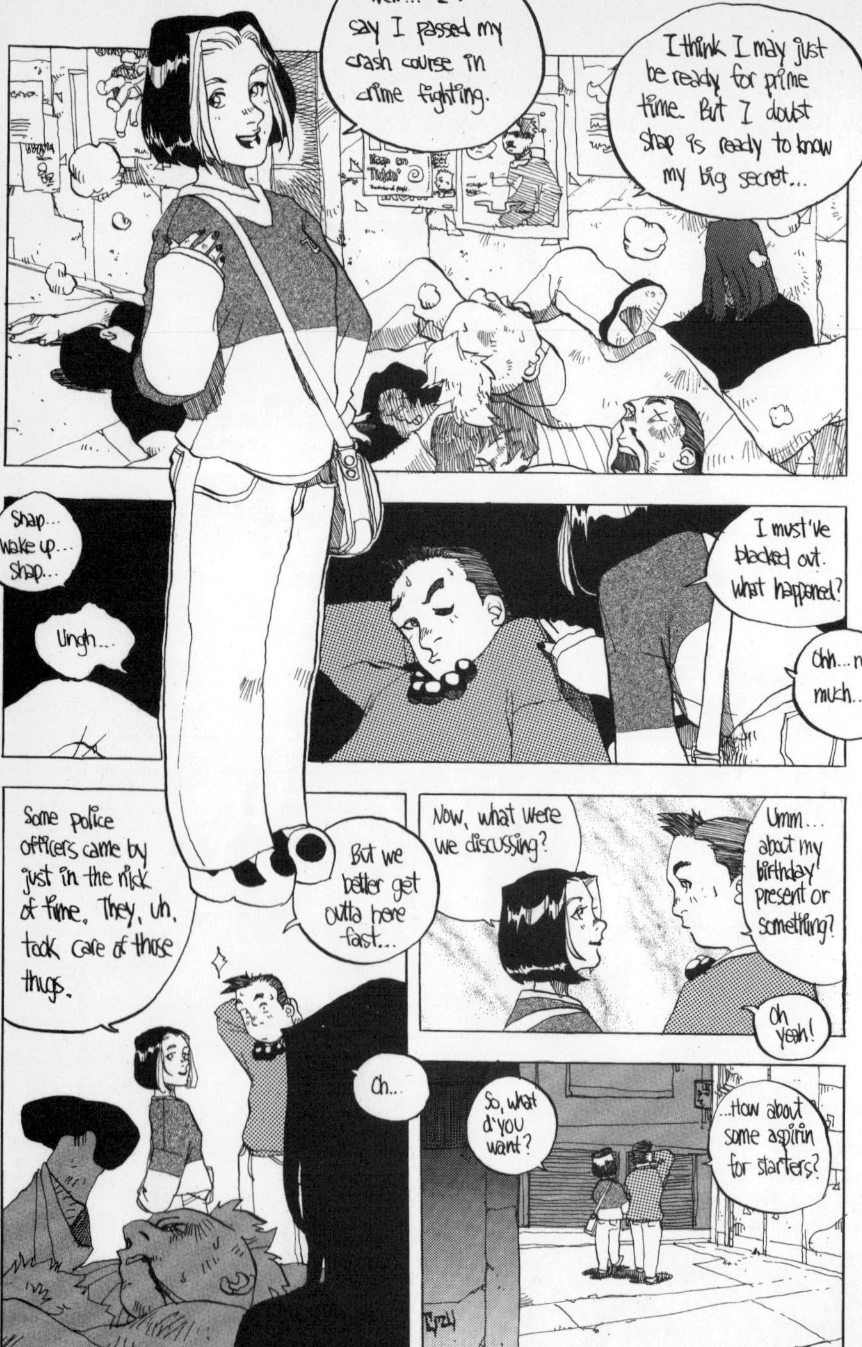
Well... I'd say I passed my crash course in crime fighting.
I think I may just be ready for prime time. But I doubt Shap is ready to know my big secret...
Shap... wake up... Shap...
Ungh...
I must've blacked out. What happened?
Ohh... not much...
Some police officers came by just in the nick of time. They, uh, took care of those thugs.
But we better get outta here fast...
Oh...
Now, what were we discussing?
Umm... about my birthday present or something?
Oh yeah!
So, what d'you want?
...How about some aspirin for starters?
End...

Sketch Gallery

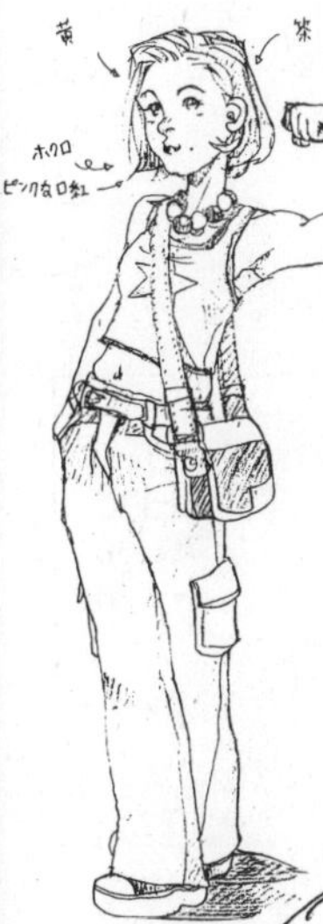

黄
茶
ホクロ
ピンクな口紅

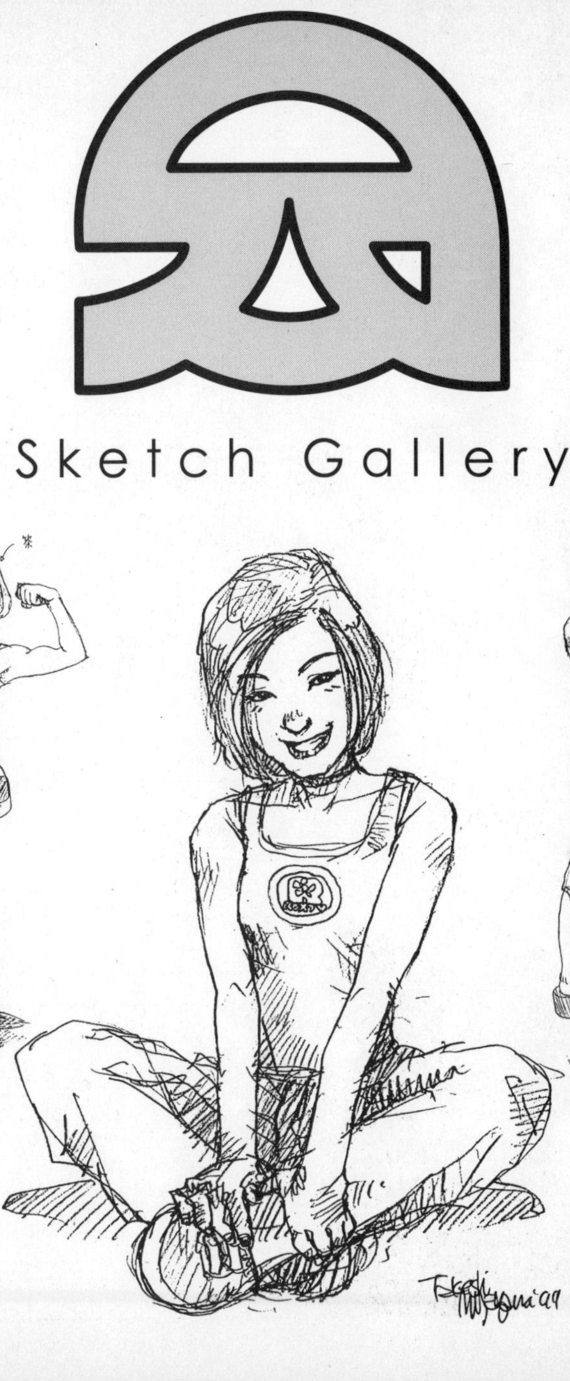

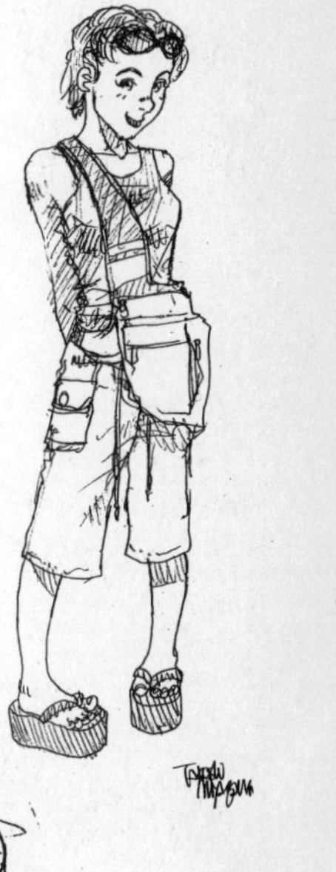

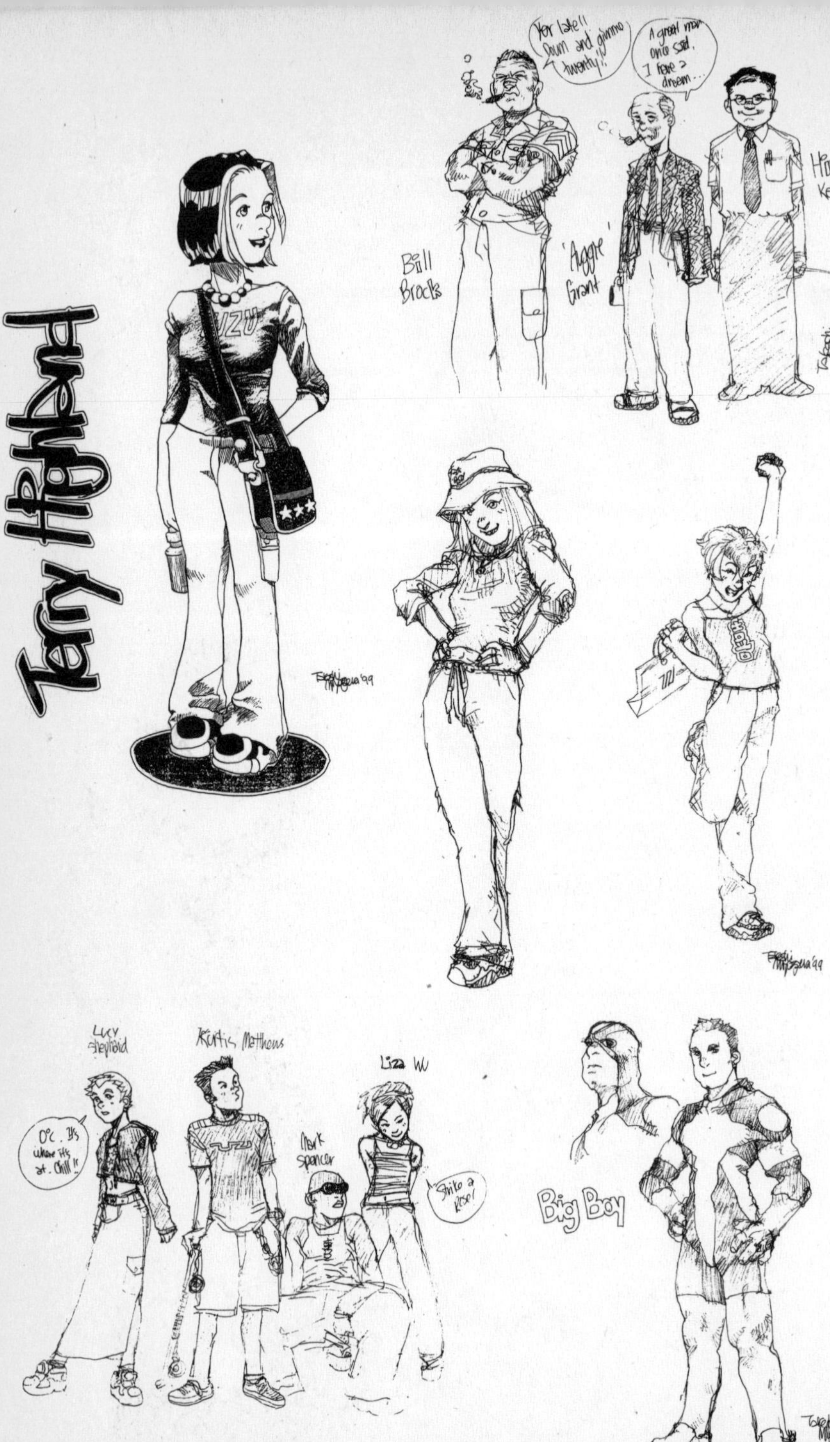
Yer late!! Down and gimme twenty!!
A great man once said, I have a dream...
Hiro Kenji
Bill Brooks
'Auggie' Grant
Terry Highland
Lucy Shepherd
Kurtis Matthews
Liza Wu
Mark Spencer
0°C. It's where it's at. Chill !!
Strike a Pose!
Big Boy

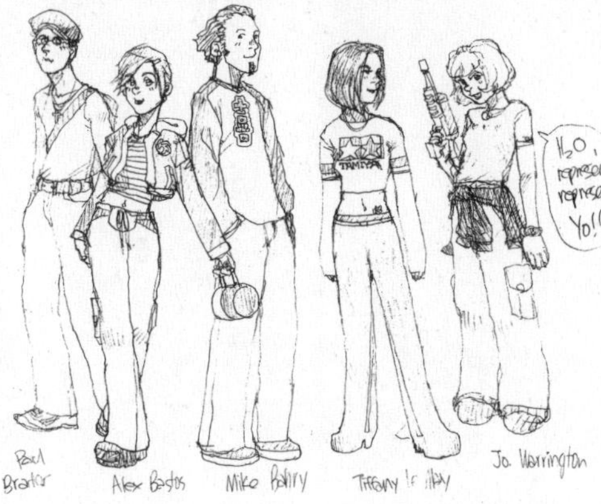
H2O, represent represent, Yo!!
Alex Bastos
Jo. Warrington

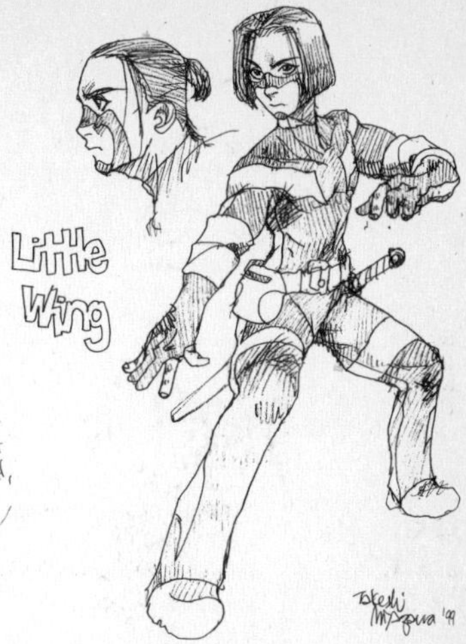
Little Wing
Takeshi Miyazawa '99

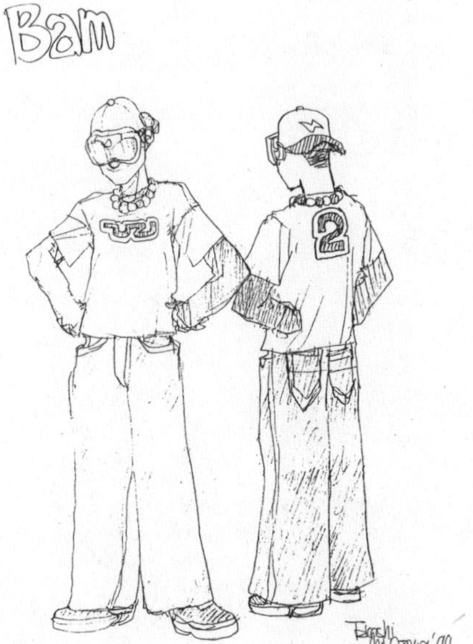
Bam
Takeshi Miyazawa '99

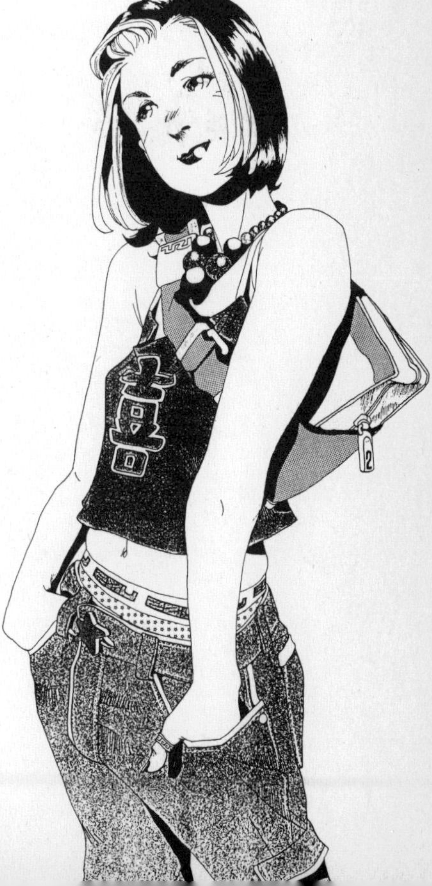

Other books from J. Torres & Oni Press...

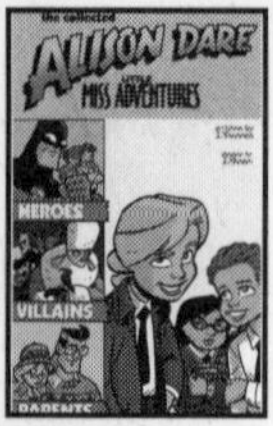
Alison Dare
Miss Adventures
Heroes
Villains

THE COLLECTED ALISON DARE™
by J. Torres & J. Bone
96 pages, black-and-white interiors
$8.95 US
ISBN 1-929998-20-1

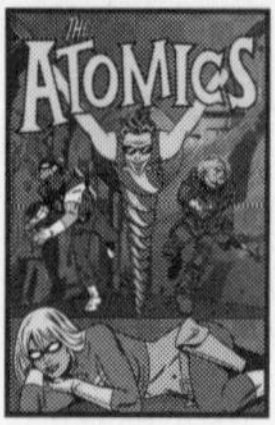
The Atomics

THE ATOMICS™: SPACED OUT AND GROUNDED IN SNAP CITY
by Mike Allred, J. Bone, Chynna Clugston-Major, Lawrence Marvit, & Martin Ontiveros
112 pages, full-color interiors
$12.95 US
ISBN 1-929998-67-8

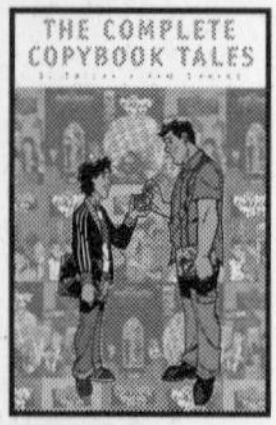
THE COMPLETE
COPYBOOK TALES

THE COMPLETE COPYBOOK TALES™
by J. Torres & Tim Levins
248 pages, black-and-white interiors
$19.95 US
ISBN 1-929998-39-2

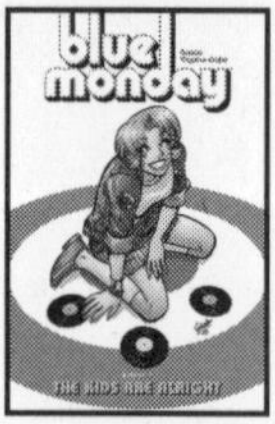
blue monday
THE KIDS ARE ALRIGHT

BLUE MONDAY™, VOLUME 1: THE KIDS ARE ALRIGHT
by Chynna Clugston-Major
136 pages, black-and-white interiors
$10.95 US
ISBN

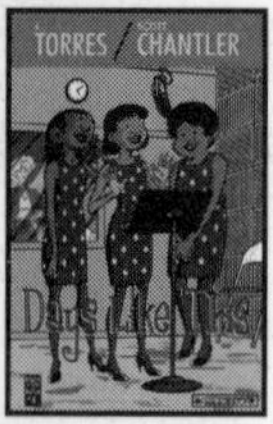
TORRES / CHANTLER

DAYS LIKE THIS™
by J. Torres & Scott Chantler
88 pages, black-and-white interiors
$8.95 US
ISBN 1-929998-48-1

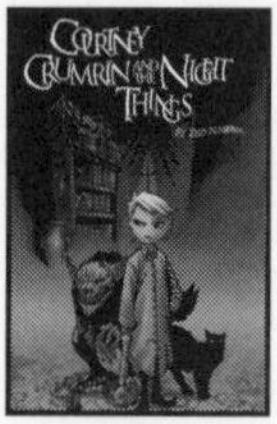
Courtney Crumrin and the Night Things

COURTNEY CRUMRIN™, VOLUME 1: THE NIGHT THINGS
by Ted Naifeh
128 pages, black-and-white interiors
$11.95 US
ISBN 1-929998-60-0

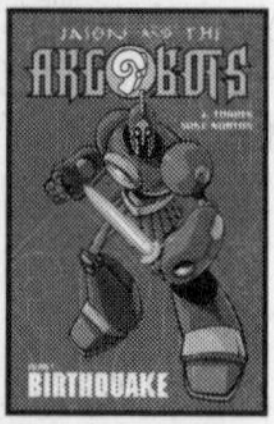
Jason and the
Argobots
Birthquake

JASON & THE ARGOBOTS™, VOLUME 1: BIRTHQUAKE
by J. Torres & Mike Norton
120 pages, black-and-white interiors
$11.95 US
ISBN 1-929998-55-4

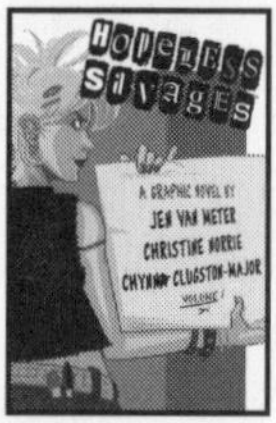
Hopeless Savages
A graphic novel by
Jen Van Meter
Christine Norrie
Chynna Clugston-Major

HOPELESS SAVAGES™, VOLUME 1
by Jen Van Meter, Christine Norrie and Chynna Clugston-Major
136 pages, black-and-white interiors
$11.95 US
ISBN 1-929998-75-9

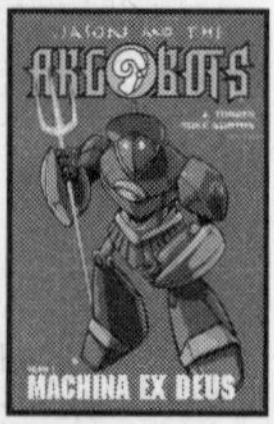
Jason and the
Argobots
Machina Ex Deus

JASON & THE ARGOBOTS™, VOLUME 2: MACHINA EX DEUS
by J. Torres & Mike Norton
112 pages, black-and-white interiors
$11.95 US
ISBN 1-929998-56-2

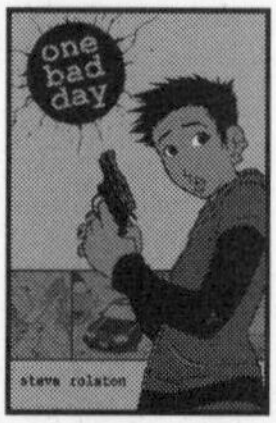
one bad day
steve rolston

ONE BAD DAY™
by Steve Rolston
120 pages, black-and-white interiors
$9.95 US
ISBN 1-929998-50-3

Available at finer comics shops everywhere. For a comics store near you, call 1-888-COMIC-BOOK.

For more information on more Oni Press titles go to: www.onipress.com